*Past and Present Publicati*

# *The English Rising of 1381*

# *Past and Present Publications*

General Editor: PAUL SLACK, *Exeter College, Oxford*

Past and Present Publications comprise books similar in character to the articles in the journal *Past and Present*. Whether the volumes in the series are collections of essays – some previously published, others new studies – or monographs, they encompass a wide variety of scholarly and original works primarily concerned with social, economic and cultural changes, and their causes and consequences. They will appeal to both specialists and non-specialists and will endeavour to communicate the results of historical and allied research in readable and lively form.

For a list of titles in Past and Present Publications, see end of book.

# The English Rising of 1381

*Edited by*

**R. H. HILTON**

*and*

**T. H. ASTON**

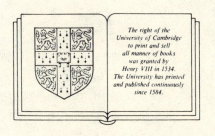

The right of the
University of Cambridge
to print and sell
all manner of books
was granted by
Henry VIII in 1534.
The University has printed
and published continuously
since 1584.

**CAMBRIDGE UNIVERSITY PRESS**

*Cambridge*
*New York   New Rochelle   Melbourne   Sydney*

Published by the Press Syndicate of the University of Cambridge
The Pitt Building, Trumpington Street, Cambridge CB2 1RP
32 East 57th Street, New York, NY 10022, USA
10 Stamford Road, Oakleigh, Melbourne 3166, Australia

First published 1984
First paperback edition 1987

Printed in Great Britain at
the University Press, Cambridge

Library of Congress catalogue card number: 84–4938

*British Library Cataloguing in Publication Data*

The English rising of 1318. – (Past and present publications)
1. Tyler's Insurrection, 1381
I. Hilton, R.   II. Aston, T.   III. Series
942.03′8   DA235

ISBN 0 521 26743 9 hard covers
ISBN 0 521 35930 9 paperback

wv

# Contents

v

# Introduction

R. H. HILTON

The papers published in this volume were, with two exceptions, presented to the annual conference organized by *Past and Present* in 1981. We were able to expand the unavoidably restricted coverage of the events of 1381 by obtaining two subsequent contributions by R. B. Dobson and A. Harding. An obvious gap remains, that is, a study of the June events in London itself, though this was almost simultaneously covered by Caroline Barron's interesting study published by the Museum of London.[1]

Our title was the 'English Rising' rather than the 'Peasants' Revolt'. It was felt that, although, as C. C. Dyer cogently argues, the main drive behind the rebellion came from the peasantry, urban involvement was of considerable importance and perhaps hitherto rather neglected. Consequently, while two contributions analyse peasant discontents and aspirations, another two deal with important instances of rebellion in provincial towns, which have been less closely studied than they deserve, in comparison, for example, with London or Bury St Edmunds. Having also decided that the rebellion should be put in the context of the wider European social conflicts of the period, we were fortunate in obtaining contributions from Raymond Cazelles on the Jacquerie – a rural rebellion much in the thoughts of England's rulers at this time – and from Samuel Cohn on the classic urban rebellion of the Florentine Ciompi.

It will be remembered that *Past and Present*'s commemoration of the rising of 1381 was by no means the only one in 1981. Popular and scholarly interest was widespread, as many meetings, conferences and festivals throughout the country bore witness. No doubt an analysis of this present fascination would be worthwhile. This lively interest also poses a problem for the historians of the event itself, for since the late nineteenth century there has been an interesting

[1] *Revolt in London: 11th to 15th June, 1381* (London, 1981).

1

shift in interpretations of the rebellion and perhaps another shift in the reverse direction is now taking place. That seventeenth-century founding father of agrarian history, John Smyth of Nibley, wrote in his *Lives of the Berkeleys*: 'Then the times began to change and he [Thomas, 4th Lord Berkeley] with them . . . much occasioned by the insurrection of Wat Tyler and all the commons in the land.' For J. Thorold Rogers, the 'solid fruits of victory rested with the insurgents of June 1381 . . . the peril had been so great and the success of the insurrection was so near that wise men saw that it was better silently to grant that which they had stoutly refused in Parliament to concede'. For William Stubbs, the rising was 'one of the most portentous events in the whole of our history . . . although the villeins had failed to obtain their charters . . . they had struck a vital blow at villeinage . . . thus indirectly the balance of power among the three estates began to vary'. William Cunningham wrote that 'although the outbreak was suppressed there is no reason to believe that the old institutions which had maintained order and enforced morality recovered an effective sway'. Nevertheless, Cunningham seems to have initiated what became the prevailing (non-Marxist) economic determinist interpretation. For he also added: 'the slow agricultural revolution which rendered their services less useful to the manorial lords, gradually set the villeins free by removing the interest their masters had in retaining a hold on them'. E. Lipson challenged Thorold Rogers's view that the landlords were afraid after 1381, so that villeinage died out because of the insurrection. May McKisack concluded: 'the Rising itself had no perceptible effect on the disabilities of peasants or artisans, nor . . . on the social and economic forces which were slowly transforming conditions of life in town and countryside'. And more recently, two eminent historians have echoed the point made by McKisack. M. M. Postan considered that 'historians are now in general agreement that it was a passing episode in the social history of the late middle ages'. R. B. Dobson wrote that the results of the revolt were 'negative where they were not negligible' – it was a 'historically unnecessary catastrophe'.[2]

[2] J. Smyth, *The Lives of the Berkeleys*, ed. J. Maclean, 3 vols. (Gloucester, 1883–5), ii, p. 5; J. Thorold Rogers, *Six Centuries of Work and Wages*, 7th edn (London, 1903; 1st edn 1884), p. 265; W. Cunningham, *Growth of English Industry and Commerce*, 5th edn, 3 vols. (Cambridge, 1910; 1st edn 1882), i, pp. 375–6; E. Lipson, *Economic History of England*, 7th edn, 3 vols. (London, 1937; 1st edn 1915), i, pp. 93–4; M. McKisack, *The Fourteenth Century* (Oxford, 1959), p. 422;

The view that the conditions of peasants, artisans and wage-labourers depended on economic factors outside human control would seem to be supported by such indices of long-term economic trends as movements of rents, wages and prices (not to speak of demographic fluctuations) as have been constructed over the years by economic historians. Nevertheless, as will appear from the contributions to this collection, the economic relationship between feudal landlord and villein tenant cannot simply be explained in terms of the supply of, and the demand for, land, or the (highly dubious) supply and demand for the benevolent protection of the lord. It emerges clearly that there was a 'political' element in the economic relationship of the main classes of medieval English society, due to the jurisdictional domination by the lord over the tenant, whether at the manorial, county or national level.

There were, of course, economic as well as political factors in the determination of rent levels. The changing land:labour ratio in the fourteenth century obviously made it more difficult for landowners to use coercion in obtaining labour services and rents. The growth of money rent, with all its implications, was clearly linked with the development of the market in agricultural produce. Nevertheless it must be obvious that the strength or weakness of manorial jurisdiction was a crucial element in deciding rent levels, whether because of the actual power of individual lords over their tenants or because of a more general weakening of lords' legal powers through the attenuation of the terms of full servile villeinage. If this is accepted, shifts in the balance of power between landlords and tenants would be as important as purely economic factors in shaping the conditions of the late medieval peasantry. This is what Stubbs implied and it restores the rising of 1381 from an irrelevancy to an event of considerable economic and social significance.[3]

It should also be borne in mind that the 1381 rising may best be regarded not so much as an unexpected explosion of popular resentment against various forms of repression but as simply a high point in the struggle between landlords and tenants which had been going on at a local and uncoordinated level for at least two hundred years and which would continue after 1381 for as long again. If it is argued that 'there was a general movement towards the commuta-

M. M. Postan, *The Medieval Economy and Society* (London, 1972), p. 154; *The Peasants' Revolt of 1381*, ed. R. B. Dobson (London, 1970), pp. 27–8.
[3] *Constitutional History of England*, 4th edn, 3 vols. (Oxford, 1896), ii, p. 485.

tion of labour services and the emancipation of serfs'[4] before the rising of 1381, earlier rebellions and protests must have contributed substantially to that 'general movement', just as it can be shown that continuing demonstrations of peasant anti-seigneurialism after 1381 helped further to push down rents and services. It might also be added that not only was the 1381 revolt a high point in a very long and historically significant conflict between peasants and landlords, but should also be seen in the European context of widespread social conflict, so well illustrated, in different ways, by the contributions here on the Jacquerie and Ciompi.[5]

One of the problems of the analysis of the events of 1381 is, as one might expect, a considerable ambiguity about the source material. This relates, in particular, to our appreciation of the rising as a coherent movement with more or less clearly defined goals. Earlier historians, quite naturally, relied on the many and varying accounts by the chroniclers. Did these writers endow the rebels with coherent aims which came out of their (the chroniclers') own fears? The chroniclers certainly give the general impression that this was a mass rising of rustics whose primary and coherent aim was the achievement of free tenure and status for all. And, as Dr Dyer shows in his contribution, this and other specific demands of the rebel leaders at Mile End and Smithfield appeared, well before the writings of the chroniclers, as issues in manor after manor in south-eastern England. Substantial evidence of a widespread ideology of freedom, even if 'conservative' in form, is produced by Dr Faith from the southern and south-western counties in the 1370s, echoing more scattered evidence which goes back to the thirteenth century. Nor can the existence of this widespread ideology of freedom be minimized by pointing to the fact that unfree villeins were a minority of the peasant population. Court rolls were burnt, evidently as a symbolic anti-seigneurial gesture in tenurially free Kent. 'Freedom' was conceived in much more general terms than freedom of tenure, being as much freedom from the tax-collector,

---

[4] Postan, *loc. cit.*
[5] For movements before 1381, see R. H. Hilton, 'Peasant Movements before 1381', *Econ. Hist. Rev.*, 2nd ser., ii (1949); for movements after 1381 see Christopher Dyer, 'A Redistribution of Incomes in Fifteenth Century England', *Past and Present*, no. 39 (Apr. 1968), pp. 11–33, and R. H. Hilton, *The English Peasantry in the Later Middle Ages* (Oxford, 1975), ch. 4. Late medieval rebellions in Europe are also described by M. Mollat and P. Wolff in *Ongles bleus, Jacques et Ciompi: les révolutions populaires en Europe au XIVᵉ et XVᵉ siècles* (Paris, 1970).

from the royal official, from the justice of the peace or of trailbaston as from the local lord. No doubt preachers like John Ball helped to knit together strands of popular demand into something approaching a coherent programme, but their moral doctrine of the freedom and equality of the descendants of Adam and Eve would not have been so readily received had it not fitted into an old demand for freedom expressed in many conflicts at law between lord and tenants.

There is another type of source material which, if uncritically used, could lead the historian towards an interpretation of the rising as an incoherent riot. I refer to the indictments against the rebels in the royal courts after the insurrection had been crushed. These were already used many years ago by André Réville and led him to describe the rebellion in Norfolk as 'an immense pillage'.[6] Although this evidence is of vital importance in tracking down named individuals, it deserves as much critical scrutiny as do the chronicles. There are few grounds for supposing that indictment juries necessarily told the truth about those whom they accused; they – the 'questmongers' so hated by the rebels – could be expected to be revengeful; and naturally they would emphasize the element of pillage and self-seeking among those they accused. Concentration on the indictments, therefore, without due concern for context and background, can too easily produce a picture of fragmented episodes which do little more than confirm prejudices that rebels are simply criminals. On the other hand, if the indictments are used with discrimination, and named individuals in them are linked with reference in other sources, a picture of, for instance, the changing pattern of social conflict can be drawn, as Dr Butcher has done for Canterbury and its region. Above all, one must perceive the judicial process not simply as a generator of documentation, but as Professor Harding shows, as one of the major elements in the widening of the social gulf which ended in rebellion.

An analysis of the tensions in rural society, of the grievances of the peasants, rural wage workers and artisans and of their social and even political aspirations, can bring us close to an understanding of the English rising. This is, to a considerable extent, due not merely to the fact that some of the best-informed chroniclers wrote intelligently from the standpoint of the landowners and of the state, but

---

[6] A. Réville and C. Petit-Dutaillis, *Le soulèvement des travailleurs d'Angleterre en 1381* (Paris, 1898), p. 85.

that the manorial documentation, especially court records, is strikingly rich as compared with that available in any other European country. This is clear from the contributions of Dr Dyer and Dr Faith, as well as from many earlier writings on the subject. In comparison, our understanding of the part played by urban societies in the rising is by no means clear. This is partly due to the fragmentary and uneven survivals of the documentation of many important medieval towns. Records of administration and judicial proceedings are often discontinuous. The records of courts leet, for example, which can be very informative on social and economic matters, do not survive on the same scale for urban as they do for rural societies. The economic activity of merchants and craftsmen (especially the latter) often has to be deduced from indirect evidence, such as urban regulation, which can be very equivocal. Conclusions are difficult to arrive at concerning the precise nature of urban discontents, as both Professor Dobson and Dr Butcher make clear. Perhaps one of the problems, in addition to gaps in the documentation, is that research into the social history of medieval English towns has lagged behind that into agrarian history, a lag which may soon be overcome.

Whatever the state of research, conclusions have been drawn about the nature of urban involvement in the rising. A view commonly held is that tensions in urban society were specific to them, and that issues such as freedom and serfdom and the burden of rent, so important in the countryside, would be irrelevant in the town. The main urban tensions were of a political character, that is, the exclusion of the craftsmen and lesser traders from participation in town government, which was dominated by faction-ridden mercantile oligarchs. Added to these would be the discontents of urban communities which were under the lordship of monastic corporations (such as Bury St Edmunds and St Albans) or which were in conflict with ecclesiastical franchises – a widespread phenomenon illustrated by some of the northern towns. The breakdown of authority which was the consequence of a peasant uprising would then act as a trigger to simmering urban conflicts.

Such an interpretation, perhaps over-simply presented here, is inadequate and its inadequacy is made clear, directly and indirectly, in the contributions to this volume. Grievances such as the operation of the Statute of Labourers, judicial and official oppression and the unequal distribution of the burden of taxation were common to both town and country. Furthermore, as Dr Butcher has implied, the above interpretation assumes a separation of urban and rural societies which hardly existed. This does not mean, of course, that there was nothing specific about large and small towns where non-agricultural occupations predominated. It does mean, however, that the differing demographic patterns of town and country led to a constant flow into towns of rural immigrants, from all social strata. These immigrants often retained connections with their native villages, not to speak of 'rural' cultural, social and political attitudes. In the demographic crisis of the second half of the fourteenth century, the interpenetration of town and country populations was even more marked. Whether there was such a shift in other towns in the nature of class relationships as is suggested for Canterbury and its hinterland cannot confidently be demonstrated, but the question is suggestive for further research.

Dr Tuck, in his essay on the reactions of the ruling class to the rebellion, suggests that, at any rate in the short term, the consequences of the revolt were 'political' rather than 'manorial'. In particular, he observes that the members of the House of Commons – representing the interests of the middling landowners – saw excessive taxation as the cause of the rebellion. In order to deal with the situation they proposed not only the abandonment of tax innovations but strong measures to enforce order and obedience. Hence the Statute of 1388 with its reaffirmation of the labour legislation and the inquiry into the guilds, regarded as being hives of subversion. But, as we have observed, the concept of the rising having political implications can be extended well beyond these suggestions.

Attention has already been drawn to the 'political' nature of the exercise of jurisdictional power in medieval society. This is observable at the manorial level (especially where lords had the combined jurisdiction of court leet and court baron); at the county level with the J.P.s; and nationally with the court of King's Bench and the various judicial commissions such as oyer and terminer and trailbaston. It could be expected therefore that the reactions of those oppressed by jurisdiction would be similarly political in character, though the sophistication of the programmes put forward in 1381 is striking, especially now that it has been demonstrated that these demands were not chroniclers' rationalizations but reflected grass-roots opinion. The advance from earlier demands for tenurial freedom to what Professor Harding has called 'civic' freedom is an interesting aspect of this increasing sophistication.

To sum up: the rising of 1381 has usually been treated as an expression of grievances which were essentially economic or social in character – the attempt of landowners to recuperate rent income in a period when the overall trend of rents was downwards; their renewed emphasis on servile villeinage; the operation of the labour legislation which attempted to counter the upward trend in wages; the attempt by the government to impose a series of taxes which were clearly discriminatory against the lower income groups. No analysis of the events could fail to place these factors at the forefront. What is interesting is that the response was so political – even though naïve. We have suggested that this was to some extent the consequence of the political character of all the essential relationships between the ruling class of late medieval England and those subordinated to it. In addition, any challenge to the authority of the state and of the class which controlled the state was bound to be political, and not only in the middle ages.

# 1. *The Social and Economic Background to the Rural Revolt of 1381**

CHRISTOPHER DYER

Was the revolt of 1381 merely a 'passing episode' in English history, an irrational aberration, or was it deeply rooted in the economic and social life of the later middle ages?[1] The frustration of historians who despair of finding a social explanation of the rising is understandable, as causes suggested in the past have been shown to be inadequate. There is little evidence to support the theory that labour services increased in the late fourteenth century, and we can no longer accept the view that the revolt was caused by the dissolution of the traditional feudal order by the advance of a money economy.[2] There is now general agreement that the conditions of peasants as well as wage-earners tended to improve after the plague of 1348–9, so that any economic explanation of the revolt

* I have received help from too many people to be able to thank them all individually. The British Academy made the research possible by providing a generous grant. I found various unpublished theses of value, notably that of D. A. Crowley, and a fellowship essay by L. Poos. I owe a special debt to Professor A. L. Brown of Glasgow University, who gave me access to his extensive researches in the public records. Abbreviations used in footnote references to manuscript sources: B.L.: British Library; Bodl. Lib.: Bodleian Library; C.C.L.: Canterbury Cathedral Library; C.U.L.: Cambridge University Library; E.R.O.: Essex Record Office; G.L.: Guildhall Library, London; H.R.O.: Hertfordshire Record Office; N.C.: New College, Oxford; P.R.O.: Public Record Office; S.R.O.B.: Suffolk Record Office, Bury St Edmunds Branch; S.R.O.I.: Suffolk Record Office, Ipswich Branch; St J.C.: St John's College, Cambridge; W.C.: Wadham College, Oxford.

[1] M. M. Postan, *The Medieval Economy and Society* (London, 1972), pp. 153–4.
[2] For older interpretations, see J. E. Thorold Rogers, *A History of Agriculture and Prices in England*, 7 vols. (Oxford, 1866), i, pp. 80–3; D. Petrushevsky, *Wat Tyler's Rebellion*, reviewed by A. Savine in *Eng. Hist. Rev.*, xvii (1902), pp. 780–2; this work is also discussed in P. Gatrell, 'Studies of Medieval English Society in a Russian Context', *Past and Present*, no. 96 (Aug. 1982), pp. 35–7. Rogers's explanation was criticized effectively in C. Petit-Dutaillis, *Studies and Notes Supplementary to Stubbs' Constitutional History*, 3 vols. (Manchester, 1914), ii, pp. 252–304. For more recent explanations, see *The Peasants' Revolt of 1381*, ed. R. B. Dobson (London, 1970), pp. 1–31; R. H. Hilton, *Bond Men Made Free: Medieval Peasant Movements and the English Rising of 1381* (London, 1973).

must be expressed in terms of rising expectations. Did the actions of landlords frustrate these expectations? Was there a seigneurial reaction in the post-plague decades? In order to consider these problems it is necessary to define more closely the groups who made up the rebel ranks, and to examine their motives and aims. These questions are too numerous to receive a full answer in a single essay. In concentrating on them here, the political and religious aspects of the revolt, which deserve to be properly considered in any full assessment of the complex events of 1381, will be unavoidably neglected.

Much of the literature on the 1381 rising was published before 1907, when most of the chronicle sources were already in print, and many of the relevant classes of public records were available for research. The main sources for investigating the social and economic background, the manorial records, lay scattered in the muniment rooms of country houses and the offices of local solicitors. This study is based on the mass of this local material which is now more readily available. Such is its bulk that it has been necessary to concentrate on the four counties of Essex, Hertfordshire, Kent and Suffolk. The method of research has been to compile an index of non-urban places affected by the revolt, and then to look for manorial records of those places, or at least for manors in their vicinity. The manorial records were used to compile biographical studies of individual rebels (supplemented by some information from the archives of central government), and to examine the changes in rural society in the forty years before the revolt. The records of more than a hundred manors have been consulted, though many more sources for the four counties are known to exist.[3]

THE RURAL REVOLT OF 1381

Accounts of the revolt naturally concentrate on the events in London and, although we cannot be sure of the precise numbers involved, the large crowds of countrymen assembled there provide some indication of the mass support that the revolt received, particularly from Essex and Kent. Much of the rebellious activity

[3] The large St Albans Abbey estate in Hertfordshire has been excluded from this study because the large numbers of records involved, and the complexities of their interpretation, deserve separate study.

took place outside the capital, and the numbers of villages involved can be calculated from sources in print as 105 in Essex, 35 in Hertfordshire, 118 in Kent and 72 in Suffolk. These are minimum figures, which will be greatly expanded when the results of research recently carried out in the public records are published.[4] The distribution of the places known to have been affected by the revolt reveals no clear geographical pattern, except for a concentration of rebellious villages in south-central Essex and central Kent, and a relative absence of recorded activity in north-west Hertfordshire and the extreme south-east of Kent.

The total number of rebels can only be guessed. It is possible to extract the names of about four hundred rural rebels for the four counties from the printed documents. The new researches in the public records could well multiply this total tenfold. Even then we can expect that these were the leaders, or people who attracted the attention of jurors or informants by notorious acts, or perhaps some who were not involved in the revolt but who had enemies among the jurors. Even as a means of identifying the leaders these lists are inadequate, as the manorial records reveal the existence of local leaders unnoticed by the royal courts, like John Cok of Moze (Essex), who 'was the first in error, seeking and taking the court rolls', or the eighteen who burnt the court rolls of King's Langley (Herts.), or John Cole who did 'damages or trespasses', and helped to burn the court rolls at Felixstowe (Suffolk).[5] The rank and file of

---

[4] The printed records that have been used are: A. Réville and C. Petit-Dutaillis, *Le soulèvement des travailleurs d'Angleterre en 1381* (Paris, 1898), pp. 175–240, 288; J. A. Sparvel-Bayly, 'Essex in Insurrection, 1381', *Trans. Essex Archaeol. Soc.*, new ser., i (1878), pp. 205–19; W. E. Flaherty, 'The Great Rebellion in Kent of 1381 Illustrated from the Public Records', *Archaeologia Cantiana*, iii (1860), pp. 65–96; W. E. Flaherty, 'Sequel to the Great Rebellion in Kent of 1381', *Archaeologia Cantiana*, iv (1861), pp. 67–86; E. Powell and G. M. Trevelyan, *The Peasants' Rising and the Lollards* (London, 1899), pp. 3–12; E. Powell, *The Rising in East Anglia in 1381* (Cambridge, 1896), pp. 126–31, 143–5; *Rotuli Parliamentorum*, 6 vols. (Record Comm., London, 1783), iii, pp. 111–13; *Cal. Pat. Rolls, 1381–5, 1385–9; Cal. Close Rolls, 1381–5; Cal. Fine Rolls, 1377–83.* Some secondary sources also make references to otherwise unpublished documents, notably in Réville and Petit-Dutaillis, *Le soulèvement des travailleurs*, and in *V.C.H. Herts.*, iv, article on social and economic history by A. F. Niemeyer. Large quantities of information about the rebels remain unpublished in manuscripts in the P.R.O. Professor A. L. Brown has helped me with additional names from these sources, and I have also received information, notably about the burning of records, from Mr A. Prescott. The new research mentioned is being carried out by these two scholars.

[5] E.R.O., D/DGh M14; P.R.O., S.C.2/177/47; S.R.O.I., HA119: 50/3/80.

the rebel bands must have been made up of many who will always remain anonymous. The indictments tell us of whole villages which rose, like 'all of the men' of three Essex vills assembled by John Geffrey of East Hanningfield.[6] The lords of manors were apparently sometimes willing to believe that their property had been attacked by outsiders, 'unknown malefactors', but at Great Bromley (Essex) 'all of the tenants of this manor in bondage' were accused of involvement, as also were the tenants of servile holdings at Bacons in Dengie (Essex).[7] At the latter place it was also stated that the revolt went on for a much longer span of time than is normally allowed – not the first three weeks in June, but from April to July.

The indictments in the royal courts and the chronicles tell us a great deal about the major acts of rebellion in 1381. Many of these had a partly or wholly political character, such as the attacks on royal officials, escheators, justices and tax-collectors, and the killing of the 'traitors', notably Sudbury, Hales and Cavendish, and the pillaging of their property, of which the best-known example was the destruction of John of Gaunt's Savoy. There were also the apparently xenophobic killings of Flemings, and the many acts of local banditry, usually involving blackmail and theft. Social grievances are more apparent in the demands presented to the king rather than in the actions of the rebels, though the attacks on the lawyers in London were presumably expressing an antipathy with a social basis, and the revolt of the tenants of St Albans Abbey is a well-documented assault on seigneurial power. Some of the indictments mention the burning of manorial documents, but many more cases are recorded in court rolls written after the revolt, and it appears that the burning of court rolls was one of the most widespread expressions of rural rebellion. Using both direct references, and the indirect evidence of surviving series of court rolls that begin at the time of the revolt, it is possible to identify some 107 incidents of destruction, including the burning of central estate archives such as those of the archbishopric of Canterbury, Stratford Abbey and Waltham Abbey that affected the records of many manors.[8] Fortunately for modern historians, the rebels were by no means comprehensive in this form of rebellion.[9]

6 Sparvel-Bayly, 'Essex in Insurrection, 1381', p. 218.
7 E.R.O., D/DU 40/1; D/DP M1191.
8 Réville and Petit-Dutaillis, *Le soulèvement des travailleurs*, pp. 188, 218; *Cal. Pat. Rolls, 1381–5*, pp. 71–2.
9 The success of the rebels in destroying documents depended on the place of

The burning of records was often combined with a variety of actions against landlords. At Berners Berwick in Abbess Roding (Essex) the rebels stole their lord's timber, firewood, hay, harrows and cattle, and drove their animals to pasture on the demesne lands. Major trespasses on the lord's demesne by tenants' stock, in one case with twenty cows and two hundred sheep, are also recorded at Bacons in Dengie (Essex), and wood was taken from the lady of the manor of Tolleshunt Major (Essex).[10] At King's Langley (Herts.), and probably also at Knebworth in the same county, customary tenants felled timber growing on their holdings in large quantities, which normally required the lord's permission.[11] The rebels of Childerditch (Essex) asserted control over demesne land by seizing an enclosed croft which they may well have regarded as rightfully common. At the same place they made the lord's servants leave their work. The tenants of West Mersea (Essex) withdrew their rents and services at the time of the revolt.[12] Actions of individuals or small groups included refusals to pay rents, rejection of election to office in the manorial and village administration, and especially refusals to serve as chief pledge, that is, the headship of a tithing which carried the responsibility of informing the lord's view of frankpledge of the offences of the tithing-men. Individuals also rejected the jurisdiction of the courts, and made violent attacks on officials or other tenants. To take an example, the view of frankpledge at Holwell (Herts.) held on 6 June, before the revolt had really penetrated into the county, showed signs of unusual agitation, with the chief pledges initially refusing to pay the common fine, a suitor contradicting a chief pledge, and another suitor uttering threats against the constable.[13] At Fryerning (Essex), a Hospitallers' manor much nearer to the starting point of the revolt, a court and view session was begun on 4 June, but after a small

deposit of their archives used by landlords. Records kept in the manor-house were most likely to be burned. Barking Abbey's archives were evidently kept at the abbey, so the rebels at Ingatestone were able to burn only the current court roll for 1381; W. M. Sturman, 'Barking Abbey: A Study in its External and Internal Administration from the Conquest to the Dissolution' (Univ. of London Ph.D. thesis, 1961), p. 121. On some estates the steward kept the previous year's rolls with him, so that although the main series of court rolls were destroyed by the rebels, the records for 1380 and 1381 were preserved.

[10] E.R.O., D/DHf M28, M45; D/DP M1191; P.R.O., S.C.2/173/94.
[11] P.R.O., S.C.2/177/47; H.R.O., K3.
[12] E.R.O., D/DP M1099; W. Gurney-Benham, 'Manorial Customs in West Mersea', *Trans. Essex Archaeol. Soc.*, new ser., xiii (1915), pp. 307–9.
[13] G.L., 10, 312/165.

amount of business had been transacted, the court roll states that 'William fitz Perys . . . was a rebel and would not do the steward's orders', and as this is the last item on the record we may speculate that the court ended prematurely.[14] It was a fortunate coincidence for the rebels that many lords in Essex and Hertfordshire traditionally held their annual view of frankpledge in the week after Whitsun, which in 1381 fell in the first week in June, just after the first outbreak in south Essex, so that officially summoned assemblies of all the adult males in many villages were meeting at a sensitive moment.

Serious personal violence against lords seems to have been unusual, with the important exception of the revolt at Bury St Edmunds (Suffolk), where among other casualties was John Lakenheath, a monk who had carried out a systematic reorganization of the abbey's archives, and who also appears in the pre-revolt court rolls making decisions about the level of seigneurial dues.[15] The lady of Great Bromley (Essex) was 'insulted', but this was probably because the rebels encountered her in the manor-house when they broke in to take the court rolls.[16] The landlords who were killed otherwise are usually found to have been serving in some official position in local government, which led to their selection for harsh treatment.

To sum up, the rural revolt in the four counties involved large numbers of people in hundreds of villages, who attacked 'political' targets, indulged in some conventional crime, but also directed themselves in both petty and large-scale acts of rebellion against the goods, lands, privileges and judicial powers of landlords.

## THE REBELS

With the exception of the handful of gentry and clergy who participated in the revolt in our four counties, notably in Suffolk, the social status and economic position of the rebels is not easily defined. We know something about their material possessions from the escheators' valuations of the goods and lands of indicted

---

[14] W.C., 44B/1.

[15] Réville and Petit-Dutaillis, *Le soulèvement des travailleurs*, p. 64; *The Archives of the Abbey of Bury St. Edmunds*, ed. Rodney M. Thomson (Suffolk Records Soc., xxi, 1980), pp. 23–33; S.R.O.B., E3/15.3/1.19(d), shows him dealing with the forfeited chattels of a felon of Chevington (Suffolk).

[16] E.R.O., D/DU 40/1.

individuals, and the records of the royal courts sometimes give the rebels' occupations. This evidence shows that 100 of 180 rebels from the whole area of rebellion owned goods valued at £1 to £5, and 15 of them were worth more than £5, including the very affluent Thomas Sampson of Suffolk and John Coveshurste from Kent.[17] The poorer rebels, and those with non-agricultural occupations, were especially numerous in Kent. This is sufficient to show that we are dealing primarily with people well below the ranks of the gentry, but who mainly held some land and goods, not the 'marginals' recently claimed as playing an important part in the revolt;[18] in other words most of the rebels were peasants and artisans.

By combing manorial and government records for the names of known rebels, it is possible to find out more about their backgrounds. This has been done for eighty-nine rebels, forty-eight from Essex, eighteen from Hertfordshire, thirteen from Suffolk and ten from Kent. Of them, forty-six are recorded as rebels in central government records, mainly indictments, and forty-three can be identified as rebels from the manorial documents. The Kentish rebels will be discussed separately because of the nature of that county's documents.

Of the remaining seventy-nine, we have information about the landholding of almost fifty of them. Thirty-eight are recorded as holding land by customary tenure; six held both free and customary land, and five are recorded only as free tenants. So the majority of our sample of rebels held land by disadvantageous tenures, often described as villein land, in a region where free tenants were very numerous. At least a tenth of our rebels (eight) were 'serfs by blood' (*nativi de sanguine*).

The economic standing of our rebels is best indicated by the size of their holdings, of which we are given some indication in thirty-six cases. Of these, fifteen had holdings of 14 acres or more, of whom only two held more than 32 acres; nine held between 7 and 12 acres; and twelve were smallholders with 5 acres or less. In some cases the information is incomplete, so the figures represent minimum landholdings. Nor should the other rebels be assumed to have been landless – the great majority can be shown from references to rent payment or their attendance at manorial courts to have been

[17] Hilton, *Bond Men Made Free*, pp. 180–4.
[18] G. Fourquin, *The Anatomy of Popular Rebellion in the Middle Ages* (Amsterdam, 1978), p. 101.

tenants. An indication of the scale of the rebels' agricultural activities and of their wealth is provided by references to their animals. We find individuals owning flocks of as many as twenty-five, twenty-eight or eighty sheep; John Hermar of Havering-atte-Bower (Essex) had four oxen and a horse, while William Smyth of Ingatestone and Fryerning (Essex) owned six *avers* (draught animals), five calves and some pigs. Robert Wryghte from Foxearth (Essex), whose holding of land is not recorded, can be assumed to have had a strong interest in agriculture from references to his possession of three horses, two cows and six pigs.[19] Rebels with smallholdings, and some sizeable amounts of land, would have had alternative sources of income from wage work or from the pursuit of crafts or trades. John Phelipp of Thorrington (Essex) was employed in fencing a park for 36½ days soon after the revolt. At least three of the rebels from his village cut wood for sale.[20] Elsewhere individual rebels are known to have sold fish, and three are recorded as traders, as a fellmonger, draper and chandler. There were two carpenters, a miller, a cook and a barber. A subgroup among the rebels were brewers or close associates of brewers, for example one of the few women to be named as a rebel, Margaret Wright of Lakenheath (Suffolk), who helped to kill John Cavendish, the chief justice, appears in the court records before the revolt as breaking the assize of ale. The wife of Robert Wryghte of Foxearth brewed a good deal, and the father of William Metefeld junior was the chief seller of bread and ale at Brandon (Suffolk).[21] Perhaps ale houses were especially suitable breeding grounds for disaffection, so that their keepers were drawn easily into rebellion, or perhaps brewers, like others involved in crafts and trades, were likely to be independent, articulate and aware.[22] At the higher end of the scale of status and wealth was a franklin (Richard Baud of Moulsham, Essex), and two others who, judging from their wealth in animals and goods, clearly belonged to the top ranks of village society, perhaps on the fringe of the gentry.[23]

[19] E.R.O., D/DU/102/1; W.C., 44B/1; E.R.O., D/DK M58.

[20] St J.C., 97.25(1), (2).

[21] C.U.L., EDC/7/15/11/2 (I am grateful to Miss J. Cripps for lending me her notes of the Lakenheath court rolls); E.R.O., D/DK M57–8; S.R.O.B., J529/1–2.

[22] On radicalism among modern craftsmen, E. J. Hobsbawm and J. W. Scott, 'Political Shoemakers', *Past and Present*, no. 89 (Nov. 1980), pp. 86–114.

[23] For Baud P.R.O., E179/107/63. The other two are William Gildeborn and Thomas Sampson.

In general, the sample seems to represent a wide spectrum of rural society, with a slight bias towards the better off. This could reflect the nature of the government sources, which tend to give the names of leaders rather than the rank and file, and the manorial records, which will tell us more about tenants than servants. The gentry will not appear in the sample because manorial documents will refer to them rarely, but rebels from this group were few in any case. There is nothing here to contradict the traditional identification of the rising as the 'Peasants' Revolt'.

The most striking common characteristic of our sample of rebels is their prominence in the government of their manor, village or hundred, either at the time of the revolt or within a few years of 1381. No less than fifty-three of them, out of seventy where we might expect to find evidence, are known to have served as reeves, chief pledges, affeerers, ale-tasters, bailiffs, jurors, constables or in other positions of responsibility. These offices were numerous, so that even a small village had to find more than a dozen officials at any one time, and we cannot regard the occupants of these positions as a narrow oligarchy. None the less every village had an élite, and it was evidently from this group that the leadership in the revolt was drawn. Office-holders in normal times and leaders in revolt both tended to have some maturity of years, and we can show that many of the 1381 rebels were middle-aged. Some estimate can be made of the age of twenty-two of our sample, and seventeen of them, judging from their appearance in the court records in the years 1359–68, or from references to their mature children in the years around 1381, are likely to have been at least approaching forty at the time of the revolt.[24] Most of the rebels came from families well established in their villages, and only two can be identified as recent immigrants, of which one was a special case. This was John Geffrey, a serf who had moved (or rather perhaps had been moved) from a Suffolk manor of the earls of Pembroke, Badmondisfield, 35 miles across the estate to their Essex manor of East Hanningfield to act as bailiff, presumably because of his administrative skills and trustworthy character.[25]

It is typical of previous conceptions about the participants in the

---

[24] It has recently been suggested that John Ball was aged about fifty in 1381: B. Bird and D. Stephenson, 'Who was John Ball?', *Trans. Essex Archaeol. Soc.*, 3rd ser., viii (1976), pp. 287–8.

[25] E.R.O., D/DP M833.

revolt that the editor of the *Essex Sessions of the Peace* has speculated that some of the criminals who were indicted before the J.P.s in 1377–9 would have joined the rising.[26] In fact none of those accused of felonies appear in the list of rebels; on the contrary, one of those helping to identify the criminals, a juror of Barstable Hundred in 1378, William Gildeborn of Fobbing, was hanged for his part in the revolt.[27] Similarly, we might expect to find some of the many labourers hauled up before the justices for offences against the labour laws among the rebels. There is one, James atte Ford of Takeley, who took excessive wages in 1378, but he was exceptional, as he bought a large holding of 18¾ acres in 1380, and so had transformed his social position by the time of the rising. The other Essex rebel known to have fallen foul of the labour laws was an employer, William Bette of Elmdon, who lured two ploughmen with high wages – he may have been acting as a bailiff at the time. Two Suffolk rebels are known to have employed servants in their own right in the decade before the revolt.[28]

The very different character of the Kentish manorial records makes similar analysis of our ten rebels from that county much more difficult. We can say no more than that three held office in seigneurial courts as borsholder (the Kentish equivalent of chief pledge), affeerer and juror; two of them were active in the land-market, though the size of their holdings is not known; and three appear in the records in the 1360s, so in 1381 they were near to middle age. This suggests similarities with the rebels north of the Thames, but it must be said that rebels are more difficult to find in the manorial records in Kent. This could result from the peculiarities of Kentish customs and documentation, or may reflect the higher proportion of landless and poor among the rebels, already noted on the basis of the escheators' valuations.

In our concern to identify and learn more about the background of the named rebels, we are in danger of ignoring the participation of humbler and poorer men. For example, manorial *famuli*, full-time servants on the demesne, joined the rebel bands, like the servants of Coggeshall Abbey at Childerditch (Essex), who departed, supposedly against their will, on the encouragement of

---

[26] *Essex Sessions of the Peace, 1351, 1377–1379*, ed. E. C. Furber (Essex Archaeol. Soc. Occasional Pubns., iii, 1953), p. 69.     [27] *Ibid.*, p. 155.

[28] *Ibid.*, pp. 162–4; P.R.O., K.B.27/479; S.R.O.B., J529/1–2; S.R.O.I., HA12/C2/19.

John Noreford, and at least five of the *famuli* at Wye (Kent) were 'ensnared by Rakestrawesmayne' according to the manorial official who had to justify extra expenditure on replacement labour for the hay-making.[29]

Although not all of the rebels were men of substance, occupying positions in seigneurial administration and as upholders of the law in their local communities, the presence of so many people of this kind must affect our assessment of the revolt. Experienced and well informed, they knew about the workings of law and government, and must have been aware of the risks of rebellion. In the event at least five of our sample were hanged, and another eight spent some time away from their homes as fugitives. Their revolt was not a temporary aberration, as some of them persisted in acts in defiance of authority long after the revolt, even to the point of personal ruin, like John Wylkyn of Fryerning (Essex), who lost his holding in 1382 for refusing to pay rent and carry out repairs after June 1381.[30] It is difficult to believe that these leading rebels were acting on mere impulse, or that they were affected by collective delusions. We must conclude that they had substantial grievances, and that their experiences of the real world drove them to embark on the revolt.

CHANGES IN SOCIAL RELATIONSHIPS, CIRCA 1340–81

The four counties had such diverse characteristics in their economy and social structure that it is difficult to identify features that made them ripe for revolt in the late fourteenth century. It should be noted that the area contained a good deal of woodland, marsh and pasture, that settlements were often dispersed, and that field systems were irregular, with much enclosure.[31] The inhabitants of such areas in later periods have been characterized as being independent and nonconformist, and their radical tradition may well date back to the middle ages.[32] However, similar landscapes

[29] E.R.O., D/DP M1099; P.R.O., S.C.6/901/5.

[30] W.C., 44B/1.

[31] O. Rackham, 'The Medieval Landscape of Essex', in D. G. Buckley (ed.), *Archaeology in Essex to A.D. 1500* (Council for British Archaeology Report No. 34, London, 1980); A. M. Everitt, 'The Making of the Agrarian Landscape in Kent', *Archaeologia Cantiana*, xcii (1976), pp. 1–31; L. M. Munby, *The Hertfordshire Landscape* (London, 1977); P. Barton, 'Manorial Economy and Society in Shenley', in *The Peasants' Revolt in Hertfordshire, 1381* (Hertford, 1981); N. Scarfe, *The Suffolk Landscape* (London, 1972).

[32] J. Thirsk (ed.), *The Agrarian History of England and Wales, 1500–1640*, series ed. H. P. R. Finberg (Cambridge, 1967), iv, pp. 109–12.

are found throughout England, and those outside the south-east were not in the forefront of the 1381 revolt. The counties are well known for their widespread rural industries, and craftsmen have often played an important role in rural revolts. In Essex and Suffolk there was an unusually high proportion of servants and labourers, who were vulnerable to the attempts to restrict wages, but as we have seen, landless wage-earners do not seem to have played a *leading* part in the rising.[33] The proximity of London may have been a factor in the rapid diffusion of news, rumours and ideas. The London market stimulated both industrial and agricultural producers in the surrounding countryside, so that those with a saleable surplus were acutely aware of opportunities for profit, and therefore perhaps particularly resentful of the restrictions imposed on them, such as the rents and dues that ate into their surplus.

The landlords of the four counties included the normal mixture of ecclesiastical corporations, lay magnates and gentry. Large church estates were prominent in western Suffolk, Hertfordshire and Kent, but not sufficiently to mark off these counties as very unusual. The peasantry of Kent enjoyed the unique privilege of the total absence of both serfdom and the normal restrictions of customary tenure. In the other three counties free tenants were numerous, but it is possible to find many manors where they were outnumbered by customary tenants, and most lords had at least a few serfs by blood (*nativi de sanguine*). Customary holdings might carry heavy burdens of rent and services, though the distinction between free and customary tenure was blurred by the existence of tenements of intermediate status, like molland, and the land-market allowed many tenants – a quarter of those at Hadleigh (Suffolk) in the early fourteenth century, for example – to hold both free and customary land.[34] Did the presence of so much free tenure increase the customary tenants' consciousness of their disadvantages? And in Kent were the tenants so privileged that they resented even the light hand of lordship that they experienced?[35]

In the thirteenth and early fourteenth centuries a feature of the rural society of the south-east, noticeable especially in Essex and Suffolk, was the very small size of most tenant holdings.

[33] Hilton, *Bond Men Made Free*, pp. 170–4.

[34] J. F. Nichols, 'Custodia Essexae' (Univ. of London Ph.D. thesis, 1930), p. 251.

[35] Réville and Petit-Dutaillis, *Le soulèvement des travailleurs*, p. 55; F. R. H. Du Boulay, *The Lordship of Canterbury: An Essay on Medieval Society* (London, 1966), pp. 181–9.

Generalization is difficult; although a few manors, like Lawling (Essex) in 1310, had two-thirds of its tenants with 30 acres or more, and on most manors the liveliness of the land-market allowed a small minority to prosper and accumulate very large holdings, it is often found that a half or even three-quarters of tenants held 5 acres or less.[36] The information available relates normally to the amount of arable land only, and the many smallholders must have made use of the pastures, wastes and woods, as well as supplementing their incomes from agriculture with wage and craft work.

The plague epidemic of 1348–9, judging from the Essex frank-pledge payments, killed nearly half of the population, and no real recovery is apparent in the next three decades.[37] We might expect to find that the number of tenants was reduced, and the size of holdings increased; these trends can be discerned, but on a very limited scale. The holdings left vacant by the plague were filled by inheritance, or taken on by survivors who were prepared to accumulate greater quantities of land, either on the old conditions or on new leasehold terms. Formerly landless wage-earners could move into the ranks of tenants, like Edmund, servant of the rector of Ingatestone (Essex), who took a 7-acre holding for a term of seven years in 1359.[38] The reduction in the number of tenants could be a slight one, so that those listed in rentals of Fristling (Essex) declined from forty-four in *c.* 1340 to thirty-nine in 1369.[39] On some manors a potential force for change came from demesne leasing in

[36] J. F. Nichols, 'The Extent of Lawling, A.D. 1310', *Trans. Essex Archaeol. Soc.*, new ser., xx (1933), pp. 173–98; G. F. Beaumont, 'The Manor of Borley, A.D. 1308', *Trans. Essex Archaeol. Soc.*, new ser., xviii (1928), pp. 254–69; A. J. Horwood, 'A Custumal, A.D. 1298, of the Manor of Wykes', *Trans. Essex Archaeol. Soc.*, new ser., i (1878), pp. 109–15; K. C. Newton, *Thaxted in the Fourteenth Century* (Chelmsford, 1960), pp. 10–16; K. C. Newton, *The Manor of Writtle* (London, 1970), pp. 37–54; Sturman, 'Barking Abbey: A Study in its External and Internal Administration from the Conquest to the Dissolution', pp. 244–51; A. Clark, 'Church Hall Manor, Kelvedon, in 1294', *Essex Rev.*, xix (1910), pp. 139–49; J. L. Fisher, 'Customs and Services on an Essex Manor in the Thirteenth Century', *Trans. Essex Archaeol. Soc.*, new ser., xix (1930), pp. 111–16; M. K. McIntosh, 'Land, Tenure and Population in the Royal Manor of Havering, Essex', *Econ. Hist. Rev.*, 2nd ser., xxxiii (1980), pp. 17–31; E. Miller, *The Abbey and Bishopric of Ely* (Cambridge, 1951), pp. 113–53.
[37] A. Clark, 'Serfdom on an Essex Manor, 1308–78', *Eng. Hist. Rev.*, xx (1905), pp. 479–83; L. R. Poos, 'Population and Mortality in Two Fourteenth-Century Essex Communities, Great Waltham and High Easter, 1327–89' (Fellowship Essay, Univ. of Cambridge, 1979), ch. 2; Newton, *Manor of Writtle*, pp. 78–82.
[38] E.R.O., D/DP M19.
[39] E.R.O., D/DP M1411, M1412.

parcels, which put further quantities of land in the hands of tenants.[40] It seems that in spite of the undoubted shift in the balance between population and land after 1348 that smallholders remained an important element in society at the time of the 1381 rising. Of the 155 customary holdings on six Essex manors restored to their tenants after the burning of the court rolls in the revolt, 81 (52 per cent) contained 5 acres or less, and only 13 were of 20 acres or more, not very different from the overall distribution of land before 1348.[41]

There is some evidence of growing prosperity among the peasantry. Smallholders would have enjoyed the benefits of rising wages. There seems to have been a general increase in the numbers of animals owned, judging from the tenant animals presented for trespassing on the lords' demesne lands. Flocks of eighty or a hundred sheep or herds of six or ten cattle were not uncommon, and occasionally even greater numbers are mentioned, appreciably larger than the flocks and herds appearing in the early fourteenth-century records. The value of land remained remarkably high, and tenants seem to have had large amounts of cash at their disposal. This is indicated by the occasional records of the sums paid for customary holdings by one tenant to another. Thomas Spryngefeld of Fristling (Essex) bought an 8½-acre holding in 1379 for £20; at Fingrith (Essex) a tenant paid £12 for 20 acres in 1378, and just after the revolt land changed hands at Havering-atte-Bower (Essex) for 13s. 4d. per acre. A rare direct piece of evidence for an accumulation of cash concerns John Henne of Earl Soham (Suffolk), who had 20s. 0d. in money to be stolen in 1370.[42] Disputes recorded in court rolls reveal a lively trade in grain, wool, cheese, animals and timber, sometimes in large quantities, like the 160 sheep sold by an East Hanningfield (Essex) tenant in 1378.[43]

The evidence for the changes in peasant fortunes in the period is fragmentary and difficult to quantify. There is no certainty that their circumstances were improving decisively, but the trends were mainly in their favour.

---

[40] For example, at Layham (Suffolk) the demesne was leased in 1379 to nine tenants: S.R.O.B., E3/1/2.7.

[41] E.R.O., D/DP M1191; D/DP M833; D/DFy M1; D/DGh M14; E.R.O. (Southend Branch), D/DMq M1; E.R.O., T/B 122.

[42] E.R.O., D/DP M718; D/DHt M93; D/DU 102/1; S.R.O.I., V5/18/1.2.

[43] E.R.O., D/DP M833. See also E. Clark, 'Debt Litigation in a Late Medieval English Vill', in J. A. Raftis (ed.), *Pathways to Medieval Peasants* (Toronto, 1981), pp. 247–79.

The landlords of the south-east, in common with those in other regions, were already experiencing economic difficulties in the second quarter of the fourteenth century. The plague epidemic opened up the prospect of sharp reductions in their incomes. Before 1348 demesnes were being cultivated with much wage labour. The labour shortage and rising wages eroded the profits of the demesnes, but most landlords continued with the old system, reducing the area under cultivation, and gaining some benefit from the high grain prices of the period up to 1375.[44] Whole demesnes were leased in the 1350s and 1360s, and there was renewed leasing activity just after 1381, but at the time of the revolt most demesnes were still under direct management.

The landlords' attitudes towards their tenants, subordinates and employees must have been coloured by the high wages and signs of increasing peasant prosperity, however embryonic. Their resentment of the changes affecting the rest of society are reflected in such literature as *Winner and Waster* and Gower's *Vox Clamantis*, and, more forcefully, in legislation like the 1351 Statute of Labourers and the Sumptuary Law of 1363. They were naturally anxious to take what advantage they could of the new developments and to tap some of the growing wealth that they saw below them.

Lords hung on to their powers after the plague epidemic. Their hold over their serfs represented the most complete form of social control available to them. In the 1330s and 1340s the *nativi* appear in the court rolls paying marriage fines and less commonly leaving their lords' manors illicitly or on payment of chevage. The degree of control exercised by one lord is indicated by an inquiry at Birdbrook (Essex) in 1338, after a 4-acre holding fell vacant, as to 'which of the neifs who have no land are most capable of taking the said land', implying that a serf could be compelled to take on the tenancy.[45]

After 1349, marriage fines continued to be exacted, up to and beyond 1381. They declined in number at Ingatestone (Essex), but at Birdbrook (Essex) they were levied in the late 1370s more frequently than before.[46] There was no fixed rate of fine and after

---

[44] On pre-1348 problems, see Miller, *Abbey and Bishopric of Ely*, pp. 105–11; R. A. L. Smith, *Canterbury Cathedral Priory* (Cambridge, 1943), pp. 126–7. For post-1348 developments, see A. R. Bridbury, 'The Black Death', *Econ. Hist. Rev.*, 2nd ser., xxvi (1973), pp. 580–6.

[45] E.R.O., D/DU 267/29.

[46] E.R.O., D/DP M15–M22; D/DU 267/29, 30.

1349, although some payments continued at the old level of 1*s*. 0*d*. or 2*s*. 0*d*., some lords demanded higher fines, 3*s*. 4*d*. or even 6*s*. 8*d*.

References to the emigration of serfs increase markedly after 1349, reflecting both the general *Wanderlust* of the period, and also the renewed concern of the lords to deal with the problem. Licensed departures might cost the serf a fine of 20*s*. 0*d*. or 40*s*. 0*d*., or a regular chevage payment which could be nominal, or as high as 3*s*. 4*d*. per annum. Permission to leave could be hedged around with conditions, to return once a year, or, in the case of a servile woman, not to marry without a licence. The lords' chief anxiety was to prevent illicit departures that might deprive them of their valuable assets. Pressure was put on relatives to bring the errants back, like the 20*s*. 0*d*. amercement demanded from Robert atte Chirch of Drinkstone (Suffolk) in 1377 because he failed to produce his two sons at the court, 'which he did not do, but refused'.[47] The lord of Aldham (Suffolk) imposed oaths on his serfs in 1369–71; Nicholas Mervyn, after a period of absence, came to the court and swore 'that he would be obedient to the lord and bailiffs and that he would come to serve the lord wherever and whenever the lord or his council wish'.[48]

Lords also attempted to control the acquisition of free land by their serfs, and to force them to pay extra rents and hold the land on customary tenure. An elaborately recorded case in 1374 at Crondon in Stock (Essex), a manor then held by Simon Sudbury as part of the estates of the bishopric of London, concerned one William Joyberd, who took a mare of his aunt's which the lord required as a heriot. It was then revealed that William, though a *nativus de sanguine*, held a messuage and 9 acres of free land which he had acquired by charter in the nearby village of Ramsden Bellhouse. An order was given for William, his family, lands, goods and chattels to be seized because 'he never gave to the lord an increment of rent, nor rendered the said lands to the lord as serfs ought'.[49] The danger of allowing such arrangements to go unchecked is shown by a discovery made by the officials of the countess of Norfolk at Walton (Suffolk) after the revolt, that two of her serfs had set themselves up as leading townsmen of Manningtree (Essex), one with 63½ acres of freehold

[47] S.R.O.B., E7/10/1.2.
[48] S.R.O.I., HA68:484/135.
[49] E.R.O., D/DP M780.

land, and the other with 21 acres and 11 messuages, shops and cottages.[50]

The lords had obvious financial reasons for maintaining control, but another motive in the post-plague labour shortage lay in the possibility of using their hold over serfs as a means of securing a supply of wage-labourers. This attempt to impose a sort of 'second serfdom' emerges from some agreements made when serfs were given permission to leave the manor. At Aldham (Suffolk) in 1368 an emigrant was required to return each year 'in the autumn to serve the lord', in other words to help with the harvest. A servile girl of Windridge (Herts.) was allowed to leave providing that she should be 'ready [to serve] the lord when he pleased to have her'.[51] The coercive power of the lord could also be used to secure employees for the demesne through the election of *famuli* in the courts, recorded at Brandon (Suffolk) and Winston (Suffolk) in the 1360s and 1370s. The hapless employees were required to take an oath on election. Needless to say, the candidates were often recruited from the unfree. Such was the lord's claim on the employment of serfs at Iken (Suffolk) that in 1372–3 the parson paid a fine in order to obtain the services of Agnes Fenman, a *nativa domini*.[52] The families of servile employees were also vulnerable to pressure to enforce labour discipline, as is recorded at Thorrington (Essex) in 1381. William Phelipp, a serf, was employed by the demesne farmer, probably on an annual contract. He broke the contract and left, but revisited the village and stayed with his mother, brother and uncle. These three were distrained by the lord of the manor for the trespass of receiving and entertaining their relative.[53]

Perhaps the term 'second serfdom' can also be applied to agreements made between lords and non-serfs, who were bound to work on the demesne as wage-earners in return for a grant of land. John Dryvere of Foxearth (Essex) was granted in 1364 a cottage, curtilage and one acre of land for life, at a rent of 5s. 0d. per annum 'on condition that the same John will serve the lord of this manor for the whole of his life . . . as a common labourer', and at Birdbrook (Essex) in 1377 Thomas Whetelee was granted 5 acres of land 'as long as he remains in the service of the lord'. In a similar case at Iken

[50] S.R.O.I., HA119:50/3/17.
[51] S.R.O.I., HA68:484/135; H.R.O., X.E.I.C.
[52] S.R.O.B., J529/1–2; C.U.L., EDC7/17/25/3; S.R.O.I., HD32:293/390.
[53] St J.C., 97.25(1).

(Suffolk) Roger Wisman took a holding in 1378 and promised 'to serve the lord as a labourer, taking for his wage what is just', which we may suspect in the circumstances involved a commitment to accept wages below the current rate.[54]

'Serfs by blood' formed a relatively small minority of the rural population of the south-east. Much more numerous were the customary tenants, many of whom still held 'servile land (*terra nativa*)', heritable by their family or 'brood (*sequela*)', and who received seizin of the holding 'by the rod (*per virgam*)'. The terminology is that of servile tenure, the obligations of which had been fixed in the very different economic circumstances of the thirteenth century. Increasingly after 1349 lords were letting customary holdings on short-term leases (ten years or less, or a single life), for a cash rent only, or for a cash rent and minimal labour service. The development of these forms of tenure affected only a minority of customary holdings, as they were more numerous than the old heritable tenures on only nine of a sample of thirty manors. For the tenants who were still in theory liable to heavy labour services the late fourteenth century saw a prevalent tendency towards commutation which meant that few tenants were expected by 1381 to perform week-work, though seasonal services and boons were commonly demanded. Kentish labour services had not been very onerous, but tenants there were sometimes expected to do their services in the late fourteenth century with little opportunity for commutation.[55] No doubt these continued demands for service were resented, as is suggested by many references to their non-performance in court records, but we may suspect that the lords' demands for cash also caused a good deal of friction. The leasehold tenancies carried a heavy burden of rent, varying from 6*d.* to 2*s.* 0*d.* per acre for arable, and commonly at a shilling per acre, or three times the universal rent demanded by the rebels at Mile End.

The leasehold tenures often carried no more than a nominal entry fine, but the traditional tenures involved a liability to pay a variable fine on inheritance or transfer. Wide differences between rates of fine, such as 22*s.* 0*d.* for a cottage and 6*s.* 8*d.* for 19 acres, on the same manor in successive years in 1380–1, suggest their flexibility,

[54] E.R.O., D/DK M57; D/DU 267/30; S.R.O.I., HD293/388.
[55] On the new forms of tenure, see B. F. Harvey, *Westminster Abbey and its Estates in the Middle Ages* (Oxford, 1977), pp. 244–67. On commutation in Kent, see Smith, *Canterbury Cathedral Priory*, pp. 126–7.

influenced by the lord's calculation of the new tenant's capacity to pay and the variable quality of the land. There was no consistent trend in the rate of entry fines, which may reflect both economic differences between manors, and variations in seigneurial policy. New tenants at East Hanningfield (Essex) paid 11*d*. per acre before the plague, and 6*d*. per acre up to the 1380s. More commonly the rate fell after the plague, but then increased until by the 1370s it was very near to its pre-plague level. For example, at Bredfield (Suffolk) fines averaged 5*s*. 2*d*. per acre in the 1340s, 2*s*. 9*d*. in the 1350s, and 4*s*. 11*d*. in the 1370s. Ingatestone (Essex) shows an unusual pattern of consistent increase from a pre-plague 5*d*. per acre to 1*s*. 1*d*. in 1379–81.[56]

The growing variety of customary tenures in the late fourteenth century must have led tenants to make comparisons. Tenants on manors which did not see any significant move towards leasehold would have cause for resentment. Those who had access to land on the new terms could well have envisaged that one major change in traditional arrangements might be followed by others.

Landlords were much concerned with the control of the market in customary holdings. Land changed hands rapidly both before and after the plague, and the lords accepted this provided that the transfer was carried out through the manor court, so that a fine could be levied and the new tenant and the conditions of tenancy entered on the court roll. The numbers of illicit transfers recorded in the late fourteenth century, either sales by charter in the manner of freeholders or sublettings for terms of years, increased, and are commonly encountered in the 1370s. This could reflect a growth in attempts to bypass the lord, or renewed seigneurial vigilance, or both. On some manors one gains the impression of some administrative slackness in the two decades after the plague, followed by more stringent controls in the 1370s. This would explain the number of cases in which former illicit transfers were discovered, like the unlicensed marriage of a widow at Arkesden

---

[56] The wide discrepancies in rates of fine are recorded at Fristling (Essex): E.R.O., D/DP M718. The other figures for fines come from E.R.O., D/DP M832–3; S.R.O.I., HA91/1; E.R.O., D/DP M15–M22. Parallels to Bredfield are Fingrith (Essex), with a rate of 1*s*. 10*d*. per acre in 1327–38, 11*d*. in 1362–4, and 1*s*. 3*d*. in 1377–81, and South Elmham (Suffolk), with rates of 2*s*. 10*d*. and 3*s*. 7*d*. before 1348, and 1*s*. 5*d*. in the 1350s, 1*s*. 2*d*. in the 1360s, and 2*s*. 6*d*. in 1372–81: E.R.O., D/DK M108, D/DHt M92, M93; S.R.O.I., HA12/C2/14–19. These rates are all calculated from fines paid on *ad opus* transfers.

(Essex) of 1366 which was revealed to the manor court in 1378, or the remarkable discovery in 1379 at Earl Soham (Suffolk) that a serf, John Hamond, had enjoyed the profits of a free tenement for ten years by granting the land into the hands of feoffees, a legal device normally associated with a more elevated section of society.[57] A tightening of administration is suggested also by the number of new rentals made in the 1370s and in 1380–1, or the order in 1380 at Aston (Herts.) 'to inquire who holds lands of the demesne and servile land, namely how many hold by copies because it is said that a great number of acres have been usurped'.[58] Unofficial transfers might lead to confusion over the exact status of particular plots of land, so that we find inquiries as to whether parcels were free or customary, again common in the 1370s.

The seigneurial courts were the key institutions for the maintenance of lordly control. They were used to enforce the obligations of tenants, such as the performance of labour services, or the repair of buildings on customary holdings. The courts disciplined manorial officials for slackness or corruption. They helped to maintain labour discipline, by amercing *famuli* employed on the demesne for poor work, and by assisting the higher courts in dealing with offences against the labour laws, ordering labourers to accept offers of work from the lord's officials, and occasionally punishing those who demanded high wages, like the three threshers at Chartham (Kent) who had obtained 2*d*. per day plus food in 1379.[59] The courts also provided lords with revenues from amercements and fines, including levies on brewers, and amercements on craftsmen such as potters and tilers for collecting their raw materials, that seem to have had the character of a seigneurial tax on trade and industry. Regular annual dues, like the common fine, or avesage (pannage of pigs), were collected through the courts.

The perquisites of courts made an appreciable contribution to seigneurial incomes; they rarely accounted for more than a tenth of manorial profits, but their value lay in the flexibility which allowed them to be increased when other sources of income were static or tending to decline. The normal pattern in the four counties was for court profits to increase between the 1340s and the post-plague decades. (See Table 1.) The amount of increase may seem

[57] E.R.O., D/Ad 122; S.R.O.I., V5/18/1.3.
[58] H.R.O., D/EAS 24.
[59] C.C.L., U15/12 48480.

Table 1. *Average annual total of court perquisites*

| Wheathampstead (Herts.) | | Chevington (Suffolk) | |
|---|---|---|---|
| 1340–7 | £6. 10s. 1d. | 1339–48 | £2. 8s. 10d. |
| 1371–81 | £7. 1s. 2d. | 1359–80 | £4. 3s. 8d. |
| Meopham (Kent) | | East Farleigh (Kent) | |
| 1340–7 | £1. 0s. 1d. | 1334–43 | £8. 3s. 7½d. |
| 1368–75 | £2. 6s. 5d. | 1372–88 | £9. 2s. 9½d. |

*Source:* Hertfordshire Record Office, D/ELw M144–Ml85; Suffolk Record Office, Bury St Edmunds Branch, E3/15.3/2.4–2.11; Canterbury Cathedral Library, beadles' rolls for Meopham and East Farleigh.

unremarkable, but to expand such revenues when the numbers of people attending the courts was declining must have involved a considerable growth in the average *per capita* payments made by the suitors. Presentments of some offences increased in number; on some manors the quantity of brewing offences and public nuisances moved slightly upwards, and on all manors the failure to repair buildings became a repetitive item of business by the 1370s.[60] Another growth point was provided by amercements for trespass on the demesne; no doubt the quantity and scale of incursions by tenant stock really increased because of the growing emphasis on pastoralism in peasant farming, but lords probably also made efforts to ensure that as many cases as possible were reported to the courts and substantial sums levied in amercements. The number and size of amercements both rose, so that the total taken from tenants for trespass offences might double between the 1340s and 1370s. Individual very high amercements could be demanded, such as 26s. 8d. from an Ingatestone tenant for selling a building from his customary holding.[61]

The rising trend in court perquisites made only a modest contribution to offsetting the overall downward movement in seigneurial incomes. The extent of that decline was surprisingly slight. Income from rents is difficult to survey in the long term because of the changes in the form in which rents were paid, such as fluctuations in the commutation of services, and the advance of leasehold tenures. Nor can we be certain as to the amount of

[60] D. A. Crowley, 'Frankpledge and Leet Jurisdiction in Later Medieval Essex' (Univ. of Sheffield Ph.D. thesis, 1971), chaps. 11, 12 (brewing offences declined after 1350 at Messing, but increased at Rickling; public nuisance presentments increased at Messing and Claret but may have declined at Rickling).
[61] E.R.O., D/DP M22.

evasion of rent payment. These complications are least problematic on the Kentish manors of Canterbury Cathedral Priory, and we find there that the reduction of total rent income on individual manors between the 1340s and the 1370s rarely exceeded 15 per cent and could be as low as 3 per cent. The most adversely affected estate with manors in the region seems to have been that of Battle Abbey, which suffered a 30 per cent drop in income between 1346–7 and 1381–2. The normal experience seems to have been a decline in revenues considerably smaller than this.[62]

We must conclude that fourteenth-century landlords defended their interests and incomes with vigour in a period of economic adversity. To emphasize one aspect of their position in the late fourteenth century, they succeeded in retaining the initiative so that they were still capable of disciplining tenants and making arbitrary demands through fines and amercements. The tenants had gained access to more land, and presumably the growth in leasehold tenure represented a concession to them, providing greater certainty in obligations. They seem to have been constantly testing the regime: serfs successfully left their manors, attempted to conceal the marriages of their daughters, and secretly acquired free land. Customary tenants also sought to evade the restrictions on the sale and leasing of land, and neglected or wasted their buildings. They failed or refused to perform labour services, four cases of which are known involving a dozen or more tenants in the years 1379 and 1380. These could be seen as leading cumulatively to the subversion of lordly authority, or merely as actions to gain short-term advantage. However, the existence of a strand of open and self-conscious opposition to seigneurial control sometimes emerges from episodes recorded in even the most routine series of court records.

The first half of the fourteenth century provides examples of protests by tenants, such as the collective avoidance of suit of mill at Ingatestone (Essex) in 1346, or the complaint of a tenant of Polstead (Suffolk) in 1340 who accused the lord and his bailiffs of corruptly protecting the manorial *famuli*, who he claimed were robbers, or the well-known Bocking (Essex) petition, apparently

---

[62] E. Searle, *Lordship and Community, Battle Abbey and its Banlieu* (Toronto, 1974), pp. 256–62; G. A. Holmes, *The Estates of the Higher Nobility in Fourteenth-Century England* (Cambridge, 1957), pp. 90–3, 109–20; Smith, *Canterbury Cathedral Priory*, p. 13; Harvey, *Westminster Abbey and its Estates in the Middle Ages*, pp. 66–7. On the demands of lords in general, see R. H. Hilton, *The Decline of Serfdom in Medieval England* (London, 1969), pp. 36–43.

made by free tenants to the prior of Christ Church, Canterbury, over the excesses of a steward. Actions against lords in the royal courts are most commonly found in the midlands at this period, but the 'poor people' of the village of Albury (Herts.) petitioned parliament in 1321–2 over the oppressions of their lord, Sir John de Patemore, who had imprisoned them and seized their cattle.[63]

Throughout the period examined here we find serfs seeking to assert their freedom, and being thwarted by their lords. Two South Elmham (Suffolk) men, John Clench and John Soule, claimed to be free in 1360. The 'whole homage' of the manor court stated that they were serfs, and they were put in the stocks. They did fealty as serfs to their lord, the bishop of Norwich, and were fined 3s. 4d. each 'for an unjust claim and rebellion'. Another tenant who had supported them (suggesting that the other villagers were by no means unanimous in their opinion) was deprived of his lands until he submitted to the lord's grace and paid a fine.[64] A similar case at Great Leighs (Essex) in 1378 concerned Joan Lyon, daughter of William Lyon, serf, who married without permission. William White and Richard Dryver, both servile tenants, and Richard Gardener, a born serf, 'conspired among themselves at Chelmsford to swear and give the verdict at the next court at Great Leighs' that Joan was free. They 'could not deny' the conspiracy, and the two tenants were amerced the large sums of 13s. 4d. and 20s. 0d. Needless to say, all three conspirators served as chief pledges at the time.[65]

A sharp reaction against a claim to freedom is revealed in the manor court of Earl Soham (Suffolk) in 1373. Alice Conyn, the daughter of John Bronnewen, was asked by what right she held land and married without licence. She produced a charter of manumission granted to her father by Thomas Brotherton, earl of Norfolk, in 1337. The court discovered a loophole in her claim to be free. Brotherton had held the manor in fee tail, by the terms of which he

[63] E.R.O., D/DP M16; B.L., Add. Roll 27683; J. F. Nichols, 'An Early Fourteenth Century Petition from the Tenants of Bocking to their Manorial Lord', *Econ. Hist. Rev.*, ii (1929–30), pp. 300–7; *Rotuli Parliamentorum*, i, p. 189. On tenants' legal actions against lords, see R. H. Hilton, 'Peasant Movements before 1381', in E. M. Carus-Wilson (ed.), *Essays in Economic History*, 3 vols. (London, 1954–62), ii, pp. 73–90.
[64] S.R.O.I., HA12/C2/14.
[65] P.R.O., L.R.3/18/3.

could not alienate property except in his own lifetime, so the charter carried no weight. Alice, and her sister, were each required to pay marriage fines at the punitively high rate of 13s. 4d.[66]

When at Flixton (Suffolk) Robert Borel denied his servile condition, 'with ingratitude', and committed a series of offences, marrying without permission, detaining a rent of a lamb, and wasting his holding, the lady of the manor, the prioress of Flixton, summoned an extraordinary tribunal in 1377, consisting of nuns, the prior of Aldeby (Norfolk), the steward and other lay advisers, who concluded an 'agreement' with Borel. He acknowledged his serfdom, swore an oath of servility 'without coercion', and agreed to render the old customs, to observe the rules governing marriage, and to reconstruct his buildings. He had to find pledges who were bound to see him carry out his obligations under penalties of £5 each. The prioress's side of the 'agreement' was to remit amercements totalling 53s. 4½d. in exchange for a fine.[67]

All of these cases show the lords using their judicial authority to assert their interests against the claims of their subordinates. However, the seigneurial courts were somewhat ambiguous institutions, which depended on the participation of tenants who presented offenders, fixed penalties, and collected dues. These petty officials can be seen ideally as performing a mediating role, moderating the harshness of the lord's rule, and making the regime more acceptable to their neighbours. In reality, especially in a period of heightened tension, the officials found themselves assailed on all sides. They were under pressure from the lord to present more cases, reveal more misdemeanours, and to collect more cash; on the other side, their friends and neighbours expected some protection and favourable treatment. They received a good deal of criticism in the courts from people who 'contradicted the chief pledges', uttered threats, and showed contempt for the courts. For example, in February 1381 William Morkyn of Fingrith (Essex) had to pay an amercement of 12d. because his wife 'was a rebel and spoke badly of the affeerers'. In 1380 at Walsham-le-Willows (Suffolk) Edmund Patyl, who had just heard that his illicitly acquired customary tenement of 9 acres had been seized by the lord, was amerced 3s. 4d. 'for contempt done to the lord, abusing the whole inquest [jury] openly in full court', directing his anger, it

[66] S.R.O.I., V5/18/1.2.
[67] S.R.O.I., HA12/C3/7.

should be noted, against the jurors who revealed his involvement in the secret sale of land.[68]

The village élite could attempt to act as spokesmen for the villagers in negotiations with the lord, as apparently happened at Ingatestone (Essex) in 1379 after a dispute over the allocation of services among tenants, when the homage offered the lord a sum of 40s. 0d. so that rents and services could be made 'certain'.[69] They might also conceal cases and shield their neighbours, but if they were found out by the lord they had to answer to him. We can sense the growing distrust between the lord of Winston (Suffolk) (a manor of the priory of Ely) and the jurors. In 1374 a jury which 'did not know' who had killed three of the lord's lambs was ordered to pay for the dead animals, and a chief pledge was amerced 1s. 0d. for concealing a case. In 1378 the reeve's failure to report the taking of wood cost him 1s. 0d., and the homage was ordered to investigate damage to the woods. In the same year a group of jurors told the steward after the court that the jury had concealed trespasses against the lord and the vill by animals belonging to the vicar, which led to another collective amercement of 3s. 4d. In 1379 the jury failed to report ruinous buildings and defaults of suit of court; in 1381 damage to the woods was concealed again.[70]

In view of the widespread difficulties arising from the ambiguous position of the officials it is hardly surprising that we find, particularly in the 1370–81 period, many refusals to serve in administrative positions, as rent-collectors, constables or ale-tasters. This could involve a collective refusal, like that of the homage of Fingrith (Essex) in 1375, to elect any rent-collector.[71] Such actions threatened the existing machinery of government, and lords reacted sharply with threats of high penalties and eviction from holdings. Similarly, refusals to take the oath as chief pledge, which occurred on a number of occasions, were regarded as acts of rebellion, and punished with such large amercements as 6s. 8d. That these amounted to more than an individual desire to escape the responsibility and expense of office is suggested by the collective denial of the common fine, paid over by the chief pledges at the annual view of frankpledge, which is found five times between 1370 and 1379.

---

[68] E.R.O., D/DHt M93; S.R.O.B., HA504/1/8.
[69] E.R.O., D/DP M22.
[70] C.U.L., EDC7/17/23/5; 7/17/25/4; 7/17/25/5; 7/17/25/7; 7/17/26/4.
[71] E.R.O., D/DHt M92.

Even if they accepted office, the chief pledges might 'spend all day making their presentments', which annoyed the East Hanning-field (Essex) steward in 1379, or not turn up to the view at all. The most remarkable case of this kind occurred at Fingrith (Essex) in 1376 when the June view was boycotted, and none of the fifteen chief pledges, and only ten of the (presumably) hundred or more tithing-men, attended, so that the business of the view had to be postponed until a court session held in the following December.[72]

Offenders against manorial discipline, such as those who failed to pay rents or other dues, might find that their goods or animals were seized in order to distrain them to pay up. At all times a reply might come in the form of a 'rescue', in which the tenant took back the distrained possessions, but cases seem to occur more frequently in the decade 1371–81. 'Rescue' was also sometimes accompanied by violence against the official concerned, like the minister of Canter-bury Cathedral Priory who was assaulted in 1372 by Thomas Creake of Adisham (Kent), for which Creake was amerced 4s. 0d.[73] An extreme case of an attack on a seigneurial official was the subject of a complaint by the abbot of St Augustine's Canterbury to the court of King's Bench in 1380. Roger Manston 'with other malefactors' assaulted the estate steward and prevented him from holding the abbot's court at Minster in Thanet, leading to disruption in the manorial administration, and a loss of income for the lord.[74]

Many lines of continuity can be seen between the events of the pre-revolt period and the 1381 outbreak. The manifestations of discontent made before the revolt, notably the insubordinate acts in lords' courts, were repeated in local incidents in 1381. The protests made before the revolt concerned issues that figured in the rebel demands to the king in 1381 – the abolition of serfdom and servile tenure, the removal of service beyond a simple cash rent, and the curtailing of lords' judicial power. In the agitations before 1381 and in the main revolt the local élite, such as the chief pledges, played a prominent role. Places that rose in the main revolt, such as East Hanningfield, Ingatestone and Thanet, had some experience of pre-revolt incidents.

Close links between the seigneurial policies of the years 1350–81 and the revolt itself can be substantiated if we return to our sample

---

[72] E.R.O., D/DP M833; D/Ht M92.
[73] C.C.L., U15/9 48357.
[74] P.R.O., K.B.27/479.

of eighty-nine rebels. In pre-revolt documents we can show that they experienced the routine incidents of manorial life: John Cok of Prittlewell (Essex) was in arrears with his rent; John Cok of Moze (Essex) was amerced for failing to repair a building; Edmund Gerneys and Thomas Gardyner of Little Barton (Suffolk), along with many others, allowed their animals to trespass on the demesne and were amerced.[75] Most of the rebels, especially those who were customary tenants, would expect to pay at least a few pence every year for such offences. Occasionally we can show that individual rebels had experienced especially harsh treatment before the revolt, notably from records of a court session held on 6 June 1381 at Thorrington (Essex), when two serfs were accused, in spite of their protests that they had already paid merchet, of having married off their daughters without permission, and Juliana and John Phelipp were punished for sheltering their own son and brother who had broken an employment contract, in an incident described above. All four people involved in these cases joined in the burning of the Thorrington court rolls a week later.[76]

Prominent among the rebels were those whose economic position was improving before 1381. John Philip of Brandon (Suffolk) accumulated at least five separate holdings of land in the 1370s as well as rising in his lord's service from warrener to bailiff.[77] Three Essex rebels, John Fillol, John Geffrey (both of Hanningfield) and James atte Ford of Takeley all acquired land in 1380. Geffrey, who had recently been appointed bailiff and moved into East Hanningfield from his Suffolk home, had bought a smallholding, and obtained the reversion of a further 15 acres. He was evidently about to build a new house, for which he had collected timber worth 8 marks. In the late 1370s Robert Wryghte of Foxearth was increasing the number of animals that he owned, and his wife became the chief brewer in the village. John Cole of Felixstowe (Suffolk) had bought a freeholding before the revolt, and John Herde of Berners Berwick (Essex) was leasing his lord's herd of cows.[78] The lords of these successful peasants were able to take advantage of their enterprise. John Fillol and James atte Ford both had to pay higher-than-

[75] E.R.O., D/DU 190/6; D/DGh M14; S.R.O.B., E7/24/1.3.
[76] St J.C., 97.25(1), 97.25(2a).
[77] S.R.O.B., J529/1–2; P.R.O., S.C.6/1304/31–36.
[78] E.R.O., D/DP M833 (Fillol and Geffrey); N.C., 3697 (Ford); E.R.O., D/DK M57–8; P.R.O., S.C.2/172/10 (Wryghte); S.R.O.I., HA119:50/3/80 (Cole); E.R.O., D/DHf M28, M45 (Herde).

average entry fines for their new purchase of land. Ford was actually in the process of paying at the time of the revolt a fine of 33*s*. 4*d*. for 18¾ acres of land (1*s*. 9*d*. per acre). Wryghte was being milked of large sums of money through the manor court; he was charged unusually high amounts for such offences as trespassing on the demesne, and his wife had to pay substantial brewing fines. Together they paid a total of 7*s*. 8*d*. in 1378, and 13*s*. 0*d*. in 1379, including an exceptionally high brewing fine of 10*s*. 0*d*. Here is direct evidence for the view that not just rising expectations, but actual achievements, were being exploited by a vigorous seigneurial administration, and that the victims were numbered among the 1381 rebels.

Rebels with a background of service in administrative positions, such as Godfrey Panyman of Mistley (Essex) and Thomas Gardyner of Little Barton (Suffolk), are known to have refused office, in the former case as a bailiff, the latter as a juror, before 1381.[79] It is tempting to see the involvement of so many local officials in the revolt as a development of such actions, leading to a widespread rejection of their ambiguous position, and an unequivocal siding with their neighbours against the constant demands of lords.

## GENERAL IMPLICATIONS

To interpret the revolt solely in terms of lord–tenant relationships is to take far too narrow a view of the events of 1381. The horizons of the rebels extended beyond their own village and manor, of necessity, because of the intrusion of the state into the lives of every rural community. The operation of royal justice had become particularly evident to the people of Essex, Suffolk and Norfolk in 1379 when the court of King's Bench made one of its infrequent journeys out of Westminster and held sessions under Sir John Cavendish at Chelmsford, Bury St Edmunds and Thetford.[80] The business of the royal courts had expanded in the mid-fourteenth century with the attempts to enforce the labour laws. Labour cases still occupied

[79] P.R.O., S.C.2/171/59, 60: the identification of Panyman is not entirely certain. The 1381 rebel was called Geoffrey, while the man who refused to act as bailiff is called Godfrey in the court rolls. If they were two individuals, they are likely to have been close relatives and the line of argument about attitudes to office-holding may still be relevant. For Gardyner's refusal see S.R.O.B., E7/24/1.3.

[80] *Proceedings before the Justices of the Peace in the Fourteenth and Fifteenth Centuries*, ed. B. H. Putnam (London, 1938), p. 32.

the attention of the Essex J.P.s in 1377–9, and cases are also recorded on the King's Bench plea rolls of 1379–81; in 1380 a long list of Suffolk outlaws includes a number of servants. Two servants of the future rebel, Thomas Sampson of Kersey, were fined in 1380 by King's Bench for taking excessive wages. Sampson acted as pledge for them, suggesting that he did not regard himself as the injured party in the case, and indeed he may have resented this interference in the competitive labour market. A cursory examination of the King's Bench records of 1379–81 reveals the names of eight other future rebels who were involved in trespasses or land disputes.[81] Their experiences with the law may well have had some influence on their behaviour in 1381. A radical dissatisfaction with royal justice in Essex in 1378 is apparent from the refusal of the constables of Dunmow Hundred to make any attempt to enforce the labour laws, an incident that was still concerning the authorities three years later.[82] Some of the victims of the rebels also had dealings with King's Bench on the eve of the revolt, such as John Sewall and John Ewell, respectively sheriff and escheator in Essex, and no doubt the progress through the courts of the cases of such influential figures was accompanied by rumours of partiality and corruption.

The king's wars also affected the lives of many people. Villagers might be involved in military activity, like the men from the hundred of Wye (Kent) who served in Calais and guarded the Kent coast in the early 1370s.[83] Taxes to pay for the war touched everyone, including the numerous smallholders and wage-earners after the introduction of poll-taxes in 1377. A reluctance to pay the conventional lay subsidies as well as the new tax is suggested by the scatter of legal disputes between collectors and non-payers found in the records of manorial courts, peace sessions and King's Bench in 1379–81. In the 1380–1 poll-tax that sparked off the revolt the lists show that future rebels contributed, no doubt with reluctance, but some rebels' names cannot be found in their village lists. Is it possible that they had evaded payment, almost as a first stage of

[81] P.R.O., K.B.27/475, 479, 480, 481.

[82] *Essex Sessions of the Peace*, ed. Furber, p. 169; P.R.O., K.B.27/481.

[83] P.R.O., S.C.2/182/21; references to service in coastal defence are rare, and the main French threat affected the whole Channel coast from Kent to Cornwall, not primarily the south-eastern counties which rebelled, so it seems unlikely that invasion fears were a major cause of the revolt, as argued in E. Searle and R. Burghart, 'The Defense of England and the Peasants' Revolt', *Viator*, iii (1972), pp. 365–89.

rebellion? A specific example would be John Fillol, a miller of Hanningfield (Essex), who appears in a list compiled by the tax-collectors in 1381 alone, without any reference to a wife. He had evidently concealed her, as after he was hanged for his part in the revolt, she recovered tenure of his holding.[84] The most important aspect of the poll-tax was, however, not its effect on individuals but its universality, shifting financial burdens everywhere on to the less well off, and taking away from every village élite their almost fifty-year-old right to assess and collect taxes, all in the cause of paying for a futile war.

While it is possible to demonstrate that individual rebels had suffered at the hands of both their lords and officials of the state, these specific frictions are inadequate to explain the whole rising. If, for example, the local tyranny of Thomas Hardyng of Manningtree and Mistley (Essex) provoked a rebellion in those places, why was it not directed solely against the offending lord?[85] The striking feature of the revolt is that it did not consist only of a mass of private vendettas; the rebels were willing to generalize their actions and demands. The rebels' behaviour was not always directly related to their personal grievances. To choose one example, Robert Wryghte of Foxearth, who had been so badly treated in his lord's court, went off in 1381 to plunder the property of the chief justice of King's Bench, Sir John Cavendish. One thinks also of the men of Kent, where there were no serfs, being provoked into revolt according to one account by the imprisonment of a serf from outside the county, or reviving the revolt in September 1381 on hearing a rumour that John of Gaunt had freed his serfs.[86] We may suspect that the rebels recognized the close connection between lordship and government, so that 'political' and 'social' grievances were linked in their minds. The seigneurial view of frankpledge enforced laws in the name of the king, including the labour laws; the royal courts were involved with social matters, villeinage cases or the enforcement of contracts between employers and employees; the same men acted as royal justices and estate stewards, and held manors of their own. Dr Maddicott has explored the long history of collusion between royal judges and landowners, represented at the time of the revolt by

[84] P.R.O., E179/107/63; E.R.O., D/DP M833.
[85] A. J. Prescott, 'London in the Peasants' Revolt: A Portrait Gallery', *The London Journal*, vii (1981), p. 127.
[86] *The Anonimalle Chronicle, 1333–1381*, ed. V. H. Galbraith (Manchester, 1927), p. 136; Flaherty, 'Sequel to the Great Rebellion in Kent', p. 76.

John Cavendish's association with the monks of Bury.[87] We can only guess at the suspicions caused by such arrangements as John Bampton doubling as an Essex J.P. and estate steward of Barking Abbey.[88] Thomas atte Ook of Suffolk, like Cavendish and Bampton, was killed by the rebels in 1381, and his property was plundered. He combined employment as steward of the bishopric of Ely with service as Justice of the Peace and on many commissions in Essex, Norfolk and Suffolk. In his role of steward atte Ook had to deal with the difficult tenants of Brandon, who on one occasion in 1370 refused to appear before him in spite of a formal summons. As a royal official, he served on commissions with such figures as Cavendish, Bampton and Belknap, including one with Cavendish and others in 1378 to deal with a conspiracy of tenants to withdraw services and customs at Framsden (Suffolk).[89] Such men represented the power of government in its many guises, and it is understandable that the rebels should have seen their superiors as involved in a single system of corrupt authority.

It is not possible to attribute any single aim to a very heterogeneous group of rebels. We need to seek no profound motive behind acts of simple pillage. A complicating factor must have been the existence of feuds and conflicts within peasant society that helped to condition attitudes and alliances before and during the revolt. The chief pledges and other officials must have been involved in such rivalries, hence some of the dissatisfaction and violence expressed against them. An example would be William Draper and his son Thomas, both of South Elmham (Suffolk). William served regularly as chief pledge in the 1370s and 1380s, and was clearly quite prosperous. In 1372 the Drapers were involved in a bitter conflict with members of the Erl family, involving both personal violence and litigation over trespass in the manor court. The dispute may well have been over land, as fourteen years earlier William Draper had some connection with a tenement called Erl's.[90] Such quarrels were frequent and other examples could be

---

[87] J. R. Maddicott, *Law and Lordship: Royal Justices as Retainers in Thirteenth- and Fourteenth-Century England* (Past and Present Supplement no. 4, Oxford, 1978), pp. 63–4.

[88] Sturman, 'Barking Abbey: A Study of its External and Internal Administration from the Conquest to the Dissolution', pp. 40, 212.

[89] S.R.O.B., J529/1–2; P.R.O., S.C.6/1304/31–6; *Cal. Pat. Rolls, 1370–4*, pp. 36, 239, 489, 491; *1374–7*, pp. 137, 276, 332, 486–7; *1377–81*, pp. 299, 305, 474.

[90] S.R.O.I., HA12/C2/14, 15, 18.

given involving individual rebels. While in no sense a cause of revolt, the decision to participate may well have been coloured by alliances and enmities created by feuds, so that the involvement of the Drapers ensured that the Erls stayed at home, ready to inform the authorities after the events had ended. Many inexplicable episodes in the revolt, especially apparently motiveless assaults and attacks, must owe their origins to long-remembered grievances and jealousies. Such factors might also solve such puzzles as the appearance of a King's Langley (Herts.) man, John Marler, as both a participant in the revolt and the victim of a rebel from Berkhamstead![91]

However, while accepting the existence of many complexities of motive, to discuss 1381 primarily in terms of rivalries within villages would reduce the rising to the absurd. The demands made in London seem to indicate an ability to think in general terms, and there is some evidence to support the view that the leaders in the capital were voicing radical opinions widespread among the rebels. The rebels came from the manors of all kinds of landlord, not just from the estates where the regime was particularly harsh, like those of the countess of Norfolk or the bishopric of Norwich. For example, the revolt found support at Havering-atte-Bower (Essex), where the tenants enjoyed the extensive privileges of a royal demesne manor.[92] And then there is the problem of Kent. At first glance the freedom of Kentish peasants and the feebleness of seigneurial authority in the county, where the manorial courts lacked many powers normally found in their counterparts north of the Thames, might be thought to have prevented the tenants of Kent developing any strong sense of grievance against their lords. Yet frictions and insubordination are recorded in Kentish court rolls before 1381, and in the revolt itself manorial documents were destroyed, and services refused. Throughout the four counties it is therefore difficult to discern evidence of much discrimination in the rebels' attitudes towards landlords, which contrasts with their highly selective choice of 'political' targets. This could be taken to mean that many rebels were hostile to lordship in general, a view that found its ultimate expression in the well-known Smithfield demand for the division of lordship among all men.

[91] P.R.O., S.C.2/177/47; Réville and Petit-Dutaillis, *Le soulèvement des travailleurs*, p. 39.
[92] McIntosh, 'Land, Tenure and Population in the Royal Manor of Havering, Essex', pp. 17–18.

The burning of court rolls, again involving no apparent selection of particular lords or types of lords, should not be underestimated as an act of radical rebellion. A view of the aims of the rebels of Wivenhoe (Essex) was given by the clerk who wrote the record of 'the first court . . . after the burning of all the court rolls'. He stated that the tenants claimed to hold land 'at their own will for ever, freely, and not at the will of the lord'. In short they wished to abolish all customary tenures, depriving the lord of a good deal of his power and wealth, 'in disinheritance of the lord' as the clerk put it.[93]

The Smithfield demands envisaged the removal of the machinery of government, so that the only law was to be the 'law of Winchester'. When we find that so many of the rebels had experience of government at village level, this aim does not seem as naïve as is often assumed. The chief pledges of Holwell (Herts.) were fully aware of the law mentioned at Smithfield when in 1377 they complained that the village constable did not summon the watch 'according to the statute of Winchester'.[94] They could imagine (as we know happened in the Flemish revolt of the 1320s) that local government of a kind could function without direction from above, with order enforced by the local militia provided for in the statute.

Finally we must allow for the millenarian enthusiasm that gave the revolt a strong impetus. The controversy over the collection of the poll-tax helped to create the volatile atmosphere of the summer of 1381. Other events may have contributed to the sense of excitement, incidents which may seem trivial to us, such as the great storm of May 1381 – we know that the gale of January 1362 had a major impact on contemporaries, who saw in such happenings warnings of imminent catastrophe.[95]

## CONCLUSION

Rural unrest in the late fourteenth century can be readily explained in terms of the tension between entrenched lordly power and the changes, or potential changes, in peasant society. These tensions were felt acutely in the south-east because of the importance of the

---

[93] E.R.O., T/B 122; W. C. Waller, 'A Note on the Manor of Wivenhoe', *Trans. Essex Archaeol. Soc.*, new ser., x (1909), pp. 320–2.

[94] G.L., 10, 312/163.

[95] Newton, *Thaxted in the Fourteenth Century*, pp. 97, 99, on the 1381 storm. For reactions to the 1362 gale, see M. W. Bloomfield, *Piers Plowman as a Fourteenth-Century Apocalypse* (New Brunswick, 1962), p. 114.

market economy in the region. Dissatisfaction with the government, especially with the administration of the law, was bound up with resentment against landlords. The outbreak of a major revolt came when the poll-tax provided the whole region with a single common grievance. The specific form taken by the revolt, in terms of its organization and demands, reflected its origins in rural society. The village élite, acting from a position of confidence and authority, gave the revolt leadership and coherence. Out of the diversity of motives found in any popular movement emerged ideas and actions hostile not just to serfdom and servile tenures, but also to the very existence of lordship, championing the realizable goal of independent and self-governing village communities.

# 2. The 'Great Rumour' of 1377 and Peasant Ideology*

## ROSAMOND FAITH

In the west Berkshire village of Coleshill the harvest of 1377 was disrupted because 'all the tenants who [should] work at harvest-time did not work on account of a great rumour (*prout magnum rumorem*) among various other tenants'.[1] It seems very likely that this 'great rumour' was, or was connected with, a little-known peasant movement involving at least forty villages in Wiltshire, Hampshire, Surrey, Sussex and Devon. It seems to have come to a head and died away four years before the great revolt of 1381 began and took place mainly in an area not generally considered to have been much affected by the events of that momentous year. It does not appear to have had any of the broad political aims of the Mile End and Smithfield programmes, being concerned rather with the local goals of achieving personal freedom and the abolition of labour services for particular groups of peasants. Its legitimizing ideas seem to have come not from egalitarian hopes of a better future but from views of an idealized past. It was conservative to the point of archaism, and the book that largely inspired it was not the Bible, but Domesday Book. In spite of its apparent differences from the 1381 revolt, however, this episode, I believe, illustrates some themes in medieval peasant ideology which played an important part in the events of that year and endured for a long time afterwards. We know very little about the episode and its leaders; no doubt much remains to be discovered.[2] It clearly made a great

* I wish to thank Dr D. Crook, Dr E. M. Hallam and Dr J. Post of the Public Record Office, Prof. R. H. Hilton, and the members of the University of Birmingham medieval graduate seminar for their interest and assistance. Since this paper was delivered, further research on the topic has been made possible by a grant from the Small Grants Research Fund in the Humanities of the British Academy.

[1] Public Record Office (hereafter P.R.O.), S.C.2/154/1 (Simon and Jude, 1 Richard II), quoted in R. J. Faith, 'The Peasant Land-Market in Berkshire in the Later Middle Ages' (Univ. of Leicester Ph.D. thesis, 1962), p. 205; *V.C.H. Berks.*, ii, p. 189; M. McKisack, *The Fourteenth Century, 1307–1399* (Oxford, 1959), p. 337.

[2] J. H. Tillotson, 'Peasant Unrest in the England of Richard II: Some Evidence from Royal Records', *Historical Studies* (University of Melbourne), xvi (1974–5),

impression on contemporaries and almost certainly gave rise to the parliamentary petition of 1377 which has often been quoted as evidence of general unrest.[3] This petition, presented to the October parliament of that year, has a distinct note of panic. It speaks of fears of civil war and treason and of the danger of a Jacquerie or general peasant rising such as had 'recently' occurred in France. These fears were caused, the petitioners say, by a specific and odd-sounding peasant movement:

in many parts of the kingdom . . . the villeins and tenants of land in villeinage who owe services and customs to the lord . . . have (through the advice, procurement, maintenance and abetting of certain persons) purchased in the king's court for their own profit exemplifications from the Book of Domesday concerning those manors and vills where these villeins and tenants live. By colour of these exemplifications and through misunderstanding them as well as the malicious interpretation made of them by the said counsellors, procurors, maintainors and abettors, they have withdrawn and still withdraw the customs and services due to their lords, holding that they are completely discharged of all manner of service both from their persons and their holdings.

This was clearly more than a spontaneous and uncoordinated uprising. It had a common aim and quite a high degree of organization: 'To sustain their errors and inventions they have collected large sums of money among themselves to meet their costs and expenses, and many of them have now come to court to secure assistance for their designs.' The petitioners asked for immediate remedies 'directed against the said counsellors . . . as well as the said villeins . . . and especially those who have now come to court'. Their fears were evidently taken seriously, for the reply enabled special commissions to be set up to inquire into withdrawals of labour services and to try the rebels and their counsellors and imprison them without bail.[4] Three such commissions had already been appointed, which provide valuable information about the location of the revolt: on 1 September concerning 'men and tenants of divers lordships in

pp. 1–16, which did not come to my notice until after this paper was delivered, discusses the evidence for the revolt that appears in the Patent Rolls; principally enrolled exemplifications (see below, pp. 71–2) and judicial commissions.

[3] *Rotuli Parliamentorum*, 6 vols. (Record Comm., London, 1783), iii, pp. 21–2. The petition is translated in *The Peasants' Revolt of 1381*, ed. R. B. Dobson (London, 1970), pp. 76–8.

[4] *Rotuli Parliamentorum*, iii, p. 22.

Wiltshire' and in the county of Southampton, on 10 September concerning the tenants of St Mary Ottery in Devon, and on 1 October for Surrey. More followed in 1378: on 8 April 'touching bond men and bond tenants of the Bishop of Winchester at Farnham', on 18 May concerning the abbot of Chertsey's men at Chobham, Thorpe and Egham (Surrey), on 20 May in respect of the abbess of Shaftesbury's tenants on eight of her manors in Wiltshire and Dorset, on 22 May in respect of the prior of Bath's tenants on two Somerset manors and the tenants of the lord of Aston Bampton, Oxfordshire.[5] It is clear from the wording of these commissions that a very specific kind of peasant strike had been troubling the authorities, of precisely the kind that the parliamentary petition referred to: the tenants of the warden and college of St Mary Ottery, Devon, had been withholding services 'under the pretext of letters patent of exemplification of an extract from Domesday Book by virtue whereof they claim to be exempt from such rents and services'; the Wiltshire tenants had done exactly the same thing, and made 'confederations' to do so. The bishop of Winchester's tenants at Farnham 'who have long rebelliously withdrawn the customary services' had bound themselves by oath to resist him and his ministers, and the abbot of Chertsey's men in three Surrey villages, similarly withholding services, 'daily congregate for further mischief'. Domesday Book is not mentioned in connection with the Farnham strike but was, it appears, very much involved at Chertsey. A petition from the abbot, associated with the parliamentary petition of 1377, describes a riot which had taken place on four of the abbey manors, Chobham, Thorpe, Frimley and Egham. Here, according to the abbot, the tenants who had paid and rendered their due and accustomed services since the abbey's foundation, had now, by the wicked counsel, alliance and confederacy of many tenants of similar condition, purchased a patent called an exemplification by which they supposed themselves to be free and of free condition and that they did not have to pay or do anything for their lords except rent and suit of court. When the abbot's ministers had tried to distrain them they had resisted with armed force and threatened to burn down the abbey and the monks in it. The abbot had obtained a writ directing the sheriff of Surrey to

---

[5] *Cal. Pat. Rolls, 1377–81*, pp. 50 (Wiltshire), 20 (St Mary Ottery), 204 (Farnham), 251 (Chobham, Thorpe, Egham; abbess of Shaftesbury's tenants; prior of Bath's tenants; Richard de Molyns's tenants).

take distraints, but the rioters had nearly killed the sheriff's men and threatened that 'a thousand men in this district would be killed' if they did not have their way.[6]

A statute was issued in response to the parliamentary petition. It repeated the gist of it and gave statutory authority to the issuing of special commissions.[7] It gives us the valuable additional information that the exemplifications of Domesday Book, which were the cause of so much trouble, had been 'caused to come in the Parliament and . . . declared in the same Parliament'. It is possible that this was the occasion referred to in the petition on which many of the rebellious tenants had 'come to court to secure assistance for their designs'. Both the statute and the reply to the petition are adamant in denying the curious association of Domesday Book and freedom on which the villeins had based their case:

> As regards the exemplifications made and granted in Chancery, it is declared in Parliament that these neither can nor ought to have any value or relevance to the question of personal freedom, nor can they be used to change the personal terms of tenure and its customs or to the prejudice of the lords' rights to have their services and customs as they used to do in the past.

The special commissions which were appointed seem to have left no traceable records[8] and it may be that they never in fact sat. The records of the King's Bench and justices in eyre for the relevant years have so far yielded very little further information. The rolls of a Wiltshire session of the justices of the peace, before whom one might expect offenders to have been brought in the first instance, have been printed by B. H. Putnam and give us the name of one of the 'counsellors, maintainors and abettors' of the movement in those parts but no more.[9] Beyond this, however, judicial records of the public courts have so far added little to our knowledge of the affair, and it may well be that once the initial panic had died down the great landlords concerned found that their own manorial courts proved adequate to deal with their rebellious tenants. The villeins of landlords of many small estates may have been involved without the fact ever coming to light: such landlords might not have been willing or able to request the appointment of a special commission

[6] P.R.O., S.C.8/103/5106.

[7] 1 Richard II, *cap.* 6, in *The Statutes of the Realm*, ed. A. Luders *et al.*, 11 vols. (Record Comm., London, 1810–28), ii, pp. 2–3.

[8] Information kindly supplied by Dr D. Crook of the Public Record Office.

[9] See pp. 60–2 below.

on their behalf, as such powerful figures as the bishop of Winchester and the abbot of Chertsey were able to do. Our knowledge of the 'great rumour' depends at present – apart from the parliamentary petition and statute, and the terms of the special commissions already quoted – on the existence of a number of documents which were the basis of the 'exemplifications from the Book of Domesday' which seem to have played so important a part in it, and on references in the Patent Rolls to the enrolment of these exemplifications.

The compilers of the 1377 petition used the word 'exemplification' advisedly, for it is a legal term to describe letters patent under the Great Seal which were certified copies of other documents – in this case of extracts from Domesday Book. Exemplifications could be made of many kinds of document: copies of legal decisions or charters were commonly obtained in this way. They were obtained by means of the writ *certiorari* (also known as *certis de causis*), most commonly used to transfer legal proceedings, and their records with them, from lower courts into King's Bench, but also available to private individuals who wished to have authenticated copies of documents in the possession of government departments or courts. In the case of exemplifications from Domesday Book the writ would go from Chancery to the treasurer and barons of the Exchequer. The return to the writ, consisting of the required extract, would be sent back to Chancery with the writ itself. It is these writs and returns which survive among the public records. A copy of the return would then be issued to the interested party in the form of letters patent under the Great Seal (and could, for a fee, be enrolled, although this was not always done).[10] The whole process, though not particularly complicated, nevertheless demanded a certain amount of legal knowledge on the part of the applicant, and a fair amount of cash. Apart from the cost of the writ, exemplification and enrolment, and the inevitable payments to officials, he would have had to meet the cost of a few nights' stay in London, for there was always a delay of several days between the issuing of the writ and its return. Yet there survive in the Public Record Office writs issued between autumn 1376 and early 1378 on behalf of the people of no fewer than forty villages, chiefly in Surrey, Hampshire and Wiltshire, who had applied for exemplifications of extracts

[10] For Domesday exemplifications, see V. H. Galbraith, *Domesday Rebound* (London, 1954), pp. 48–9.

from Domesday Book relating to the manors of which they were tenants.

There was of course nothing new about appealing to Domesday Book; recorded examples of such appeals appear to have become more common from the time of Edward I with the increased emphasis on the need for written verification for claims to rights and property.[11] People appealed to Domesday, or, in the legal phrase, 'vouched' it, for a variety of reasons. Questions of lordship over particular lands were settled in this way. Townspeople applied to Domesday over questions of borough status and burghal privileges: the years immediately after 1381 saw a small outbreak of boroughs requesting copies of Domesday entries. Very occasionally – and this is an aspect which loomed very large in 1377 – questions of dues and services were the subject of an appeal when people thought, we would say mistakenly, that Domesday could decide the issue. However, as is well known, the overwhelming majority of recorded appeals were made by tenants seeking to establish that the manors in which they held land were part of the 'ancient demesne of the Crown'.[12] To hold land as a privileged villein or 'villein sokeman' on such a manor brought definite advantages to the tenant. Even though he was not technically a free man: he was not obliged to attend the hundred and county courts, to pay geld or toll or contribute to the *murdrum* fine, and he only had to pay tallage – even when the manor was no longer held directly by the king – when the rest of the king's tenants were tallaged. Although, like other villeins, he could not bring an action concerning his land against his lord in a public court, he had his own legal forms which he could use in the manorial court or before visiting royal justices: the 'little writ of right close' and the process known as *monstraverunt*. The aspect of his special status which came to assume the greatest importance by far, however, was that the rents and services of the 'villein sokeman', as he was called, were fixed and certain, and could not be increased.

The whole question of 'ancient demesne' – land held by the crown at some time in the past and considered to have retained its special character and special protection for its tenants, ever since –

[11] M. T. Clanchy, *From Memory to Written Record: England, 1066–1307* (London, 1979), p. 19.

[12] R. H. Hilton, 'Peasant Movements in England before 1381', in E. M. Carus-Wilson (ed.), *Essays in Economic History*, 3 vols. (London, 1954–62), ii, pp. 73–90.

is a complicated one. We have to bear in mind not only what ancient demesne actually was – and scholarly opinion has changed radically about that – but also what people in the past thought it was; not only what lawyers and legal writers thought, but what peasants, often quite mistakenly, thought. Summarizing crudely a century of scholarly work on the subject, one can say that the earlier modern view, held by Vinogradoff and Maitland, was that the comparatively privileged legal position of tenants on manors held by the crown at the time of the Conquest, 'on the day that King Edward was alive and dead', or in 1086, and which continued when these manors were subsequently alienated, 'was connected in principle with the conditions of things in Saxon times' and preserved a certain degree of Anglo-Saxon freedom. R. S. Hoyt radically challenged this view, showing that the whole idea of 'ancient demesne' was itself 'the creation of the Angevin monarchy' and that the king, far from preserving ancient freedoms because he was, in Maitland's words, 'the best of landlords', was rather the most prudent of landlords, interested in preserving and protecting the tenantry on his manors chiefly in order to safeguard their ability to pay tallage. The notion of the 'ancient' demesne of the crown is itself a thirteenth-century innovation, in which 'ancient' simply meant 'former'.[13]

The question of whether particular manors were or were not ancient demesne was at first settled by local juries, but from the mid-thirteenth century people also began to appeal to Domesday Book to settle it and from the reign of Edward I (and in particular, Hoyt suggests, in response to the articles of inquiry about royal demesne in the 1274 inquest) this became the normal method of proof.[14]

---

[13] P. Vinogradoff, *Villainage in England* (Oxford, 1892), pp. 89–126 at p. 123; F. Pollock and F. W. Maitland, *The History of English Law before the Time of Edward I*, 2nd edn, 2 vols. (Cambridge, 1968), i, pp. 383–486; R. S. Hoyt, *The Royal Demesne in English Constitutional History, 1066–1272* (Ithaca, N.Y., 1950). M. K. McIntosh, 'The Privileged Villeins of the English Ancient Demesne', *Viator*, vii (1976), makes an important new contribution to this discussion, showing the importance to tenants of access to the royal courts, access which became denied to the generality of villeins but vestiges of which were preserved for villeins on manors which were, or had been, the king's. Paul R. Hyams, *Kings, Lords, and Peasants in Medieval England* (Oxford, 1980), pp. 246–8, follows Hoyt in regarding ancient demesne doctrines as an aspect of 'royal estate management', and concludes that 'Royal self-interest . . . urged the protection of tenants of former royal demesne' (*ibid.*, p. 247).

[14] Clanchy, *From Memory to Written Record*, p. 19.

Domesday Book would seem to make things clear enough: the very layout of entries for particular counties, which begin with 'The King's land (*Terra Regis*)', gives such information pride of place. Yet the Soviet historian M. A. Barg has shown that for the jurors who provided the information which went to make up the Hundred Rolls, for instance, 'there was no single universal criterion underlying the establishment of ancient demesne status', although they most usually took inclusion among the royal lands of 1086 as the test. Moreover, and this is particularly interesting in the present context, they counted as ancient demesne some manors which Domesday had not numbered as among the royal lands in either 1066 or 1086. They were also capable of stretching legal memory back as far as the reign of Aethelstan in the tenth century to settle the question.[15] The more we investigate the ideas current in the movement of 1377 the less out of the way will such attitudes seem.

Barg's study of individual legal cases shows that even when Domesday Book seemed to give a clear answer 'yes' to the question 'Is this manor ancient demesne?', the lawyers tended to shift the ground of the argument to ask the question 'Are these tenants entitled to privileged status?', and to answer, as a rule, 'no'. He concluded from an examination of thirty ancient demesne cases in the collection known as *Placitorum Abbreviatio*[16] that in only one did the tenants win their case, in spite of the fact that the Domesday evidence established ancient demesne in over half the examples.

'Domesday does nothing for them (*nil fac' pro eis*),' said the defendant when his tenants of the ancient demesne manor of Tavistock claimed security of tenure by doing fixed services, 'because in those ancient demesne manors where the tenants have "certain status (*certum statum*)" it is found that there are so many sokemen and so many of a different condition, but in this manor it is not found that there are any sokemen, but all are serfs and villeins.'[17] Vinogradoff thought that the argument in this case, in focusing on tenants and tenures rather than on the nature of the land, was a legal aberration; Barg found it typical of a legal trend.[18]

[15] M. A. Barg, 'The Villeins of Ancient Demesne', in *Studi in Memoria di Federigo Melis*, 5 vols. (Rome, 1978), i, pp. 213–37.
[16] *Placitorum in Domo Capitulari Westmonasteriensi Asservatorum Abbreviatio*, ed. W. Illingworth (Record Comm., London, 1811).
[17] *Ibid.*, pp. 270–1.
[18] Vinogradoff, *Villainage in England*, pp. 119–20; Barg, 'Villeins of Ancient Demesne', p. 230.

The upshot of this recent work on ancient demesne has been to show that it was not an old and fixed legal concept, but one that was new and developing, influenced by pressures from groups with conflicting interests. Chief among these groups were landlords and tenants. The majority of cases in which ancient demesne was an issue came to comprise those in which tenants complained of increased services or customs, or the imposition of new ones; R. H. Hilton has shown how these are a response to increased seigneurial pressure.[19] During these conflicts each side was prepared to interpret the 'law' in its own interest and in its own way, and according to its own conceptions, or misconceptions, of what the 'law' actually was. Barg has shown how the 'law' that customs on ancient manors could not be increased was on occasion set aside in the landlord's interests, and concluded that, apart from a tiny group of privileged sokemen, 'the tenants on the manors of ancient demesne . . . found themselves, in the legal practice of the thirteenth century, just as defenceless as did their fellow-villeins on ordinary manors'.[20] However the belief that the king's own tenants – or tenants on lands which had once been the king's – were owed special protection continued among the peasantry, many of whom continued to place their trust in Domesday Book.

The painstaking work of generations of Domesday scholars has accustomed us to valuing Domesday Book primarily as a historical source; less attention has been paid to the part it played in the popular imagination. The very fact that what was essentially an Anglo-Norman fiscal document had acquired its imposing biblical name in the vernacular by the 1170s, long before it was apparently put to any extensive practical use, shows that it was known to, and revered by, the English-speaking population. FitzNeal, from whose *Dialogue of the Exchequer* the earliest use of the name comes, tells us a little about the folklore that had grown up round it by his day:

> This book is metaphorically called by the native English, Domesday, i.e. the Day of Judgement . . . when this book is appealed to on those matters which it contains its sentence cannot be quashed or set aside with impunity. That is why we have called the book 'the Book of Judgement', not because it contains

---

[19] Hilton, 'Peasant Movements in England before 1381', pp. 78–82.
[20] Barg, 'Villeins of Ancient Demesne', pp. 236–7.

decisions on various difficult points but because its decisions, like those of the Last Judgement, are unalterable.[21]

(Even today it retains its hold over the popular imagination: the staff of the Public Record Office can testify to the number of visitors who trustingly expect any number of questions about their home villages to be answered by 'searching Domesday Book'.)

Bearing in mind, then, that even for professional lawyers the concept of ancient demesne was not an entirely fixed one, that a tradition had been established of 'vouching Domesday', and that the book itself had its own charisma, perhaps it will not seem so inexplicable to us that in 1377 large numbers of people pinned their hopes of freedom, however mistakenly, on an appeal to Domesday Book. It is not even quite clear that the tenants who applied for exemplifications from Domesday in 1377 *were* in fact claiming ancient demesne status. The writs which were issued on their behalf certainly imply that they were: the majority contain the phrase 'to ascertain whether the vill of X is of the ancient demesne of the crown or not'. It is just possible, however, that this phrase was inserted by the Chancery clerks, on the grounds that it represented a recognized reason for applying for exemplification. However, if this claim was made in good faith, in the majority of cases the tenants must have been disappointed: in almost none of the manors involved did Domesday in fact say anything which would support it. The following summary of the claims makes this clear and shows, too, the extent and chronology of the movement.[22]

Two writs *certiorari* were issued in late 1376 (18 October and 14 November) to ascertain whether the bishop of Chichester's manor of Amberley (Sussex) and the church of Lambeth's manor of

---

21 *Dialogus de Scaccario*, ed. C. Johnson (London, 1950), p. 64. Domesday Book was also sometimes referred to as 'the book of Winchester'. This has led to the suggestion that there may have been a connection between ancient demesne claims and the mysterious demand of Wat Tyler at Smithfield that 'there should be no law but the law of Winchester (*qe nulle lay deveroit estre fors la lay de Wynchestre*)': *The Anonimalle Chronicle, 1333–1381*, ed. V. H. Galbraith (Manchester, 1927), p. 147. The present essay argues for giving such claims more importance and wider implications among peasant ideas than has previously been done. However, the phrase 'the book of Winchester' seems only to have been used infrequently: it does not figure in any of the ancient demesne cases in the *Placitorum Abbreviatio*, where 'the book of the Exchequer called Domesday' or a similar expression is used, as in the case of the writs *certis de causis*.

22 References for applications for exemplifications, the enrolment of exemplifications, and the Domesday holders of the manors concerned are given in the Appendix, pp. 71–3 below.

Lambeth (Surrey) were ancient demesne or not. Both manors had been in the hands of their 1377 owners in 1066. On 7 March writs were issued 'at the supplication of the tenants' of the bishop of Winchester's manor of Farnham (Surrey) and 'at the request of the tenants of Crondall (Hampshire)'; Farnham was a bishopric manor in 1066, Crondall 'was always the church's (*semper fuit in ecclesia*)'. On 8 April writs were issued inquiring whether four more manors of the bishopric of Winchester in Hampshire – Highclere, Ecchinswell, Woodhay and Ashmansworth – were ancient demesne or not. All had belonged to the bishop in 1066. Writs of 14 April and 20 April made the same inquiry about Froyle (Hampshire), then the property of the nunnery of St Mary's, Winchester, and, according to Domesday Book, 'always so held', and four Chertsey Abbey manors in Surrey: Thorpe, Egham, Chobham and Cobham, all listed as among the abbey's lands in 1066. The next writ, of 10 May, for exemplification of the entry regarding Whitchurch (Hampshire) – St Swithun's, Winchester, and so held in 1066 – was not specifically an ancient demesne inquiry. On 5 June a writ was issued 'at the request of the men of Warfield, Berkshire to ascertain whether the tenures (*tenure*) and lordships (*dominia*) within the hundred of Ripplesmere in the county of Berkshire are of the ancient demesne of the crown of England or not'. The Domesday text for Ripplesmere hundred, exemplified in reply to this, was complicated: only the vill of Warfield itself appears in the *Terra Regis*, but four other vills, *Ortone*, Losfield, Clewer and Dedworth, were held from the king in the time of either King Edward or King William. On 12 July writs were issued to inquire whether the manors of St Mary's, Winchester, at All Cannings and Urchfont (Wiltshire) were ancient demesne. These were followed during the next four weeks by requests for exemplifications from the tenants of sixteen more manors in Wiltshire and one just over the Berkshire border, as follows (their Domesday holders are given in parentheses): 16 July, Stanton St Bernard and South Newton (St Mary's, Wilton); 25 July, Bishops Cannings (bishop of Salisbury); 1 August, Manningford Abbots and Pewsey (St Peter's, Winchester); 2 August, Melksham (lands of the king); Bradford-on-Avon (church of Shaftesbury) and Steeple Ashton (church of Romsey); 3 August, Christian Malford (St Mary's, Glastonbury); 6 August, Kintbury (church of Amesbury); before 5 August, Sutton Mandeville and Wroughton (St Swithun's, Winchester); 8 August, Badbury (St Mary's,

Glastonbury), Chisledon (St Peter's, Winchester) and Liddington (St Mary's, Shaftesbury); 10 August, Chilmark and Wylye (St Mary's, Wilton). (All these manors were in Wiltshire except for Kintbury, which was in Berkshire.) Apart from Bensington or Benson (Oxfordshire) on 13 December, and two Sussex manors of St Peter's, Winchester, at Southease and Donnington – all of which were ancient demesne inquiries – requests for exemplifications seem to have come to a sudden stop in the middle of August, doubtless as a result of the swift retaliation of the authorities. Yet of all the manors known to have been the subject of ancient demesne inquiries in 1376–8 and all those whose tenants took action on the basis of Domesday exemplifications, only three would have satisfied the conventional legal criteria for ancient demesne status. These three were Melksham, Benson and Warfield. It is a striking fact, however, that very many of the places involved had been royal property *before* the Conquest, in some cases long before.[23] Several had been given by the king as part of the original or

---

[23] The earliest evidence for the grant of the manors mentioned in the text, pp. 52–4, to their Domesday holders is given below. The abbreviations used are *A.S.C.*: P. H. Sawyer, *Anglo-Saxon Charters, an Annotated List and Bibliography* (Roy. Hist. Soc., London, 1968); Finberg, *Wessex*: H. P. R. Finberg, *The Early Charters of Wessex* (Leicester, 1964). *All Cannings*, Wilts.: *V.C.H. Hants.*, ii, p. 122; *V.C.H. Wilts.*, x, p. 23. *Amberley*, Sussex: *A.S.C.*, nos. 232, 1291. *Ashmansworth*, Hants.: Finberg, *Wessex*, no. 42. *Badbury*, Wilts.: Finberg, *Wessex*, nos. 222, 273. *Bensington* or *Benson*, Oxon.: *A.S.C.*, no. 887. *Bishops Cannings*, Wilts.: *V.C.H. Wilts.*, vii, p. 187. *Bradford-on-Avon*, Wilts.: Finberg, *Wessex*, no. 1001. *Bromham*, Wilts.: *A.S.C.*, no. 887. *Chilmark*, Wilts.: Finberg, *Wessex*, no. 235. *Chisledon*, Wilts.: H. P. R. Finberg, 'The Churls of Hurstbourne', in H. P. R. Finberg, *Lucerna* (London, 1964), pp. 131–43. *Chobham*, Surrey: *A.S.C.*, no. 1165, and see nos. 420, 752, 1035, and 1094 for spurious charters recording the grant of Chobham to Chertsey Abbey. *Christian Malford*, Wilts.: Finberg, *Wessex*, no. 251. *Clewer*, Berks.: no pre-Domesday information. *Cobham*, Surrey: no authentic charter survives recording the grant of Cobham to Chertsey Abbey, but see *A.S.C.*, nos. 1181, 420, 752, 1035, and *A.S.C.*, no. 1165, recording the grant of Chobham. *Crondall*, Hants.: Finberg, *Wessex*, nos. 25, 85, 120, 122, 128, 129 and p. 242. *Dedworth*, Berks.: no pre-Domesday information. *Donnington*, Sussex: *A.S.C.*, no. 746. *Easthampstead*, Berks.: B. F. Harvey, *Westminster Abbey and its Estates in the Middle Ages* (Oxford, 1977), p. 27, n. 1. *Ecchinswell*, Hants.: Finberg, *Wessex*, no. 48. *Egham*, Surrey: *A.S.C.*, no. 1165, and see *ibid.*, nos. 420, 752, 1035, 1093 and 1094 for spurious charters recording royal grants of Egham. *Farnham*, Surrey: *A.S.C.*, nos. 235, 382, 818, and see Finberg, *Wessex*, nos. 109–19. *Froyle*, Hants.: no pre-Domesday information. *Highclere*, Hants.: Finberg, *Wessex*, nos. 5, 46, 77, 112. *Kintbury*, Berks.: *A.S.C.*, no. 1533. *Lambeth*, Surrey: *A.S.C.*, no. 1036. *Liddington*, Wilts.: Finberg, *Wessex*, no. 252. '*Losfelle*', Berks.: no pre-Domesday information. *Manningford Abbots*, Wilts.: Finberg, *Wessex*, nos. 323, 326. *Melksham*, Wilts.: no pre-Domesday information. '*Ortone*', Berks.: no pre-Domesday information. *Ottery*

very early endowment of the early minsters or monasteries: for instance Caedwalla gave Farnham to the church of Winchester and Amberley to the church of Selsey in the 680s. Highclere was given to Winchester in 749 by Cuthred. Other lands were given to endow the ninth-century royal foundations at Winchester: the New Minster (later Hyde Abbey) and Nunnaminster, founded by Alfred and his queen and continued by Edward. Chisledon is an example of such endowment. The tenth century saw a flood of royal donations to monastic houses. This was when the New Minster received Pewsey from Edmund and St Mary's, Wilton South Newton, while Farnham, which the monks of Winchester had lost, was restored to them by Edgar. It was in Edgar's reign (959–75) that the monastic revival received especial impetus. The gift of Steeple Ashton to Romsey Abbey dates from this time, and it was no doubt the traditional role of Edgar as benefactor of the monasteries that led to later charters being forged purporting to come from his reign, as did one granting Thorpe to Chertsey Abbey. Examples of later royal gifts are Bradford-on-Avon to Shaftesbury Abbey (Ethelred) and East-hampstead to Westminster Abbey (Edward the Confessor). In many cases, of course, it is impossible to determine when and how a particular place first came into the hands of its Domesday holder. The strong archival tradition at Winchester means that the Winchester estates are particularly well documented, but in the case of many other religious houses, particularly smaller ones, no relevant pre-Conquest evidence survives. In the face of this evidence it is initially puzzling that the tenants of these places evidently held such high hopes of proving them to be ancient demesne and even more puzzling that it was 'by colour of' the Domesday exemplifications they obtained that they felt emboldened to claim their freedom. It is here that Barg's evidence that in practice the criteria for ancient

St Mary, Devon: *A.S.C.*, no. 1033. *Pewsey*, Wilts.: Finberg, *Wessex*, no. 248. *Southease*, Sussex: no authentic charter survives recording the grant of Southease to the New Minster, but see Finberg, *Wessex*, no. 300. *South Newton*, Wilts.: *A.S.C.*, no. 766. *Stanton St Bernard*, Wilts.: Finberg, *Wessex*, no. 286 (to bishop of Ramsbury). *Steeple Ashton*, Wilts.: *A.S.C.*, no. 727; *V.C.H. Wilts.*, viii, p. 202. *Sutton Mandeville*, Wilts.: no information. *Thorpe*, Surrey: *A.S.C.*, no. 1165, and see *ibid.*, nos. 353, 420, 752, 1035, 1093 and 1094 for spurious charters recording the grant of Thorpe to Chertsey Abbey. *Urchfont*, Wilts.: no pre-Domesday information, but see *V.C.H. Hants.*, ii, p. 122. *Warfield*, Berks.: no pre-Domesday information. *Whitchurch*, Hants.: *A.S.C.*, no. 378. *Winkfield*, Berks.: *A.S.C.*, no. 482. *Woodhay/East Woodhay*, Hants.: Finberg, *Wessex*, no. 42. *Wroughton* (*Ellandune*), Wilts.: *V.C.H. Wilts.*, xi, p. 238. *Wylye*, Wilts.: Finberg, *Wessex*, nos. 254, 65; *V.C.H. Wilts.*, iii, 232.

demesne were not fixed but elastic, embracing not only lands held by the crown after the Conquest but long before it, provides a new perspective. There are indications that it was in just such a light that the peasant rebels of 1377 viewed the matter, and that their view, on occasion, could receive official sanction.

The Hampshire manor of Crondall was bequeathed to the Old Minster at Winchester in 972 and the gift was confirmed by King Edgar shortly afterwards: that is to say it belonged to the prior and convent of St Swithun.[24] It is listed under the bishop's lands in Domesday, 'and it always belonged to the Church'. Nevertheless in 1280 the people of Crondall, together with those of 'Hesseborne' and Whitchurch, made a complaint which seems to have been based on a claim to ancient demesne status:

> [They] complain . . . that they were granted to the Prior and Convent, and to his Church . . . by the ancestors of the Lord King . . . and that the Prior and Convent exact from them other services which they were not accustomed to do in the time that they were in the hands of the aforesaid predecessors.[25]

This dispute came to a head again – or perhaps had continued until – 1364, when the tenants of Crondall again complained by *monstraverunt* to the king of 'additional services which had not been demanded of their ancestors', again basing their case on the fact that the manor had anciently been in royal hands.[26] An extraordinary aspect of this episode is not only that the claim was made but that it was accepted by the crown in the teeth of the Domesday evidence. Edward III wrote to the prior of St Swithun's that:

> The tenants of the manor of Crondall, which is of the ancient demesne of the crown of England, as we have heard (*a ceo que nous avons entenduz* [perhaps 'understood'?]), have shown us how you have demanded from them other services than those which their ancestors used to do at the time when the manor was in the hands of our forebears, the kings of England.[27]

Edward prohibited further exactions. One of the manors associated with Crondall in the petition of 1280 was 'Hesseborne'. This is the 'Esseborne' or Hurstbourne Priors of Domesday Book, and it *had*

---

[24] *A Collection of Records and Documents Relating to the Hundred and Manor of Crondal in the County of Southampton*, ed. F. J. Baigent (Hampshire Rec. Soc., Winchester, 1891), p. xv.

[25] *Ibid.*, p. 43, n. 1.

[26] *Ibid.*, pp. xx, 43.

[27] *Ibid.*, pp. 43–7.

in fact once been 'in the king's hands', but long before. Originally given to the church of Abingdon in the eighth century, it then went through a period of royal ownership, held first by Egbert (802–39), then by Ethelwulf (839–55) who bequeathed it to Alfred (871–99), with remainder to the church of Winchester. The church held it briefly during Alfred's reign, but returned it to the king, and it did not come back into the possession of the monks of Winchester until the reign of Edward the Elder (899–925).[28] When the people of Crondall and Hurstbourne Priors referred to 'the time when they were in the hands of the king's predecessors', therefore, they must have been referring to a period which cannot have been nearer to their own time than the tenth century, and may have been as far back as the ninth. That this was not merely a hopeful fantasy but a concept which passed the scrutiny of professional lawyers is surely testified by Edward III's acceptance of it.

An equally impressive feat of memory is a petition of the tenants of the abbey of Chertsey's manors of Thorpe, Egham, Chobham and Cobham in *c.* 1410. Claiming that they 'formerly held directly from your most noble forebears the kings of England and from the crown and showing how one of your said predecessors King Edgar, as it is said (*come est suppose*) gave the said manors . . . to the abbey', they protested to the king that the abbot had increased their services and charged them tallage since that time and, on their refusal to pay, 'had distrained them and harried them against the form of their tenure and the wish of the said donor'. Many of them were 'men of free birth (*francs de sanc*)' able to alienate their lands and goods at will: if the abbot was allowed to have his way he would have as much of their possessions as he pleased. They pleaded to be able 'to hold their lands and tenements as freely from the abbot as they had held from the crown before the said grant'.[29] (Interestingly, the tradition that these four manors came to Chertsey as a royal gift rests on a series of forged charters at Chertsey, variously attributing the gift to Alfred, Athelstan, Edgar and Edward the Confessor. The only authentic charter relating to them shows that the abbey had actually acquired it much *earlier*: it records that Frithuwold, sub-king of Surrey, granted it to the abbey in 672–5.)

---

[28] H. P. R. Finberg, *The Formation of England* (St Albans, 1976 edn), pp. 131–3, and 'The Churls of Hurstbourne', pp. 131–43.
[29] P.R.O., S.C.8/144/7173. See also *Cal. Pat. Rolls, 1408–13*, p. 310, and pp. 45–6, above.

Of these manors, whose tenants extended the idea of ancient demesne so far back beyond the Conquest – Crondall, Hurstbourne Priors, Whitchurch, Thorpe, Egham, Chobham and Cobham – six were places where tenants applied for exemplifications from Domesday Book in 1377. We can see that in these cases the events of that year were simply one episode in long-drawn-out disputes involving repeated claims to real or imagined ancient demesne status. The problem remains, however, of explaining why, if these claims went back to a time well before the era that Domesday Book records, it was on Domesday Book that so many tenants pinned their hopes of freedom. It may be that the answer in part lies in the very reverence in which Domesday Book was held; possibly people thought that it would indeed settle all matters 'because its decisions like those of the Last Judgement, are unalterable'.

For if wide-ranging ideas of what constituted ancient demesne certainly played an important part in the events of 1377, another element was also present, a notion that Domesday Book would in some way vindicate the peasants' claim, not only to protection against increased services, but to personal freedom.

By colour of these exemplifications and through misunderstanding them as well as the malicious interpretation made of them by the said counsellors . . . they have withdrawn . . . the customs and services due to their lords, *holding that they are completely discharged of all manner of service both from their persons and their holdings.* (my italics)

This was to go much further than simply to resist increases in services as Domesday appeals had traditionally done, and although one must allow for the possibility that the petitioners exaggerated the peasants' claims, this looks very much like a widespread claim to a complete end to villeinage in the manors concerned. Certainly the statute, by implication, interprets it in this sense. It denies that the Domesday exemplifications 'can or ought to have any value or relevance to the question of personal freedom', or that they 'can be used to change the personal terms of tenure'.

It is difficult to see what support even a 'mistaken' or 'malicious' interpretation of Domesday entries could be held to give such a claim. Oman, who briefly discussed the references to exemplifications in the parliamentary petition of 1377, thought that they were used as 'proofs that in particular manors there were in 1085 free men and socmen, where in 1377 villeins were to be found'.[30] This is substantially the same argument put forward in the Tavistock case already quoted and, as far as the majority of manors was concerned, one would have to agree that as far as the peasants were concerned, 'Domesday does nothing for them.' None of the Wiltshire tenants, for instance, who acquired exemplifications would have found free men or socmen mentioned in any of them, even on the indisputably royal manor of Melksham. Unless we suppose that they would have considered the *villani* who regularly appear on the Wiltshire manors in Domesday to have been free men – and it seems much more likely that contemporaries would have translated this word as *villeins* – we must conclude that there was actually nothing in the Domesday entries to support their claims.

Paradoxically, it may have been the absence of something from Domesday that they thought would do so. It is possible that tenants may have thought that any rents or services which they legitimately owed for their holdings would be written down in Domesday Book. The idea that specific services could be traced back three centuries would not in itself have seemed at all out of the way to a peasantry with long memories for rights and duties. Fourteenth-century tenants were able themselves to list what they thought they had owed at the time of the Conquest: the people of Acle (Norfolk) did this in 1364. On the basis of a claim to be tenants in ancient demesne which was heard in the court of King's Bench, they listed the services 'whereby their ancestors held their tenements at the time of William the Conqueror and have ever since held the same until the manor came into the seisin of the abbot [of Tintern]'.[31] The tenants of the abbey of St Albans in 1326–7 thought that they should have their rights to 'have common in lands, woods, waters, fisheries and other commodities as are contained in Domesday Book' as they used to.[32] As we have seen, the Chertsey Abbey tenants thought that their services should not have been increased since the tenth century, when they had been 'free men by blood', and the people of Crondall, Hurstbourne Priors and Whitchurch thought of their 'accustomed services' as those due possibly as far back as the ninth.

Cherished traditions such as these may not have been historically

---

[30] C. Oman, *The Great Revolt of 1381*, new edn (Oxford, 1969), p. 11.

[31] *Cal. Pat. Rolls, 1345–8*, pp. 162–3.

[32] *Gesta Abbatum Monasterii Sancti Albani, a Thoma Walsingham . . . Compilata*, 3 vols. (Rolls Ser., London, 1867–9), iii, p. 157.

accurate in detail, but there is no reason to reject the peasants' assertion that conditions had worsened since their ancestors had become tenants of religious houses rather than of the king. It was the view of H. P. R. Finberg that the grants to the church of regalian rights over land, which frequently followed or accompanied royal grants of the land itself, tightened the church's control over tenants and were at the root of seigneurial jurisdiction.[33]

The idea, absurd to present-day scholars, that Domesday Book contains an authoritative statement of villein labour services, may well have appealed to a largely illiterate peasantry who had been accustomed for generations to viewing it as a kind of secular Book of Judgement. The exemplifications themselves, which were issued as letters patent with the Great Seal attached, must have been impressive-looking documents, thought to carry royal authority as they took the form of official letters 'from the king'. Nor should we forget the power of rumour in an unstable political situation. A few years later, during and after the rising of 1381, some equally implausible rumours circulated, and were believed and acted upon: among them that John of Gaunt had freed all his serfs and that all the men of Somerset would receive manumission by the king's charter.[34] The facts that the rising of 1377 flared up so quickly, and that tenants from neighbouring villages co-operated to purchase exemplifications suggest a situation in which rumour might well play an important role.

Who were the 'counsellors, procurors, maintainors and abettors' who are said by the parliamentary petitioners to have been hired by the rebellious tenants and were thought of as being responsible for the 'malicious interpretation' of Domesday? (The tenants themselves were guilty merely of 'misunderstanding' it.) Petition and statute are both tantalizingly vague about this. They are not described as professional lawyers, although they took 'hire and profit' from the peasants to help them, and it seems most likely that they were the people who actually obtained the writs in Chancery which applied for the exemplifications. By chance, we know the name of one such 'counsellor' and a little about him. John Godefray

---

[33] *Wessex*, p. 229, and see H. P. R. Finberg, *The Formation of England*, pp. 138–41.
[34] '. . . pilgrims from the Northern ports who had come to Canterbury said that John, Duke of Lancaster, had freed his bondmen in divers counties': *Cal. Pat. Rolls, 1381–5*, p. 237. For Somerset, see B. Harvey, 'Draft Letters Patent of Manumission and Pardon for the Men of Somerset in 1381', *Eng. Hist. Rev.*, lxxx (1965), pp. 89–91.

appeared before the justices of the peace at Melksham (Wiltshire) some time between June 1382 and June 1384. It was stated that in the first and second years of Richard II's reign he had 'counselled (*consultor fuit*)' various unfree tenants in Wiltshire:

> by exemplifications which he wished to procure to be made for them by record from the book [? of the king called D(omesday)] that they should be free, to the grave damage of the lords and magnates of the county, and an open and pernicious example to the villeins and other tenants in villeinage of the lord king.[35]

The manuscript of the justices' roll is partly damaged, and the exact reading is not quite clear, but Godefray must surely be counted among the 'counsellors' of 1377. With another man, John Donam or Donham, he is known to have intervened in a dispute between the precentor of Salisbury Cathedral and the parishioners of West-bury, altering the date of a notarial instrument which the precentor had produced and delaying the case 'to his manifest . . . damage'.[36] He was involved with his brother Thomas in abducting another man's wife at Bradford-on-Avon, forcing her to divorce her husband illegally and as illegally marry Thomas.[37] With another brother, Nicholas, and two other men he was accused of breaking and entering a close belonging to the prioress of Deptford at Norton Bavent, stealing hay and attacking her servants.[38] John Donham, who was also involved in this affair, was elsewhere described as *clericus*.[39] Godefray and Donham are described in the indictment relating to the abduction as having formed 'many such confeder-acies and conspiracies' and having bound themselves to support one another. It is hard to get a clear picture of them. They were clearly violent men with some kind of gang or local following, for 'others leagued with them' took part in the abduction. The attack on the prioress of Deptford's men and servants included 'wounding them and shooting them with arrows'. Yet Donham was a 'clerk', one of them was knowledgeable enough about the law to alter successfully a notarial document, and Godefray had enough influence with the Wiltshire peasantry to be one of the instigators of the Domesday

---

[35] *Proceedings before the Justices of the Peace in the Fourteenth and Fifteenth Centuries*, ed. B. H. Putnam (London, 1938), p. 385. See also P.R.O., J.I.3/221/ 18, m. 4.

[36] *Proceedings before the Justices of the Peace*, ed. Putnam, p. 386.

[37] *Ibid.*, p. 8.

[38] *Ibid.*, p. 392.

[39] P.R.O., K.B.27/490, M.T. 7 Richard II, Rex, m. 11v.

appeals of 1377. All this suggests something more than simply the leaders of a local criminal gang, though of course such men are common enough figures in fourteenth-century society.

Other than this, we know as yet nothing about the 'counsellors' of 1377. Three groups from which they might have been drawn suggest themselves: lawyers, gentry and clerks. They must have been literate, and familiar enough with the law to know how to go about obtaining writs, so it is possible that they were, or included, professional lawyers. It was not uncommon for groups of peasants to hire lawyers: tenants of the abbey of St Albans quite frequently did so.[40] Peasant movements in medieval England on occasion received support from local gentry. The tenants of the abbey of Bec's Wiltshire manor of Ogbourne, who carried out a 'thoroughly organized peasant revolt', on the basis of a claim to ancient demesne, which began before 1309 and continued throughout the fourteenth century, were supported by 'Hildebrand of London, knight' and John Strympel of Hungerford.[41] Hilton has drawn attention to the involvement of minor clergy in the revolt of 1381,[42] and a case from Suffolk, of 1385, shows what a leading part they could play in local disputes. The tenants of Little Haugh (Suffolk), who claimed to be 'free and of free condition', had formed a league and collected £6 for a common purse and had also obtained Domesday exemplifications under the Great Seal, 'but these were of no use in the matter'. They had been 'acting with the counsel and advice of Robert the parson of Thurston church, Simon his chaplain, John Aubrey and four others'.[43]

We may now turn to a more general consideration of the ways in which the ideas current in these peasant rebellions of 1377 relate to the ideology of the revolt of 1381 and to peasant political thought in England. Three notions seem to have been of particular importance in the 'great rumour'. First is the claim, based to some extent on the common law, that a tenant on royal land, or on land that had at one time been royal land, was entitled to special privileges, ranging from protection against increases in services to personal legal freedom. Second is the great reverence for, and trust in, documents

---

[40] A. E. Levett, *Studies in Manorial History*, 2nd edn (London, 1963), p. 192.

[41] M. Morgan, *The English Lands of the Abbey of Bec* (Oxford, 1946), p. 106.

[42] R. H. Hilton, *Bond Men Made Free: Medieval Peasant Movements and the English Rising of 1381* (London, 1977), pp. 124–5.

[43] E. Powell, *The Rising in East Anglia in 1381* (Cambridge, 1896), pp. 64–5. See also *Cal. Pat. Rolls, 1385–9*, p. 88.

that were thought to guarantee privileges or liberties. Third is the emphasis placed on local traditions of ancient rights.

The first of these are clearly related in some way to a view of the king as protector of the people, a concept in key with Hilton's summary of the peasant political ideal in 1381 as 'a popular monarchy, a state without nobles, perhaps without churchmen, in which the peasants and their king are the only social forces'.[44] (An early European parallel to the appeals to ancient demesne in 1377 appears in Hilton's account of the tenants of the monastery of St Ambrose, Milan, who in the ninth century claimed to be liable only for those services which were due when their villages had been part of the imperial estates.[45]) The account given by St Albans chronicler, Thomas Walsingham, of the long dispute between the abbey of St Albans and its tenants in the town and on its nearby estates, which came to a head in 1381 but was by no means resolved then, illustrates very well the themes that have been discussed so far.[46] Two issues dominated the dispute: the townspeople's claim to borough status for the town, and the refusal of the abbey's tenants to accept the abbot's seigneurial monopoly on milling. These two groups, townsmen and peasants, overlapped, and at various stages in the dispute they were prepared to co-operate in order to achieve their objectives, but essentially the opposition to the abbey came from a heterogeneous group: part peasant, part artisan, part urban bourgeoisie. For this reason, its demands were of a mixed character, as were the legitimizing ideas put forward to justify them. In the crisis of 1326–7, for instance, the townspeople's list of demands included both parliamentary representation and common rights in 'lands, woods, waters and other commodities',[47] the one justified by an appeal to precedent ('as we used to do'), the other by an appeal to Domesday Book. Domesday Book was also searched in the townspeople's interest for its evidence – apparently confirming their claim, but rejected by the abbot – of the town's former borough status. A charter of Henry I, and a charter granted by the

---

[44] R. H. Hilton, *The English Peasantry in the Later Middle Ages* (Oxford, 1975), p. 15.

[45] Hilton, *Bond Men Made Free*, pp. 66–7.

[46] Lord–tenant relations on the St Albans estates, and the revolt in St Albans itself in 1381, are discussed in Rosamond Faith, 'The Class Struggle in Fourteenth Century England', in Raphael Samuel (ed.), *People's History and Socialist Theory* (London, 1981), pp. 50–80, on which the following section is largely based.

[47] *Gesta Abbatum Monasterii Sancti Albani*, ii, p. 158.

abbot under duress in 1327 but later revoked, also played an important part in the dispute and were periodically appealed to. The most striking piece of local political tradition, however, was the legend of King Offa.

What chiefly instigated the townsmen (*villanos*) to rebel and to seek liberties were the lies of certain old men of the said town, who led the younger people on to this by false stories (*falsas fabulas*) so that they believed that they had once (*quondam*) had liberties and privileges granted by King Offa but that afterwards these had been taken away by force by the abbot and monks, and unjustly made void. Of these wicked old men, the ringleader was a certain Richard Bude, and Henry de Porta, and next in order a certain Benedict Spichfat, and others. William atte Halle followed them in lying, and others; who, continuing these lies until our own time, incited the community of the town and consequently led them into misfortune. For they alleged that the most illustrious King Offa, when he assembled craftsmen, smiths, carpenters, cementers and stonemasons with their workshops to build the monastery, gave the said town to the stonemasons and other workers (*operariis*) to live in, and honoured it with liberties and privileges provided by his royal munificence.[48]

The idea that a 'charter of liberties' existed, with initial letters decorated alternately with gold and azure, that was kept somewhere in the abbey, played a crucial part in the rising in St Albans in 1381. The townspeople and peasants demanded that the abbot produce it, and although the abbot repeatedly denied its existence, he was eventually obliged to write out a document granting concessions in its stead.[49]

This 'charter of liberties' and King Offa's grant to the original inhabitants of St Albans were important and striking pieces of local political folklore. Offa had been a local hero from the late twelfth century at least, and probably from a much earlier time: the writer of the hagiographical *Lives of the Two Offas* drew on local informants and legends when he started to collect material.[50] Henry de Porta, one of the wicked old men whom Walsingham describes as leading the young people of St Albans astray with their tales about

---

[48] *Ibid.*, iii, p. 365.

[49] *Ibid.*, pp. 308ff.

[50] E. Rickert, 'The Old English Offa Saga', *Mod. Philology*, ii (1904–5), pp. 29–76, 321–76.

Offa, is known to have been active in the struggle against the abbey in the 1290s, and Benedict Spichfat was a prominent leader of the townspeople and probably one of the 'greater men' of the town in the crisis of 1327.[51] Here we see traces of a live local political tradition.

However, as well as these large and public themes involving kings and royal charters, small-scale and essentially local traditions of protest also played a part in the revolt at St Albans. It is only in the light of these – and the suggestion is that they were widespread and typical of late medieval society – that one can understand the very limited nature of some of the peasant demands in 1381. While the Smithfield and Mile End programmes proposed radical changes in society, and while the preaching of John Ball was of a thorough-going fundamentalist Christian egalitarianism, when specific groups of peasants actually, though briefly, achieved power, their aims seem by contrast strikingly limited and local. The charters issued by the abbey under duress to the tenants of its Hertfordshire manors, for instance, granted them carefully defined hunting rights, freedom from specified miscellaneous payments and from work on the abbot's parks and bridges – but not from labour services or payment of rent. Above all they conceded the tenants the right to have hand-mills in their own homes and thus avoid 'suit' to the abbot's mill.[52] The main concession granted to the men of Barnet – who continued in dispute with the abbey well into the fifteenth century – was the liberty to transfer their lands by charter.[53] These peasants seem to be concerned with limited and local goals. In the 1377 risings too, the tenants who claimed their freedom on the basis of Domesday did so only on their own behalf; they made no such wide claim as Tyler's 'an end to villeinage'. Yet if we look at these seemingly limited goals in the context of long traditions of conflict between peasants and lords, they take on a different significance. So too do the actions, often symbolic or ritualistic in nature, sometimes rather inexplicable, that are attributed to the peasant crowds in 1381. At St Albans, for instance, there was a solemn procession 'with great pomp' to destroy enclosures and gates in the abbey woods, and a mass meeting at which townsmen and peasants swore an oath of fealty to each other,

[51] *Gesta Abbatum Monasterii Sancti Albani*, ii, p. 167.
[52] *Ibid.*, iii, pp. 324–7.
[53] *Ibid.*, p. 324.

'joining their right hands', and a 'giving of seisin of the warren and common woods and fields' by handing round branches taken from the trees. Then members of the crowd took a live rabbit which some of the crowd had caught in the open field near the town and fixed it on the pillory in the town as a sign of the free warren they had won.[54] From this point most of the events at St Albans conform more to conventional political behaviour – a mass meeting, negotiations with the abbot, the concession of charters, and so on. A final episode, however, also had a ritualistic and symbolic character, emphasized by the chronicler. To understand it one must bear in mind a crucial episode in the abbey's dispute with its tenants; a previous abbot had confiscated the millstones from the tenants' illegal hand-mills and had then had them cemented into the abbey floor:

> Some ribald people, breaking their way into the abbey cloisters, took up from the floor of the parlour doorway the millstones which had been put there in the time of Abbot Richard as a remembrance and memorial of the ancient dispute between the abbey and the townsmen. They took the stones outside and handed them over to the commons, breaking them into little pieces and giving a piece to each person, *just as the consecrated bread is customarily broken and distributed in the parish churches on Sundays*, so that the people, seeing these pieces, would know themselves to be avenged against the abbey in that cause. (my italics)[55]

What gave these episodes significance to contemporaries is the fact that they expressed through symbolic means victories, albeit temporary ones, for the peasants in essentially local struggles that had gone on for generations and which must have been the subject of local tradition.

On the St Albans manor of Park (Herts.), for instance, labour-rent strikes, which were particularly extensive in the 1270s and in 1318–27, involved continued refusals of service by the same tenants. Of the twelve men presented to the court in 1265 for this offence, for instance, six were involved in similar successive cases in the 1270s. In the almost continuous labour disputes of the 1320s, about a third of the tenants involved were presented in court in more than one year, and in several cases the son or grandson of a tenant who had refused services acted in the same way when he in his turn took over

[54] *Ibid.*, p. 303.     [55] *Ibid.*, p. 309.

the family holding. These protracted and deliberate refusals of labour service (as opposed to the incidental and casual non-performance, or poor performance, which were inherent in the labour service system) formed part of a tradition of non-co-operation or outright resistance in the village. Two other issues which loomed large in the peasants' demands in 1381 had been important in the village for at least a century before that: game and mills. The first is revealed in the long series of prosecutions for poaching in, and taking timber from, the abbot's woodland.[56] Although poaching obviously has an economic aspect, it seems to have had in the middle ages, as later, a vital though largely unspoken ideological aspect as well. The idea that the peasantry were entitled to what the land naturally provided conflicted with the seigneurial notion that lordship implied *dominium* over all the assets of the manor. Hilton has shown how important this issue was in medieval peasant movements.[57] Poaching, primarily of deer, was a political issue in the late fourteenth century, and was seen as such by contemporaries. The Patent Rolls of the 1360s to 1380s are crowded with reports (in the form of instructions to special commissions of *oyer* and *terminer*) of large-scale poaching raids on the property of the gentry, the aristocracy and the royal family, in which taking deer was combined with attacking manor houses, claiming common rights and burning manorial rolls.[58] A parliamentary petition of 1390, which led to a statute in the same year reserving hunting rights to those with lands of 40 shillings a year or more explicitly associated poaching with insurrection:

> artisans and labourers . . . go hunting in the parks, *conyers* and warrens of the lords . . . and thus they make their assemblies at such times to make their conferences (*entreparlance*) covins and conspiracies to make insurrections and disobedience against your majesty and laws, under colour of such hunting (*souz coulour de tiele manere de chacer*).[59]

At Park, poaching the abbot's game, trespassing, hedge-breaking

[56] Material relating to the manor of Park is drawn from Brit. Lib., Add. MS. 40625 (court book of the manor of Park).

[57] Hilton, *Bond Men Made Free*, p. 72.

[58] See, for instance, the series of commissions of *oyer* and *terminer* appointed in 1373–85 in connection with attacks on the property of Margaret, the Countess Marshal: *Cal. Pat. Rolls, 1374–7*, pp. 53, 326; *Cal. Pat. Rolls, 1377–81*, pp. 95, 304; *Cal. Pat. Rolls, 1381–5*, pp. 260, 352; *Cal. Pat. Rolls, 1385–9*, p. 85.

[59] *Rotuli Parliamentorum*, iii, p. 273.

and taking wood from his private woodland were endemic, but reached a peak in the years immediately after the Peasants' Revolt, when seigneurial prohibitions seem virtually to have broken down and the tenants *de facto* enjoyed the free rights of access to woods, warrens and fisheries that they had demanded in 1381 and that their pilloried rabbit had symbolized.

The issue of private hand-mills was partly a conflict between two technologies and economies; between the large-scale, technically sophisticated, capital-intensive economy of the abbey estates and the small-scale, low-cost economy of the peasants. It was essentially a conflict over feudal rent, of which seigneurial *banalités* such as the milling monopoly were an important part, but it also involved conflicting ideas of right. Events in Park were less dramatic than the long series of disputes in St Albans itself over the tenants' rights to hand-mills, chronicled by Walsingham, which began in 1274 and continued sporadically throughout the fourteenth century. Resistance at Park, however, to using the abbot's mill had begun as early as 1237 when the court records begin, and may well have started earlier than this. It continued almost ceaselessly through the fourteenth century. The right to use hand-mills clearly seemed of crucial importance to the peasants, and although its exercise was by nature a private affair, the need for secrecy must have involved a certain amount of communal solidarity to conceal hand-mills from the eye of beadle or bailiff or abbey official.

These three areas of conflict between peasants and the lord on the St Albans estates must, one would guess, have created local traditions of resistance.[60] The strikes of the 1320s were part of, and no doubt also a product of, the disastrous conditions of those years, and would no doubt have been remembered in the village for some time. Hand-mills remained a live issue. Poaching was endemic in rural life. The people who had been involved in these conflicts, and whose parents and grandparents had been involved in them before them, were among those who made up the armed crowd who marched on the abbey in 1381, and it was their accumulated day-to-day experience which accounts for the seemingly limited, seemingly conservative, nature of the concessions which they obtained from the abbot, and which also gives weight and significance to the symbolic acts which they performed during the days of the actual rebellion.

[60] Levett, *Studies in Manorial History*, pp. 203–5.

The peasant risings of 1377–8 clearly had much in common with the revolt of 1381: a belief in liberties granted or guaranteed by a revered ruler, reliance on long-standing traditions and old documents, direct appeals to the king. Such ideas have been characterized as 'naive monarchism' by one writer on European peasantry.[61] The notion that medieval peasants blindly revered the king himself but thought that he was surrounded by evil counsellors is one that is very commonly encountered among scholars and non-scholars alike. Hilton has effectively criticized this point of view, showing that criticism, not to mention execution, of 'evil counsellors' was 'a commonplace of medieval politics', a political programme not by any means confined to the peasantry.[62] While the patriotism and loyalty to the king shown by the rebels in 1381 cannot be denied – their password after all was 'With King Richard and the true [that is, loyal] commons', and the St Albans crowd, at least, marched under the banner of St George[63] – one should not exaggerate these feelings into an idea that Richard was in any way idolized or seen as a 'sacred' figure. Two chroniclers make a point of the deliberately familiar, even comradely, way in which Tyler addressed the king, 'half-bending' his knee and then, as if to counteract any impression of deference that even this half-gesture may have made, clasping him by the hand shaking it 'hard and strongly (*durement et fortement*)' and addressing him as 'brother'.[64] Similarly the crowd which broke into the queen's apartment in the Tower made quite a point of not showing her any respect: 'They arrogantly lay and sat on the king's bed while joking and several asked the king's mother to kiss them.'[65] The rebels intended to *use* Richard, it was shrewdly said by a contemporary; they 'would lead him round the whole of England with them and would force him to grant all their desires'.[66] Though we have no means of knowing whether this was so, it is quite consistent with their actions. It would

---

[61] J. Blum, *The End of the Old Order in Rural Europe* (Princeton, 1978), p. 335. F. Graus, 'Social Utopias in the Middle Ages', *Past and Present*, no. 38 (Dec. 1967), pp. 4–19, at pp. 16–17, takes a similar line and emphasizes the magical and mythological elements in peasant views of the monarchy.

[62] Hilton, *Bond Men Made Free*, p. 225.

[63] *Gesta Abbatum Monasterii Sancti Albani*, iii, p. 304.

[64] *Peasants' Revolt of 1381*, ed. Dobson, pp. 123–31.

[65] Thomas Walsingham, *Historia Anglicana*, ed. H. T. Riley, 2 vols. (Rolls Ser., London, 1863–4), i, pp. 456–67, trans. in *Peasants' Revolt of 1381*, ed. Dobson, pp. 168–81.

[66] *Peasants' Revolt of 1381*, ed. Dobson, p. 131.

surely have been a sign of political acumen rather than of 'naive monarchism'.

Important as the millenarian and egalitarian ideas of such as John Ball undoubtedly were in the ideology of medieval peasant movements, there is a case for saying that traditional and conservative ideas were equally important, were more firmly rooted in peasant culture, more widespread, and longer lasting: that more peasants looked back to an idealized past than forward to an idealized future. Yet their traditionalism, in its own way, could present just as much as a challenge to the established order as did Ball's Christian egalitarianism. In claiming 'ancient rights', and in keeping alive the idea of 'ancient liberties', real or imagined, they resisted feudal lordship as they experienced it, and to do so invoked not only the sanction of ancient and revered texts such as Domesday Book but also the traditions of struggle of preceding generations.

APPENDIX

| Place | Date of issue of writ | At whose request | Holder in 1086[1] | Letters patent enrolled[2] |
|---|---|---|---|---|
| *Amberley (Sussex) | 18 Oct. 1376 (P.R.O., C.260/87) | | Bishop of Chichester | |
| *Lambeth (Surrey) | 14 Nov. 1376 (P.R.O., C.260/87) | | Church of Lambeth | |
| *Farnham (Surrey) | 7 Mar. 1377 (P.R.O., C.260/88) | Tenants of Farnham | Bishop of Winchester | 26 July 1377 (p. 9) |
| Crondall (Hants.) | 7 Mar. 1377 (P.R.O., C.260/88) | Tenants of Crondall | St Swithun's Winchester | 12 Mar. 1377 (p. 452) |
| *Highclere (Hants.) *Ecchinswell (Hants.) *Woodhay (Hants.) *Ashmansworth (Hants.) | ?8 Apr. 1377 (P.R.O., C.260/88) | | Bishop of Winchester | |
| *Froyle (Hants.) | 14 Apr. 1377 (P.R.O., C.260/88) | Men and tenants of Froyle | St Mary's Winchester | |
| *Thorpe (Surrey) *Egham (Surrey) *Cobham (Surrey) *Chobham (Surrey) | 20 Apr. 1377 (P.R.O., C.260/88) | Men and tenants of Thorpe, Egham, Cobham and Chobham | Chertsey Abbey | |
| Whitchurch (Hants.) | 10 May 1377 (P.R.O., C.260/88) | | St Swithun's Winchester | |

| Place | Date of issue of writ | At whose request | Holder in 1086[1] | Letters patent enrolled[2] |
|---|---|---|---|---|
| *Hundred of Ripplesmere (Berks.) | 5 June 1377 (P.R.O., C.260/88) | Men of Warfield | Warfield: the king<br>Winkfield: Abingdon Abbey<br>Easthampstead: Westminster Abbey<br>*Ortone*: Walter son of Other<br>Losfield: Eudo Dapifer<br>Clewer: Ralf son of Seifrid (Earl Harold held it)<br>Dedworth: Albert | |
| *All Cannings (Wilts.)<br>*Urchfont (Wilts.) | 12 July 1377 (P.R.O., C.260/89) | | St Mary's Winchester | |
| *Stanton St Bernard (Wilts.)<br>*(South Newton (Wilts.) | 16 July 1377 (P.R.O., C.260/89) | Tenants | St Mary's Wilton | 20 July 1377 (p. 12) |
| *Bishops Cannings (Wilts.) | 25 July 1377 (P.R.O., C.260/89) | Tenants | Bishop of Salisbury | 27 July 1377 (p. 16) |
| *Manningford Abbots (Wilts.)<br>*Pewsey (Wilts.) | 1 Aug. 1377 (P.R.O., C.260/89) | Tenants | St Peter's Winchester | 5 Aug. 1377 (p. 10) |
| *Melksham (Wilts.)<br>*Bradford-on-Avon (Wilts.)<br>*Steeple Ashton (Wilts.) | 2 Aug. 1377 (P.R.O., C.260/89) | Tenants | King<br>Church of Shaftesbury<br>Church of Romsey | 7 Aug. 1377 (p. 18) |

| | | | | |
|---|---|---|---|---|
| *Christian Malford (Wilts.), *Sutton Mandeville (Wilts.) | 3 Aug. 1377 (P.R.O., C.260/89) | Tenants | St Mary's Glastonbury; Richard son of Gislebert | 5 Aug. 1377 (pp. 15, 16) |
| *Kintbury (Berks.) | 6 Aug. 1377 (P.R.O., C.260/89) | Tenants | Church of Amesbury | 10 Aug. 1377 (p. 15) |
| *Wroughton (Wilts.) | 7 Aug. 1377 (P.R.O., C.260/89) | Tenants | St Swithun's Winchester | 10 Aug. 1377 (p. 15) |
| *Badbury (Wilts.), *Chisledon (Wilts.), *Liddington (Wilts.) | 8 Aug. 1377 (P.R.O., C.260/89) | Tenants | St Mary's Glastonbury; St Peter's Winchester; St Mary's Shaftesbury | 13 Aug. 1377 (p. 23) |
| *Chilmark (Wilts.), *Wylye (Wilts.) | 10 Aug. 1377 (P.R.O., C.260/89) | Tenants | St Mary's Wilton | 11 Aug. 1377 (pp. 18, 19) |
| *Bensington (Oxon.) | 13 Dec. 1377 (P.R.O., C.260/89) | | King | |
| *Southease (Surrey), *Donnington (Sussex) | 18 Jan 1378 (P.R.O., C.260/89) | | St Peter's Winchester | |
| Lands of Chertsey Abbey in Surrey and Berks. | 5 Feb. 1378 (P.R.O., C.260/89) | | | |

*Notes:* All the exemplifications from Domesday Book in P.R.O., C.260, C.47, C.89, C.202 and the Calendars of Patent Rolls have now been listed by Dr E. M. Hallam of the Public Record Office.

*denotes an ancient demesne enquiry

[1] Information about holders of manors in Domesday Book is drawn from the translations of the Domesday text in the appropriate volumes of the *Victoria County History*.

[2] Page references in parentheses refer to *Cal. Pat. Rolls, 1377–81*, except in the case of Crondall, where the reference is to *Cal. Pat. Rolls, 1374–7*.

Entries grouped together formed the subject of the same writ.

# 3. *The Jacquerie*

RAYMOND CAZELLES

One of the most striking antecedents of the Peasants' Revolt of 1381, anticipating it by twenty-three years was the French Jacquerie of 1358. Let me briefly recapitulate the events: on 28 May at Saint-Leu d'Esserent, not far from Creil and Chantilly, an incident brought about a clash between nobles and country-folk. The nobles were either killed or expelled from Saint-Leu. There were immediate uprisings in neighbouring villages and the manor-houses and castles of the nobles were attacked. The Jacques failed in their attempts to enter Compiègne and Senlis. Then, having acquired a leader, Guillaume Cale, they attacked the Marché de Meaux, and on 9 May they were defeated there. The king of Navarre placed himself at the head of the nobles of Picardy and having treacherously seized hold of Guillaume Cale crushed the Jacques, between Mello and Clermont, on 10 May. From beginning to end, the revolt lasted exactly two weeks. It was a brutal and savage affair, as was the repression which followed it. The chronicles describe frightful scenes, which, it would seem, really happened.

The Jacquerie surprised contemporaries by its violence and intensity, as it continues to astonish us today. It happened suddenly, not preceded by anything like it. The nearest approach was the insurrection in the countryside around Laon, twenty years earlier, in 1338. We know exactly the reasons for this rising: it was a protest against the abusive imposition of a tallage by the cathedral chapter of Laon. With some considerable exaggeration, the chronicler Jean de Noyal estimated about 40,000 rebels. Only twelve were hanged by royal commissioners and the Canons of Laon no longer had the right to tallage at will.

What caused the Jacquerie? So far, economic causes have been stressed, either fiscal oppression or bad harvests and peasant misery.

Should we see it, as in the Laonnais, as a revolt against heavy taxation? But it could not have been sparked off by tallages, imposed either by lay or ecclesiastical lords. The countryside of the Beauvaisis was in fact divided into many lordships and there is no evidence of this sort of exaction in 1358.

Could it have been a tax imposed at the king's command? At a meeting of the Estates at Compiègne it had been decided to demand tax to give daily support to a man-of-arms from every seventy hearths in the towns and from every hundred in the countryside. So the towns were more heavily assessed than the rural areas. But it was the country people who rebelled. A hearth tax at this level was not unprecedented and had been levied the preceding year with the agreement of the Estates. As for the tax on commercial transactions, this mainly affected the urban markets, not so much the countryside. In any case hardly any documents concerning the Jacquerie mention the tax burden as a cause of the rebellion. It clearly did not play a significant part.

Could an unfavourable conjuncture in the agrarian economy have been responsible for the Jacquerie? In May 1358 the harvest was still far off and the peasants could hardly have been worrying about yields and profits. The harvests during the previous years do not seem to have been disastrous – and the region of the Jacquerie was among the most fertile in the French kingdom. Etienne Marcel even wrote to the *échevins* of Ypres saying that 'the year was fertile both for corn and the vine'.

One could, of course, also consider harvests which were too good and presented problems for the sale of agricultural produce. It is true that these prices were stable, even falling, and this over a period of years. But this fall in grain prices goes back for decades and was no more serious in 1358 than before. Low agricultural prices, then, could hardly have caused the Jacquerie.

Was the French peasantry so miserable that no escape other than by rebellion would have seemed possible? Nothing suggests that this was the case. The Black Death, ten years before, had severely depopulated the country. The supply of agricultural labour diminished and it became dearer. But the Black Death also reduced the number of tenants; the size of holdings increased and the conditions of the peasantry improved.

Let us also note that serfdom had virtually disappeared from the area affected by the Jacquerie except for a few ecclesiastical lordships in Valois, Brie and Champagne.

The Jacquerie cannot therefore be explained by the economic conditions of the peasant class. In reality the movement did not emerge from among the cultivators themselves. Chronicle descriptions emphasize that the Jacques were inhabitants of the countryside rather than of the towns, but they do not insist that they were agriculturalists. In subsequent letters of remission the term 'homme de labour' appears frequently, but 'labour' had in France at that time, as it does in England today, the implication of manual labour without any agricultural specificity. The 'laboureurs', 'laboureurs de bras' are manual workers; they could well be labourers using the hoe, or the spade, – that is working the land – but they could also be carters ('charretiers laboureurs'); or labourers unloading wine ('qui déchargent les vins'); or workers on the riversides.

Thanks to these letters of remission we know a good deal about the occupations of many of those who became compromised by participation in the Jacquerie. These are shoemakers, coopers, masons, sellers of eggs, poultry, cheese, butchers and cartwrights. It would seem that there were more rural artisans than peasants. Furthermore, another decisive argument would seem to exonerate the peasantry from the responsibility of launching the Jacquerie – its date. The end of May and the beginning of June would never be a period when the cultivator would do anything to damage the crop which he would hope to gather and to store. If he were to rebel, he would wait until the end of the summer or autumn.

Research into the occupations of those involved in the terror springs other surprises. These are clerks, priests, incumbents of rural parishes and even a canon from Meaux. One finds among the Jacques well-to-do, even rich people, owning 'hôtels', like nobles. An associate of Jean de Boulogne, count of Montfort, uncle of the queen, was compromised in the affair and lost his belongings, estimated at 3,000 *moutons d'or*. The brother of a president of the Parlement had reason for some anxiety because of participation in the Jacquerie.

It is even more surprising to find some royal officials among the Jacques – of rather low rank, it is true: a gate-keeper, and a fair number of royal sergeants, mounted sergeants from the Châtelet and from the Paris watch. A royal sergeant living near Noailles agreed to become the captain of the militia of four villages. We find ourselves here in the presence of minor functionaries whose presence at the centre of the Jacquerie shows that it could not have been, in any way, a rebellion against royal power. On the contrary, the Jacques proclaimed their loyalty to the crown; their banners sported the fleur-de-lis and 'Montjoie' was their battle-cry. The first act of the Jacques in the region of Montmorency was to ask for instructions from the royal provost, captain of Beaumont-sur-Oise, who gave them authority to choose their own leader.

The Jacquerie, then, did not only issue from among the cultivators, but from a complex milieu where the rich found themselves side by side with the poor, the royal official with the lord's subject. Here we have valuable insights into rural society, in all its diversity from the well-to-do and respected proprietor to the petty artisan.

Rather than from economic conditions, the Jacquerie emerged from the encounter of three political purposes and two mental attitudes.

The first of the three political purposes was that of the nobles who were with the regent, Charles, and supported him in his struggle against Etienne Marcel and the town of Paris. The regent tried to blockade the rivers upstream from Paris with the intention of preventing supplies from reaching Paris along the Seine and its tributaries. In this way he hoped to strike a major blow against the Parisian bourgeoisie whose fortunes had been founded on the river trade ('marchandise de l'eau'). He already occupied Melun on the Seine, and from 9 May was in control of Meaux on the Marne. All that remained was to block the Oise which was not only a route for the provisioning of the Parisians but also a link between Paris and the northern towns which supported Etienne Marcel.

At which bridge on the Oise should the river route be cut? Compiègne was a town which had, for a time, supported Marcel and in addition it was somewhat too far from Paris. Creil belonged to Beatrix of Bourbon, former queen of Bohemia. Beaumont-sur-Oise was not safe, because its captain was involved with the Jacques. There remained Saint-Leu d'Esserent and its bridge. This was the object of the operation of 28 May, which failed, but gave the impetus to the Jacquerie.

To occupy Saint-Leu would also have ensured the control of the important stone-quarries there and in the surrounding area. For stone was in those times an essential commodity, for towns to rebuild their walls and for castles to organize their defences. So the occupation of Saint-Leu d'Esserent, for the regent, would have been a profitable operation from many points of view.

The second political purpose was that of Etienne Marcel and the burgesses associated with him.

Following the defeat at Poitiers and the capture of King John, two parties organized themselves in connection with the Estates of the kingdom meeting in Paris: a reformist nobility and an activist bourgeoisie. Agreement between these two parties resulted in the policy statements of March 1357 and the measures which put them into operation. Nevertheless, under the influence of various factors, the agreement between the two Estates was undone, bit by bit. After the murder of the marshals of Champagne and Normandy in February 1350, and the departure of the regent in March, the nobility began open warfare against the bourgeoisie of Paris and the towns which were its allies. Having seen what were the actions of the nobles, let us now see how the bourgeoisie reacted.

They undertook to dismantle and destroy what was both the symbol and the foundation of the strength of the nobility: its castles. With their help, a very speedy operation was undertaken, the reduction of the fortresses which encircled Paris and a number of the towns of the Parisian basin. Etienne Marcel took the lead in the destruction of manor-houses and strongholds of his noble enemies, at all points of the compass. In order to relieve the north of the capital city, he entrusted a certain Jacques de Chenevières, originally from Taverny, with the mission of putting out of action all strongholds within what he called 'the country between the two rivers' that is between the Seine and the Oise, especially castles dependent on the lord of Montmorency. In the north-east, Pierre Gille, a grocer of southern origin, led three hundred Parisians to Bonneuil where he burned the manor-house of a squire, then to Gonesse where he burned that of Pierre d'Orgemont. From there they marched on Ermenonville.

It is at this point that one perceives the involvement of the provost of the merchants of Paris with the Jacquerie. Pierre Gille's troops joined up with Guillaume Cale in order to attack the castle of Ermenonville which belonged to Robert de Lorris. Meanwhile, another Parisian leader, Jean Vaillant, provost of the mint, joined up at Silly-le-Long with the Jacques under Cale's leadership and marched on Meaux to help its mayor, Jean Soulas, and to attack a fortress built on an island of the Marne, the Marché de Meaux. However they were repelled and defeated.

To the east, the Parisians destroyed the tower at Gournay-sur-Marne and tried to join up with the burgesses of Meaux. To the south of Paris, the troops of Etienne Marcel dismantled the castles of Palaiseau and Chevreuse, an action that was felt as far away as La Ferté-Alais and Etampes. To the west, the Parisian initiative did not go so far. They sacked the manor-houses of Simon de Bucy at Vaugirard, at Issy and at Viroflay; and the manor-house of Jean de la Villeneuve at Bailly. They took over the fort at Trappes.

This action by the Parisians against the castle had its counterpart in a number of towns associated with Paris. At Amiens, the mayor and the *échevins* helped the people of the surrounding area and sent some hundred men to help with the destruction of the castles of the nobility, up to four to six hours' journey from the town. The mayor, *échevins* and inhabitants of Montdidier took part in the destruction of castles in the neighbourhood and helped in the massacre of some nobles. The common people of Beauvais put to death nobles who had sought refuge in the towns. The burgesses of Clermont-en-Beauvaisis were later sued by Robert of Lorris for having taken part in the destruction of his castle at Ermenonville, having already sacked a number of nearer castles. The inhabitants of Senlis accepted the help of the Jacques in attacking the castles and manor-houses of Sottemont, Brasseuse, Fontaine-les-Corps-nuds, Thiers, Courteuil and Chantilly. The burgesses of Meaux acted similarly against the fortresses at Charny, Thorigny, Villeparisis and Pomponne, which hindered their communications with Paris. Even towns further away, such as Rouen, Orleans and Gien, sympathizers with the Parisian cause, followed their example.

Coming immediately after the affair at Saint-Leu, this coalition of towns against their neighbouring castles must have required some planning and it is impossible to believe that it happened by chance. In his famous letter to the people of Ypres, written two months after the Jacquerie, Etienne Marcel only dissociated himself from the excesses of these actions in the Beauvaisis. He did not deny a previous understanding with the *échevinages* to weaken the nobility by destroying their castles. I am even inclined to think that the planning by the towns must have been some time before 28 May and the fighting at Saint-Leu, that the nobles had got some wind of the intentions of the burgesses and had wanted to forestall them.

The third political purpose intervening in the Jacquerie was that of the king of Navarre.

Freed from detention in Cambrésis by the people of Amiens and region in November 1357, Charles of Navarre played such subtle and complicated games that it is difficult to reconstruct his political conduct, except in so far as concerns his territorial and possibly his monarchical ambitions. Having flattered Etienne Marcel and having reasserted his ascendancy over the future Charles V, the king of Navarre withdrew to his retreat in the Seine valley. The regent tried to associate him with the policies he had adopted in April and May 1358, but Charles the Bad slipped away. It does not seem possible to accuse him of having helped the rising of the Jacques. On the contrary, it was around him that the Picard and Norman nobility rallied; it was he who laid a trap for Guillaume Cale; it was he who butchered the band of country-folk he found in front of him. He seems then to have tried to pacify the Beauvaisis, with simultaneous decrees of punishment and amnesty, but without success. Senlis welcomed the king of Navarre and made him its captain. He then went to Paris, and in June left with armed men from the town. He tried to take Compiègne, which remained out of his reach, and then Senlis which now refused him. Charles the Bad now used his prestige with the nobility, whom he had rescued from the Jacques, and with the Parisians, for his own purposes. In fact, it was the regent to whom he was opposed and if his campaign had succeeded he would undoubtedly have replaced the future Charles V and possibly his father-in-law, John II.

The map of the areas of the Parisian basin affected by the Jacquerie shows that there was a region where the movement had scarcely any support. This was the Beauce, Yvelines and the fringes of the Perche. This was a region where the English and other *routiers* had been operating for many months and against which the union of the towns of Langue d'oil had tried to act, without much success. But Charles of Navarre had taken these *routiers* on to his pay-roll in December 1357. This king was not only playing a double, but a triple game and seemed to lose himself in too subtle manoeuvres which escaped the understanding even of his contemporaries.

These political moves would not have assumed their particular character had they not contained within them a crystallization of mentalities – of non-nobles against nobles and of nobles against non-nobles. Anti-noble feelings were not new in the French kingdom. But they were strongly reinforced by military set-backs which were blamed on the nobility. The function which justified its privileges was to engage in warfare. Crecy had already produced deep disillusion. With Poitiers, the cup overflowed. Literary works such as the *Complainte de la Bataille de Poitiers* or the *Tragicum Argumentum* of François de Montebelluna expressed generally held feelings.

It was a feeling which seems to have been partly forgotten in 1356 and 1357 when nobles and non-nobles alike, in the sessions of the Estates, searched together for the means of reforming the monarchy and defending the kingdom. The feeling however remained, latent; and exploded again following the assassination of the marshals of Champagne and Normandy. From then on, it was war between the castle and the town, a war the relentless character of which can be attributed to the pride and contempt felt by many of the nobles. During this period central authority was enfeebled; an ordinance of May 1358 went so far as to authorize the owners of castles to make requisitions – without payment of course – in order to make their castles defensible. The burgesses feared that their towns would be pillaged by the nobles and resisted all their attempts. The country people had no walls to protect them and hoped that by killing the castellans and their families they would be no longer haunted by the daily fear of being robbed and ill-treated. The horrors of the Jacquerie in the Beauvaisis have much to do with this fear.

It is easier to understand the hate felt by the non-nobles for the nobles than the opposite feeling on the part of the nobility towards the non-nobles. The horrors inflicted by the long counter-Jacquerie are explicable in terms of those inflicted by the Jacques. All the same, it was not so much against the country people that the nobles bore ill will, but against the town bourgeoisie. For these in effect were trying to supplant the nobility in its traditional functions.

Commerce had, of course, long ago brought wealth to the merchant class of the towns. This wealth enabled them to enter the royal entourage, and to aid the crown's financial administration, including making the loans necessary for the functioning of the machinery of the monarchy. Their wealth enabled them not only to acquire urban real property, but noble fiefs. In obtaining noble status they became exempt from paying tax on their *francs fiefs*. Such ennoblement, since the end of the thirteenth century, had meant the penetration of the nobility, by merchants and lawyers whose luxurious living contrasted with the misery of many of the noble class.

Furthermore, the rich bourgeois, the urban patriciate even began to usurp, with royal permission, the essential privilege of the nobility, the practice of arms. The sons of the great bourgeoisie of Paris, of Reims, of Tours, as well as of other towns in the Paris basin were to be seen organizing jousts and tournaments, and what is more, excelling at them. As they exercised the military craft it was often only their status which differentiated them from the nobility. When the towns contributed their contingents to the king's army, they were not simply composed of serjeants, but of bourgeois men-at-arms. The bourgeoisie, having ascertained that the nobility failed in battle, estimated that it could do no worse. This opinion was clearly expressed in the final ordinance of the Estates of February 1358 – the men-at-arms of bourgeois origin were placed on the same footing as those belonging to the nobility.

A phenomenon appeared which was even more dangerous to the nobility. This was the attitude of the great jurists, the doctors of law. They considered that the doctorate assimilated them to knighthood, entitled them to wear golden spurs. So the nobility, feeling that, attacked from all sides, they risked losing their exclusive status, reacted with violence against those whom they considered fake men-at-arms, false knights. The nobles, reacting to the Jacquerie, eliminated this dangerous parallel nobility.

So the Jacquerie was not, as has often been said, a peasant movement produced by the circumstances of the agrarian economy. But it was certainly a rural movement, involving country artisans, well-to-do proprietors, petty officials and some members of the country clergy. It was complex as a movement. These country people were prompted into action consequent upon the ambitions of various groups in search of power; the regent with his noble entourage; Etienne Marcel urged by the bourgeoisie of several towns; Charles the Bad, relying on the *routiers*, rallying a nobility in distress and reaching out his hand to the provost of the merchants of

Paris to help his personal revenge against the Valois. But this triple action would not have had such bitter consequences had it not been fed by a twofold rage; that of the non-nobles against the nobles who, they thought, had demonstrated their incapacity; and that of the nobles, jealous of the merchants who were supplanting them. The Jacquerie, then, was a collision between nobles and non-nobles. The nobles were to be the victors in the short battle in the two weeks of May to June 1358 – and were to ensure their domination for a long time to come.

# 4. *English Urban Society and the Revolt of 1381*

## A. F. BUTCHER

The mayor and burgesses of London asked the citizens if they wished to lock the city [against the rebels]. They replied that they would not do this in the face of their neighbours and friends.[1]

## *I*

The role of towns and townsmen in the revolt of 1381 has long been recognized. The provincial centres of Scarborough, York, Beverley, Norwich, Ely, Peterborough, Cambridge, Bury St Edmunds, Yarmouth, Northampton, Dunstable, St Albans, Winchester, Bridgwater, Rochester and Canterbury, as well as London, all provided stages for violent display; and the use of broader criteria for urban status might add other smaller communities to this list. Urban allies in a rural cause, it has been argued, townsmen found self-interested opposition to local lords and local oligarchs transformed into revolt against the king's government. Providing a geographical focus and regional stronghold for widespread rural grievance, the town played an important part in the mobilization and organization of the rebels. Yet though there has been much speculation about urban involvement there has been remarkably little detailed investigation of the activities and motivation of townsmen at this time; there has indeed been little detailed study of fourteenth-century English urban society at all. There has been even less examination of the complex interaction of town and countryside, a better understanding of which is vital to an analysis of the events of 1381.

Those who have examined urban unrest in this year, while setting London apart as a special case, have sought to distinguish between two main kinds of involvement and disorder. Oman, for example, saw the divide as between those townsmen struggling to establish municipal liberties in monastic boroughs for whom the rural rising provided an opportunity to press long-held grievances, and those lower classes caught up in the struggles between *inferiores* and

[1] *Eulogium Historiarum*, ed. F. S. Haydon, 3 vols. (Rolls Ser., London, 1858–63), iii, p. 352.

84

*potentiores* who took advantage of revolt in the countryside to fall upon their local oligarchs. Among the former towns would be St Albans, Dunstable and Bury St Edmunds, and among the latter Winchester, Beverley and Scarborough: 'troublous times of any sort suited the townsmen'. For Dobson and Hilton, the division is to be made between those towns in which conflict was exclusively urban, such as York, Winchester, Beverley and Scarborough, and those where 'a new situation emerged', and revolt became a product of alliance between townsmen and villagers in 'a temporary coincidence of revolutionary interests' in towns such as St Albans, Bury St Edmunds, Cambridge and possibly Canterbury. While both analyses have their uses, it is however the contention of this essay that both perpetuate a false dichotomy between town and countryside, both conceal the considerable diversity of English urban society, and both neglect, in these descriptions and in arguments subsequently developed, the profound changes experienced in English urban society and in rural–urban relations between 1348 and 1381.[2]

Whatever the trigger of urban revolt in 1381, and whatever the local manifestation of that revolt, the origin of social conflict lay in the response of urban social and economic processes and relations to rapid demographic change and the demands of sustained warfare. Particular social and economic structures made manifest this post-plague reconstruction in their own terms and though they might speak the language of traditional oppositions, many of which reached back into the early fourteenth century and beyond, they spoke it in a new context: old words took on new meanings. The conflict in monastic boroughs and the opposition between 'lower classes' and the oligarchs were transformed by the changed social composition of the participants, by new opportunities, expectations and uncertainties; and this transformation was critically affected by changes in rural–urban relations. This being so, the description of conflict in 1381 as 'purely' or 'exclusively' urban, or 'simply the continuation, or revival' of past struggles may well be seriously misleading, the 'new situation' of alliance being more readily explicable than that in which the intervention of villagers did not

---

[2] C. Oman, *The Great Revolt of 1381*, new edn (Oxford, 1969), pp. 13–19; *The Peasants' Revolt of 1381*, ed. R. B. Dobson (London, 1970), pp. 13–14; R. H. Hilton, *Bond Men Made Free: Medieval Peasant Movements and the English Rising of 1381* (London, 1973), pp. 186–207.

take place. Before such analysis may be undertaken, however, the fundamental reconstruction and transformation of urban processes developed by the early fourteenth century must be considered. These processes and the changes they underwent have been little considered elsewhere and their neglect has resulted in descriptions of urban social structure at the time of revolt, especially for provincial towns, which are often overly static and even anachronistic.

The precise nature of urban demographic change has still to be established. The impact of plague mortality is still only guessed at. Though rates of mortality are reckoned to be higher in town than in the countryside, perhaps nearer 50 per cent than 30 per cent in 1348–9, no clear figures are available for the Black Death or subsequent epidemics. Equally, though the evidence of the numbers of freemen admissions and the level of rents is suggestive of rapid and substantial immigration, the important problem of replacement has scarcely been investigated. The extent of changes in rates of fertility, sex ratios, age distribution and marriage patterns is no more known that the implications of such changes for family, kinship, household, neighbourhood and community in these years. Yet the profound dislocations which must have occurred and the conflicts which arose in urban society, not only in 1381 but in the decades preceding that outbreak, are not to be understood without an appreciation of the complexity of demographic response.

The condition of the urban economy in the late fourteenth century has received greater attention, but as yet only in very general terms, and in respect of those three decades which followed the Black Death the least detailed analysis. Suggestions made as to late fourteenth-century urban and industrial buoyancy, and even expansion and prosperity, may best be applicable to the last two decades of the century. Changes in the structure and organization of business and the relations of production and consumption in the period 1348–81 have yet to be carefully examined. The disruption of trading contacts and of marketing and credit arrangements deserves attention as, equally, does their reconstruction. The disintegration of accumulated capital and its redistribution have important implications not only for trade and craft structure and the volume of production but also for the economic and social constituency of urban government, the extent of the power and control which its members possessed and the number, prosperity and independence of those lesser enfranchised men or licensed traders and craftsmen who were governed. Changes in the levels and distribution of demand and, especially, the rising cost of labour not only brought the beginnings of realignments between particular economic activities but significantly influenced relations between free and unfree, and between labour and employer.

Whether it is demographic or economic considerations that are in question or whether it is changes in social structure or in urban government and the maintenance of law and order, the relative neglect of urban activities in those decades between the Black Death and the revolt of 1381 severely restricts the analysis of widespread social unrest. Most particularly, the absence of any attempt to set the actions of the rebels within a regional framework may limit an understanding of mobilization and organization. The social and economic role of provincial centres in relation to their dependent hinterlands needs further consideration, whether in examination of the multiple functions of markets and fairs, the networks of credit, the extent of investment by townsmen beyond their home community, the significance of family connections, the role of townsmen in local administration, or the place of the town as an ecclesiastical centre: and this at a time when a progressive and sometimes drastic reorganization of rural–urban and inter-urban relations was in progress. If to this range of investigations is added the problem of determining the effects of the various influences of the demands of warfare, then some idea of the necessary range of inquiry may be appreciated.

To some extent the lack of such study is a function of the survival of sources and to some extent it is a reflection of the nature of the archive for the provincial town. Even where survival is good the difficulties of constructing a full survey of urban activities are considerable. More often accounts, taxations, rentals, town and craft ordinances, court materials, testamentary evidence and sources for religious activities provide evidence for particular liberties and jurisdictions only; the normal life of the majority of townsmen remains elusive, especially as it involves rural–urban relations. The available information, moreover, is predominantly concerned with the formal sector of the economy and its enfranchised participants. As always, and at this time perhaps most critically, the lesser members of the community and those involved in the informal sectors of the economy are most difficult to investigate. The nature of the evidence tends to ensure that continuity and success are more readily identifiable than the numerous failures, instabilities and discontinuities. Yet patient reconstruction in urban and rural archives, especially in pursuit of individual and family interests, may prove illuminating and permit a reassessment of the role of the towns in 1381.

What follows is a limited attempt to explore the archives and themes indicated above in respect of one provincial town and its region whose role in the revolt of 1381 has been little considered, in the expectation that such a case-study will not only demonstrate the problems of investigation from limited sources but will also contain much of general application to urban society at this time.[3] More important still, it may force some reconsideration of the nature of the revolt of 1381 as a whole.

## II

Canterbury before the Black Death was a populous and prosperous city. In the taxation of 1334 its quota ranked fourteenth among provincial towns in England, and the number of its tax-paying population in 1377 (2,574) placed it twelfth in order of size. Both these rankings are probably underestimates. The exclusion of suburban developments from the tax assessments, especially that outside the Westgate, significantly impairs the usefulness of both the quota and the number of the taxed populations as a reliable guide. Working with a maximum possible population calculated from the poll-tax return of 1377 for Canterbury of 6,240, and adjusting for suburban omissions, the size in the early fourteenth century may well have been in excess of 7,000. A major monastic and religious centre on the principal overland route between London and Europe, a Staple town possessing mint, exchange and Statute Merchant seal, the city attracted not only pilgrims to Becket's shrine but also an international traffic of merchants. Its social and economic structure reflected a rich variety of functions. A small but wealthy group of merchant-tradesmen, possessing significant London connections and dealing especially with merchants from Italy and the Low Countries, exercised a considerable influence within the town and even attracted alien merchants

[3] It is intended to provide comparative materials in introducing this essay.

permanently into their ranks. A substantial body of tradesmen and craftsmen supplied and provisioned local needs as well as those of the hinterland, and were especially numerous in food and drink trades, the manufacture of leather goods, and in clothing and textile production. Below the ranks of those permitted to practise trade and craft, subdivided tenements and sprawling extramural suburbs give evidence of population pressure and suggest poverty.[4]

The extent of the city's hinterland may be estimated from a variety of sources. Evidence for the field of rural–urban migration must be derived principally from place-surnames. The lists of taxpayers for national and local taxations and the surviving lists of freeman admissions provide materials for the more prosperous townsmen, and these may be partially supplemented by reference to city court rolls. Within Kent, following the usual pattern of distribution, migrants came from within an area which corresponded broadly with the extent of the archdeaconry of Canterbury, bounded to the north by the river Medway, reaching to the coast in the east and south, and reaching into the Kentish Weald to the west. Some Kentish immigrants did come from beyond this area, from Dartford, Otford, Sevenoaks, Tilbury, Westerham and Wrotham, for example, but their numbers were relatively few. From beyond Kent, place-surnames suggest, there was migration from a wide variety of counties: from Berkshire, Cambridgeshire, Cheshire, Cornwall, Derbyshire, Dorset, Durham, Essex, Gloucestershire, Hampshire, Hertfordshire, Lancashire, Leicestershire, Lincolnshire, Middlesex, Norfolk, Northamptonshire, Northumberland, Nottinghamshire, Oxfordshire, Suffolk, Surrey, Sussex, Warwickshire, Wiltshire and Yorkshire. There were also a few from France, Germany, Italy, the Low Countries and Scotland. Despite the limitations of this evidence for an understanding of the dynamics of migration the general picture it conveys is impressive testimony to Canterbury's influence and tends to be confirmed by other sources.[5]

---

[4] W. G. Hoskins, *Local History in England* (London, 1959), p. 176. For calculations from poll-tax, see M. M. Postan, *The Medieval Economy and Society* (London, 1972), pp. 29–30. An indication of the social and economic structure of Canterbury in the early fourteenth century may be derived from Canterbury Cathedral Archives and Library (hereafter C.C.A.L.), B/C/A 3; JB/100–11, 117–46; R/F 1–5; R/S 1–22; Chartae Antiquae, *passim*; Public Record Office, London (hereafter P.R.O.), E.179/123/43.

[5] C.C.A.L., B/C/A 3; P.R.O., E.179/123/43; C.C.A.L., JB/100–11, 117–46 and R/F 1–5.

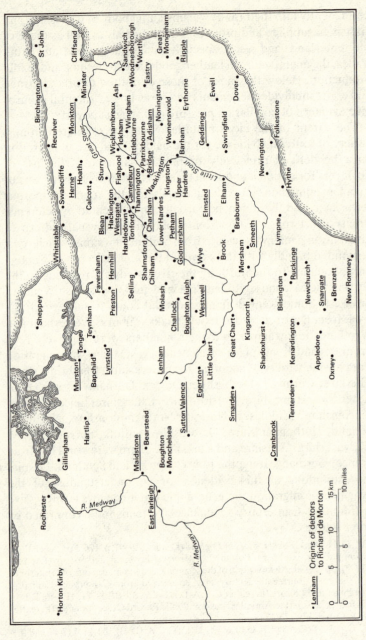

Kent origins of debtors to Canterbury men, c. 1336–49

The surviving recognizances enrolled under the Statute Merchant seal between 1336 and 1349 almost all indicate the place of origin of creditor and debtor, and thus provide some indication of the range of Canterbury's economic attraction. Once again, while many recognizances of Canterbury creditors so enrolled bore the names of parties from places beyond Kent, including London, by far the majority were Kentish and indicated origins south and east of the Medway. (See map.) The evidence of city court rolls suggests a pattern of trading contacts and market pull which confirms the picture supplied by the recognizances. The centralizing pressures of the estate management of Canterbury Cathedral Priory and St Augustine's Abbey, in particular, reinforced this regional structure. And as an ecclesiastical, religious and cultural centre the city attracted visitors not only to attend courts and work out their punishments but to observe and take part in a variety of festivals and entertainments when the town became a central place for public display.[6]

These intimate interconnections created a social structure which in many respects was essentially regional. If marriage patterns among the urban élite tended to become endogamous, for the majority of townsmen the opportunities were continuous with those of the village. Prosperous village families sent representatives to become tradesmen and craftsmen in town. Lower strata supplied recruits whose business lives were often short and who may soon have returned to the village or been swallowed up among labouring groups, unemployed and under-employed, who moved between town and country; and there were probably those in poverty whose desperation drove them to town in the hope of alms or the benefit of marginally greater and seasonally more constant employment opportunities. Family contacts and rural investments, especially within the core of the field of migration, were not necessarily broken by urban residence and often continued to be important. Townsmen, and not just the most prosperous, sought rural investment outlets. For some it was a matter of securing rent income, for some it was a matter of constructing or enlarging upon a family holding which might be subsequently bequeathed to an eldest son, and for a very few, acting on behalf of religious institutions, it was part of a policy of covert action in the land-market designed to evade the strictures of the Statute of Mortmain. Some villagers

[6] C.C.A.L., R/S 1–22.

owned property in Canterbury, as also did Londoners and other townsmen. The circulation of capital via the mechanisms of migration and investment followed the business life-cycles of individual townsmen. Those more prosperous citizens of some years' standing whose trading or manufacturing interests had enabled the creation of a rural as well as an urban holding might finally, though not invariably, seek to establish a surviving widow in urban surroundings while providing for children in the countryside, thereby inhibiting the growth of urban dynasties and completing the circular passage which their own imagination or that of their father or even grandfather had begun. For those less prosperous the fluctuation of demand and the instability of business made the journey shorter. Yet it seems that in the first half of the fourteenth century a prosperity, perhaps stimulated by institutions designed to facilitate merchant activity and perhaps sustained by the opportunities which warfare permitted, gave a continuity and stability to Canterbury's economy which encouraged the permanence of families such as Lincoln, Chicche, Cokyn, Stablegate and Tiece, and even threatened to create marked economic and social distinctions between the city and its hinterland.[7]

The government of Canterbury was principally in the hands of two annually elected bailiffs and six aldermen, each of whom represented a different ward of the city. In the first half of the fourteenth century there also existed a council of twelve jurats, whose powers were extensive, and a council of thirty-six elected citizens. The hierarchy of courts (excluding those of particular liberties, such as the prior's and the archbishop's) included at the lowest level the aldermanic courts, next the bailiffs' court, and finally the burghmoot. Servicing the principal officers and representatives were a host of minor officials from town serjeant to ward constable. Other institutions besides that of the burgesses also possessed courts and officers, including trade and craft organizations though these were never of major influence in the town; and the parish churches too, and their fraternities and chantries, possessed numerous offices. The management of this administrative structure tended to be concentrated in relatively few hands; responsibilities interlocked and overlapped. And the responsibilities of office did not stop at the city boundary: leading citizens such as

---

[7] For the rural holdings of Canterbury men, see C.C.A.L., Chartae Antiquae, *passim*.

Edmund de Stablegate, Nicholas Horn and William de Waure served on the councils of local lords and were also active in the royal administration of the county, and others were involved with the collection of national taxation and the provision of supplies and the means of defence for purposes of warfare. The power and status of this élite in Canterbury were reinforced by the peculiar nature of its franchise, since from at least as early as the 1340s the right to practise trade and craft was not confined to freemen alone. A substantial number of licensed tradesmen and craftsmen (perhaps as many as seventy or eighty in any one year) paying annual fines were a distinct non-free element within the community, while a narrow group of freemen enjoyed the privileges of their status which included the right to practise freely trade and craft. The selection of this narrow group, drawn, as far as may be judged, for the most part, not from within the town but from surrounding villages, is an obscure process but one which must have done much to maintain the power and influence of the upper stratum of a regional society.[8]

## III

Little direct indication of the impact of the Black Death upon Canterbury now survives. Rentals and chamberlains' accounts for the cathedral priory provide some indirect evidence, as do national taxation returns, freeman admissions and surviving wills. The effect upon the monastic community at Christ Church was probably greater than once thought and the much-praised preventive powers of an excellent drainage system and the water-supply provided by Prior Wibert must be disregarded – numbers may have fallen by as much as 30–40 per cent, and by 1376 they amounted to no more than 46 per cent. Comparison of pre- and post-plague taxation returns, both local and national, for 1346–7, 1348–9 and 1351–2, though giving only a crude guide, suggests that no more than one-third of all families within the taxable population survived; and comparison of pre- and post-plague rentals suggests a substantial turnover of

8 *Cal. Charter Rolls, 1257–1300*, pp. 472–3; *Cal. Charter Rolls, 1226–57*, p. 404; *Cal. Charter Rolls, 1341–1417*, pp. 84–5. See also W. G. Urry, *Canterbury under the Angevin Kings* (London, 1967); W. G. Urry, *The Chief Citizens of Canterbury* (Canterbury, 1978); A. F. Butcher, 'Canterbury's Earliest Rolls of Freemen Admission, 1297–1363', in F. Hull (ed.), *A Kentish Miscellany* (Kent Records, xxi, Maidstone, 1979).

tenants while indicating that vacancies were very soon filled. Relatively high enrolments of freemen in 1349 and 1350, here as elsewhere, may suggest replacement as urban opportunities suddenly became available (though it seems likely that the replacement was far from being simply on a one-for-one basis). More indirectly still, the extraordinary rise in receipts at the shrine of St Thomas in 1350 may also speak for devastation in town and countryside as survivors sought forgiveness and protection.[9]

For nearby Rochester, however, the survival of detailed and direct evidence permits a better understanding of the response of urban processes to the sudden and severe increase in rates of mortality. Rochester, itself later to be involved in the risings of 1381, was a town perhaps a little more than half the size of Canterbury whose ranking on the basis of taxation evidence, as with Canterbury, is probably unduly low since it too possessed extramural suburbs which have been omitted in the calculation of its population. The administrative centre of the Rochester diocese, it has left in bishops' registers and court proceedings valuable materials for an analysis of the extent of disruption. But even without such testimony the description of the consequences of the Black Death by the priory chronicler would be impressive enough: the disruption of the bishop's household, by the loss of personnel and the failure of supplies, and the digging of mass graves is reported by William de Dene and provides a vivid counterpoint to the statistics of the many institutions to benefices. Most important, however, is the evidence of the prior's 'Almerye' manor, a holding of some hundred properties in the city of Rochester and its suburbs. Drawn up in c. 1364, there survives a book of extracts from the manor court materials concerning the history of individual holdings between c. 1318 and 1364. The very existence of the book is probably witness to an administrative confusion brought about by the mortalities and the disorder of the property market, and it contains within it a survey carried out in 1355 by seven surviving tenants into those who had died during the Black Death, their tenancies and obligations. Much seems to have escaped official attention and in establishing the succession of tenants it seems that the priory may have been seeking to recover through new tenants the reliefs which they had earlier failed to collect. In all, it would

---

[9] C.C.A.L., MA 20; Priory Chamberlains' Accounts; R/F 6–7; OA/1 and 2; P.R.O., E179/123/23 and 123/24.

appear that about 50 per cent of the tenants had died of plague in 1348–50, to say nothing of subtenants. A little more than half of those who died were succeeded by their heirs, wives, children, siblings or kin, though some of the children were orphans or under legal age and needed the support of family and neighbours. The turnover of tenancies was remarkably rapid but there was, however strained, an identifiable family continuity – at least before 1361–2 when the second major epidemic struck both in Rochester and Canterbury. And comparison of family names in pre-plague taxation returns for Rochester with those in the manor court confirms this.[10]

It must be imagined that in Canterbury as in Rochester the impact of a mortality of the order of 50 per cent and subsequent immigration brought discontinuities and confusion at all levels of society. Of the 136 new freemen admitted to the city between 1349 and 1351, 70 were by redemption, 43 were by marriage, and 23 were by favour. The relatively high numbers for marriage and favour may reflect the response of the urban élite to crisis. Only 40 of the 136 are identifiable in the taxation returns for 1351–2 and, even allowing for the undoubted problems of identification and tax evasion, this low number may indicate a high degree of mobility and business instability in these years: if the tax assessments are any guide to business success then comparison of the returns of 1348–9 with those of 1351–2 would seem to indicate that this was not a profitable time for newcomers and very few seem to have risen to high office. Only two of those identifiable would seem to have been able to trace their families in Canterbury back across the Black Death and, strikingly, the flow of entrants by patrimony seems to have dried up. The urban élite would seem to have been in some disarray. Traditional relationships between wealth, status, age and office were severely threatened. The mutual interests of business and craft fellowship both within the town and between town and countryside must frequently have broken down; the network of credit must have become torn and ragged; the influx of migrants must have given an emphasis to new rural connections at the expense of older urban ones; the organization and performance of religious activities in parish church and cathedral must have suffered marked changes;

[10] Hoskins, *Local History in England*, p. 176; Kent Archives Office, D/Rc/F 1A and D/Rc/R 4; F. R. H. Du Boulay (ed.), *Medieval Kentish Society* (Kent Records, xviii, Maidstone, 1964), pp. 130, 160–1.

relations between leading citizens and their families and local landlords must often have been destroyed; and the whole business of government and administration in the town must have presented considerable problems to bailiffs, aldermen, jurats, councillors and the many minor officials. On 20 September 1351 the twelve jurats of Canterbury with the assent of the bailiffs, aldermen, council of thirty-six, and 'tote la commune' published ordinances in the burghmoot which rehearsed a number of standard customary procedures for the courts and the actions of officials, the need for the publication of which may well indicate prevailing uncertainties in these matters. Economically the sudden, large-scale disintegration and dispersal of the accumulated capital of townsmen in town and country may have proved beneficial to immigrants, but it was probably destructive of the economic power of that élite formed in the first half of the fourteenth century. The mechanism of such processes is suggested in the wills of contemporary townsmen. The dispersal of the property and cash of Richard de Morton provides an example. Morton, who was a prominent member of Canterbury's élite in the 1330s and 1340s, actively involved in town government and administration as well as royal administration in the county, closely connected with the cathedral priory, part of a family one of whose members had been sheriff of Kent, seems to have acted as a local money-lender both independently and jointly with other leading townsmen. When he died in 1349 his will provided for the distribution of his wealth in town and countryside between his wife, his three male children, the three male children of a kinsman, and the prior and monks of Christ Church. The subsequent fortunes of his wife and children may be followed in national tax assessments and other local archives: the influence and distinction of the father seem not to have been repeated in the sons, one of whom, William, was cited as a rebel in 1381. Not that such a dispersal was unusual; rather it represents an extraordinary quantity of such actions in so short a space of time.[11]

Nevertheless in Canterbury as in Rochester there were significant continuities and they must not be underestimated. They may indeed provide some explanation for subsequent social tension and con-

[11] C.C.A.L., R/F 6–7; P.R.O., E.179/123/24, 123/23, 123/43; C.C.A.L., B/C/A 3, Burghmoot Ordinance beginning 'Ceux sont les ordinances des xij Juretz de la Citee de Canterbirs', Chartae Antiquae W 245 r; W. E. Flaherty, 'The Great Rebellion in Kent of 1381 Illustrated from the Public Records', *Archaeologia Cantiana*, iii (1860), p. 75.

flict. Of the 252 persons taxed in 1351–2 perhaps as many as 80 appeared in local and national taxations for Canterbury in the 1340s before the Black Death, and some of these were from families of some local standing. Between 1346–7 and 1348–9 the constitution of the wealthiest group in the city, measured by tax assessments, changed considerably. Only men such as Hugh le Wodour, the moneyers William Broun and Robert Lapyn, John Poukel the taverner, John Elham and William Frenshe remained; and by 1351–2 still more had disappeared from the pre-Black Death lists. The greatest continuities existed among the middling groups of tax-payers and for many of these the immediate post-Black Death years seem to have been years of prosperity: of the 80 persons who survived, some 60 per cent recorded rising assessments, in marked contrast to the experience of the newcomers discussed above. Many of these survivors came to occupy the upper ranks among the taxpayers, and their new wealth in many cases brought new status and office. From this group were elected the bailiffs in the 1340s and 1350s, men associated with the old forms of city government who must have felt increasingly uncertain of their position at a time of rapid social mobility and the collapse of traditional means of social control when new and unfamiliar social groupings emerged within the city. As these families became identified with reactionary national legislation both in town and countryside, tensions rose and their position grew even more insecure.[12]

## IV

In the 1360s and 1370s the links with the early fourteenth century grow still weaker. Of 188 tenancies in the city held by the cathedral priory in 1366–7, when the rentals begin to provide detailed annual information after some years of formulaic repetition in the 1350s, only 34 individuals or families may be traced back to the 1351–2 taxation, and no more than 8 of these had survived the Black Death. Whatever the economic difficulties of the 1350s and early 1360s the consequences of the second major plague epidemic of 1361–2, remembered with other famous dates on the fly-leaf of one of the city's fourteenth-century memoranda books, must be reckoned responsible for further dislocation. A Christ Church obituary book gives evidence of high mortality in the monastery: twenty-five

12 C.C.A.L., B/C/A 3; P.R.O., E.179/123/43, 123/20, 123/22, 123/23, 123/24 and 123/27.

monks died in 1361–2, all but three of their deaths being concentrated in the months of July and August. The chamberlains' accounts for the priory suggest that numbers of monks in the 1360s and 1370s were frequently 30–40 per cent below earlier expectations. In the city archives only the lists of freemen admissions survive to provide indirect evidence of this plague year. Numbers of admissions rose again. No more than one of their number may be found in the taxation returns of the 1350s, and in both 1361–2 and 1362–3 there were no admissions by patrimony. Of the eighty-eight admissions in 1361–2 and 1362–3, ten were by marriage and seven by favour. Acting upon a population probably significantly restructured in terms of age composition and radically altered in its social organization, it may well be that this epidemic with the subsequent outbreaks in the remaining years of the 1360s and 1370s was decisive in transforming the city of the early fourteenth century and preparing the way for social conflict – all the more because this 'mortalite des enfauntz' struck at the hope of any natural, internal regeneration.[13]

The national epidemic of 1369 left no clear mark on the limited sources which survive for Canterbury's history in that year, and rentals show no significant turnover of tenancies, but the less well-known national outbreak of 1374–5 seems to have had a considerable impact. In the priory rentals more than 40 per cent of the 188 tenancies changed hands in this year, three times the normal annual rate for the undoubtedly unstable period between 1366 and 1381. It is no coincidence that it was in 1376 that St Augustine's Abbey chose to write a new rental for its city properties, and that rental bears evidence of the confused condition of the property market in the preceding years. This same year, too, saw Archbishop Sudbury seeking to restore numbers in the cathedral priory. The sixties and the seventies saw the further erosion of the traditional élite and, with the death of men such as Edmund Cokyn in 1361–2 and Edmund Stablegate (the father) in 1372, and others in 1374–5, the destruction and dispersal of the accumulated wealth and influence of still more of those families with pre-Black Death origins in the town. These decades saw the beginning, in the town and nearby villages, of the abandonment of attempts to maintain the traditional patterns of inheritance by the search for family and kin to provide

---

[13] C.C.A.L., MA 20, 21, 22; P.R.O., E.179/123/24; C.C.A.L., OA/1, Lit. MS. D 12, Priory Chamberlains' Accounts 40–4, 67, R/F 11 ii and 11 iii.

heirs, and they saw the beginnings of a demographic imbalance between town and countryside which was to have far-reaching implications for provincial urban society – the depopulation of the countryside was, temporarily, to the benefit of the towns.[14]

The evidence of the urban rent rolls undoubtedly points to a high turnover among tenancies, in the majority of cases being held for no more than three or four years with a substantial number for only one. Concentration of economic activities in trading quarters in the town was no longer apparent and is only tentatively to be identified again in the last decade or so of the century. A fluid occupational distribution in the town and a constantly changing composition of neighbourhoods is the prevailing picture; and this condition may well reflect a marked instability of business and a short duration of business lives similar to that to be found in the 1390s and the early fifteenth century when more abundant documentation permits closer examination. But for all the high rate of turnover the numbers of vacancies, especially those which lasted more than a few weeks, were very few. Everything points to sustained levels of population despite the repeated epidemics and the uncertain quality of business. What is more, between 1366 and 1381 the priory seldom thought it necessary to lower any of the rents it demanded, though there were a series of temporary adjustments in 1374–5; and real levels of payment seldom fell below the asking price. Demand for property was sustained and there was even new building work set in motion. Immigrant capital, however, quickly dissipated, and the redistributed wealth of the victims of epidemic disease seem to have combined to present opportunities to those fortunate enough to survive, despite high prices and rising wages. At this moment also, when the links between town and countryside were closer than at any time in the early fourteenth century in the persons of the immigrants who sustained levels of population and production in the towns, the invasion of the rural property market by townsmen seems to have quickened, and new estate policies by local landlords opened up to citizens the opportunity of acquiring a leasehold estate, an opportunity some Canterbury men readily seized.[15]

---

[14] C.C.A.L., MA 21, 22, Lit. MS. E 19; *Concilia Magnae Brittanie*, ed. D. Wilkins, 3 vols. (London, 1737), iii, p. 110; C.C.A.L., OA/1 and 2; Urry, *Chief Citizens of Canterbury*, p. 39; C.C.A.L., Court Rolls for Ickham, Adisham and Chartham.

[15] C.C.A.L., MA 21, 22, FA/1, Beadles' Rolls for Ickham, Adisham, Chartham, Godmersham, Eastry, Lydden, Monkton, Great Chart, Little Chart, etc., *Chartae Antiquae, passim*; Court Rolls as above.

*V*

If demographic changes in the sixties and seventies prepared the way for social conflict by transforming the urban social structure and opening up a gap between the form and the reality of urban government and the exercise of economic and social control then there were other developments which combined intimately with those demographic changes to determine the precise character of the conflict. Weather conditions and the demands of warfare were particularly important. The level of grain prices in the fifties, sixties and early seventies may have done much to sustain landlord policies and frustrate the expectations of their rural tenants, and in the towns it may have helped to worsen relations between labour and employers. Though monetary factors may have been in part responsible it is clear that in the sixties and early seventies on Christ Church manors near to Canterbury the poor quality of the harvests was the cause of much concern. Locally this concern was no doubt exacerbated by the frequent need to supply the households of king and queen, various purveyors, as well as the troops of the king, the duke of Lancaster and even Sir Robert Knolles.[16]

Such demands were a source of potential grievance and they were part of a whole series of demands made directly and indirectly upon town and country in the sixties and seventies which set these two decades apart. The fear of invasion pervades royal administration in the county. Commissioners drawn from the ranks of local worthies, regularly including leading citizens of Canterbury, are set to work to improve defences in town and castle and on the coast, and to maintain a military readiness. In June of 1363 a commission of William Halden, William Wauer, Thomas Everard and Nicholas atte Crouche, all Canterbury men, are set to work to repair the city's walls and ditches, the walls 'for the most part fallen on account of old age and stones thereof carried away', and the ditches obstructed; they were to hold an inquisition into who had stolen the stones and who had blocked the ditches; and they were to remove the houses, buildings and enclosures of gardens which had been built within and without the walls so that repairs might be carried out. In 1371, especially in 1377, in 1379, 1380 and early in 1381 there were a series of commissions to improve coastal defences. In 1378, 1379 and 1380 attention was again turned upon Canterbury's walls.

16 C.C.A.L., Beadles' Rolls for Ickham, Godmersham, Adisham and Chartham.

The bailiffs of the city were to take stonemasons to work to repair walls, turrets, gates and dykes, and also to carry out work on the cathedral. The city was granted murage for ten years in 1379, and in 1380, the old Westgate having been razed, a new one was to be built with the assistance of the archbishop of Canterbury. Commissions of array in town and countryside were numerous and grew more frequent in the 1370s. In 1369, 1370 and 1374 they were associated with injunctions to further enforce the Statute of Labourers; in 1377 they were issued in the belief that the French were about to land or had landed in great force, and the system of warning beacons was to be held in readiness; in 1379 and 1380 they continued to be associated with fear of coastal attack; and as late as 14 May 1381, following earlier commissions in the county, William Elys and Edmund Horn, bailiffs of Canterbury, were to array all between the ages of sixteen and sixty in the town. The burden of these commissions and grants added to the burden of national taxation. Grants of murage in Canterbury meant regular taxation on rents in the city and market tolls on townsmen and villagers. Other local taxations were also periodically imposed for work on city property. Complaints against the officers of the crown heard in the 1360s were specifically investigated in 1378 when accusations were made as to the oppression and corruption of collectors of subsidies. In January 1381 a commission of inquiry headed by the sheriff and escheator of Kent was to examine the number, names, abode and condition of all lay persons over the age of fifteen, men, women and servants, excepting notorious beggars, without waiting for or communicating with the collectors or controllers of the subsidy granted to the king and was asked to report to the Exchequer by 28 April of that year; and on 16 January collectors of the subsidy of three groats were appointed for Canterbury and its suburbs. On 20 May a further commission was appointed to enforce collection of the subsidy in the city. Canterbury citizens, in many ways also closely associated with village life, became identified with government policies all the more oppressive because they might be connected with war failure and frustrated opportunities. Frequently arrayed in town and countryside into a defensive military force, the townsmen and their neighbours possessed the organization for widespread insurrection should discontent coalesce and violent defensive action seem inevitable. For those who came to see the ceremonial which surrounded the interment of the Black Prince in Canterbury Cathedral at

Michaelmas in 1376 the occasion must have been highly and even dangerously charged. The close association of his tomb with the shrine of Becket powerfully reinforced the sense of military loss which his death conveyed at a time when invasion was feared, rumours of Gaunt's designs on the throne were rife and when stories of the corruption of the court and its allies among the London merchants were doubtless in circulation. Perhaps the subsequent demolition of the nave of Canterbury Cathedral before rebuilding did not seem to local men and women the obvious act of benefaction by Archbishop Sudbury that retrospectively it may appear.[17]

## VI

When violence came in 1381 the way had been prepared for it by other disturbances in the city and its environs. What is more there may be other indications of protest which deserve attention. Before the Black Death, however, there had been two major periods of urban unrest in the late 1320s and the early 1340s which may usefully be compared with what took place in the second half of the fourteenth century. The riots of the late twenties, and especially those of 1327, seem to be part of a widespread anti-monastic feeling in defence of local privileges which was inspired by national political conflicts. In the 1340s anti-monastic feeling was again apparent, though there were attacks on individuals in the countryside which involved Canterbury men and suggest more complex issues in the period between 1341 and 1344. Conflict with the priory, however, seems to have been a central issue and in August 1343 an attack on the prior's close and houses resulted in the accusation of the theft of forty horses, twenty oxen, twenty cows, and assaults on the prior's men and servants. According to the terms of the royal commission issued on 16 August Thomas Everard and Edmund Stablegate, bailiffs of the city, at the instiga-

---

[17] *Cal. Pat. Rolls, 1361–4*, p. 373; *Cal. Pat. Rolls, 1370–4*, p. 108; *Cal. Pat. Rolls, 1377–81*, pp. 4, 7, 38, 350, 471, 574, 629, 596, 274, 335, 450, 370, 460; *Cal. Pat. Rolls, 1367–70*, pp. 264–5, 446–7, 473; *Cal. Pat. Rolls, 1370–4*, p. 34; *Cal. Pat. Rolls, 1374–7*, pp. 321, 497; *Cal. Pat. Rolls, 1377–81*, pp. 38, 359, 471, 574; *Cal. Pat. Rolls, 1364–7*, p. 287; *Cal. Pat. Rolls, 1377–81*, pp. 301, 622, 426; *Cal. Fine Rolls, 1377–83*, pp. 248–9; C. E. Woodruff and W. Danks, *Memorials of the Cathedral and Priory of Christ in Canterbury* (London, 1912), pp. 159ff.

tion of the commonalty of the city, were guilty of unduly usurping royal power having caused:

> public proclamation to be made in the liberty of the city that all persons avouching themselves to be of that liberty, within the ages of sixty and sixteen years, should assemble on a certain day at a certain place to hear certain matters to be laid before them and lend their assent, council and aid to what would be treated of there, at which assembly they entered into divers unlawful confederacies prejudicial to the king and his royal power, binding themselves by oath to maintain the same and threatening some men and fellow-citizens who refused to join in these excesses and misdeeds with the overthrow of the houses wherein they dwell and all their buildings in the city unless they will consent to maintain their confederacy according to an ordinance made amongst themselves.

So difficult had conditions become indeed that the archbishop and the prior were granted royal permission on 26 August to take as many armed men with them as they might need for their protection on their forthcoming journeys to Canterbury. As late as February 1344 action was being taken against disturbances. A commission of 7 February accused several Canterbury men of:

> assembling a great number of evildoers, from the city of Canterbury and other parts of Kent, aided and abetted by bailiffs and others of that city, to prevent the men put on the panels as well on assizes as on other juries before the king's justices appointed to take the assizes from daring to come before the justices and find the truth and so terrified them with threats that the assizes and juries have not been taken, and that the said persons and others under that colour have committed assaults on others on divers parts of the county, killing some, mutilating or robbing others, and perpetrating outrages.

Whatever the source of grievance and division in these cases their manifestations, despite the similarity of rural involvement, are significantly different from what took place in 1381, for what is clear in the 1320s and 1340s is the central involvement of the urban élite as instigator in these conflicts. Not only do the bailiffs seem to be implicated, but other participants are drawn from among the leading citizens. The causes here involve the town as an identifiable political unit even though there are those citizens who would disagree with the actions taken. The conflicts seem to be, at root, or at least in the way they are articulated, conflicts between liberties. In Canterbury and its environs in 1381 the divisions are not expressed in this way.[18]

Not that such conflicts were unknown in the period between the Black Death and 1381. The removal of the corn-market by the citizens into the city from the extramural suburb of St Paul's during the period of high grain prices in 1365 was just such an incident, involving the city and St Augustine's Abbey in a dispute over jurisdiction which was only partially resolved by the abbey's production of charters going back to the grants of Ethelbert and Cnut. The most significant areas of conflict, however, are indicated by incidents which may be found in the records of the city's bailiffs' courts for the 1370s and for 1381. Such courts were, in part, the place where Canterbury citizens recorded and worked out business transactions with townsmen and villagers. Here may be found in the seventies the trading connections between, for example, Canterbury men and villagers out on the Isle of Thanet or nearby Chartham and Petham. The connections are essentially local, especially after the removal of the Staple from Canterbury to Queenborough in 1368, though those with London and dealers from more distant markets still occur. But alongside these matters are those referred up to the bailiffs' courts by the six ward courts of the aldermen, cases which reflect the tensions of this urban society and suggest the formation of lines of social division between groups in the city. A limited comparison between the courts of the seventies and those of the forties suggests, perhaps, qualitative and quantitative changes, a growth in the number of clashes and in their kind. Most noticeable are the frequent entries concerning the attempts of employers to control labour and especially its mobility and terms of contract. For the leading citizens such as Edmund de Stablegate, moreover, it was not just a question of controlling labour in the town but also of controlling agricultural labour on their estates, and they sought to use the bailiffs' courts to enforce their control. The competition for labour too bred resentment and when Christine Boghiere brought an action under the Statute of Labourers against Thomas Everard for attracting her servant from her service, she was voicing a common complaint against inequalities in the labour market and the hypocrisy of those in government.

---

[18] *Cal. Pat. Rolls, 1340–3*, pp. 365–6; *Cal. Pat. Rolls, 1343–5*, pp. 166, 167, 115, 184, 284, 278.

The gap which opened up between the leading citizens and the labouring population and between the leading citizens and the unstable, middling ranks of tradesmen and craftsmen (many of whom in Canterbury were denied the advantages of the franchise) may be seen to have grown as prosecutions were made of those who took stone from the city walls and disputes arose over the payment of local taxation. From the middling ranks, moreover, there are signs of opposition and resistance. The order to the bailiffs and community of the city of 15 September 1376 to desist from dissensions and brawls newly moved in the city indicates disorders of which the courts give some evidence. Violent outbreaks between representatives of city government and lesser men such as John Lukke, John Balsham junior and Henry Bongay the armourer are illustrative of growing tension in the last years of Edward III's reign. Shortly after the burial of the Black Prince, when Thomas Oterington the bailiff, on behalf of the city and with many citizens present, was concluding negotiations with representatives of St Augustine's Abbey concerning the construction of fish-shambles by St Margaret's church, the butcher John Horn spoke out against him, causing a confusion in which he resisted arrest by striking Oterington on the arm. In the previous year Henry Bongay had been arrested and imprisoned by the bailiffs, John Tyece and John Taunton, for assisting in the escape from gaol of a prisoner and his reaching sanctuary in a nearby church. On 16 July 1378 a commission was issued to the bailiffs of Canterbury and to John Tebbe, William Preston and Thomas Oterington to inquire into information that:

> certain malefactors and disturbers of the peace, citizens and other inhabitants of the city and suburbs, have assembled in great numbers and stirred up strife, debates and contentions therein, sowing great discord amongst the citizens, and so obstinately holding together that they will not in any way submit to justice but combine by insurrection to resist the king's ministers in the execution of their office.

However effective the bailiffs were in arresting the malefactors, the evidence of the courts makes it clear that trouble continued through 1379 and 1380. John Breche, the constable of Newyngate ward, was twice attacked in the performance of his duty in 1379–80; on 24 June 1380 a similar attack was made on Stephen Taverner in Burgate ward; and John Chalker and Stephen Taverner, acting as town serjeants, were attacked in Newyngate ward on 1 August 1380. The mandate to arrest and imprison the citizens and other inhabitants who gathered in large numbers and caused daily disturbances in the early months of 1380 seems to have had little success.[19]

The impression of mounting violence is inescapable, as is its direction; it was against those members of the urban community who were representatives of a social stratum whose interests were inextricably linked with local landlords and whose influence was felt in town and country whether as royal officials, the administrative officers of the local estates of lay and ecclesiastical magnates, or in the management of their own businesses and property holdings. In Canterbury they sought to re-establish the authority which demographic turmoil had eroded. The custumal compiled in the late fourteenth century bears witness to an assertion of their legal rights and obligations. It also indicates a determination to come to terms with the turbulence of the city by the imposition of curfew, the control of the carrying and drawing of arms, and measures against malefactors. But in the sixties and seventies the social and economic confusion combined with repressive and unsuccessful policies and a near constant state of military preparedness created antagonisms between social groups which could not be contained.[20]

## VII

On 10 June 1381, at a time of the year when many might have come to the city for the feast of Corpus Christi, the rebels came south to Canterbury from Maidstone and the Weald ('ad Maydston et Waldam et inde Cantuariam'). Froissart claimed that 'When Wat Tyler and Jack Straw entered into Canterbury, all the common people made great feast, for all the town was of their assent' and he, with others, tells the story of the entry of the rebels into the cathedral, apparently either in search of Archbishop Sudbury or to issue a warning of his murder to the monks, adding that they attacked and damaged the cathedral priory and St Augustine's Abbey as well as robbing and damaging the archbishop's palace ('the bishop's chamber'?). The account in the *Anonimalle*

---

[19] *Cal. Pat. Rolls, 1346–7*, p. 203; C.C.A.L., JB/170, 174, 176, 178, 181; *Cal. Close Rolls, 1364–8*, p. 478; C.C.A.L., JB/146; *Cal. Close Rolls, 1374–7*, p. 412; *Cal. Pat. Rolls, 1377–81*, pp. 304, 471, 574.

[20] Bodleian Lib., Oxford, MS. Tanner, clxv.

*Chronicle* speaks of the rebels successfully summoning and examining the mayor, bailiffs and commons to enlist their support and to search out traitors in the town: 'three were mentioned and their names revealed, to be immediately dragged out of their houses by the commons and beheaded'. On the following day, some remaining to guard the city, a substantial force left for London. For all their circumstantial detail these descriptions must be said to omit much and telescope events where they are not clearly inaccurate. The picture that may be pieced together from the jurors' presentments is more complex.[21]

On 10 June, according to the presentments, there were attacks in Canterbury by men from the city, from Lydd, Thanet, Lenham, Newington, Bearsted and Malling, on the houses of William Medmenham, Thomas Holt (in the extramural suburb of the Westgate hundred), Thomas Oterington, John Tebbe, Sir Richard de Hoo, Sir Thomas Fog and Thomas de Garwynton. Henry Bongay raised an assembly to attack the house of Robert Sherman in the town, and John Hales of Malling, who came with a great multitude to Canterbury, led attacks not only on houses but also upon the castle and the town hall. William Septvantz, the sheriff of Kent and local landlord, was forced to go to his nearby manor of Milton to collect and deliver up the plea rolls and writs to be burned. At nearby Tonford Sir Thomas Fog's property was attacked and townsmen and villagers ransacked Thomas Garwynton's property some three miles to the south at Welle. At Preston by Faversham rebels broke into the property of William Makenade, another man with Canterbury interests. Just to the south of Canterbury, at Otehelle, John Tebbe was murdered. The involvement of Wat Tyler in these episodes is repeatedly attested but, with the exception of Henry Bongay's intervention, the organization of this phase of the revolt is unclear.[22]

On 11, 12 and 13 June there is no evidence of activity in the town, though on 11 June Canterbury men seem to have accompanied others in the assault on Maidstone gaol and men from Canterbury and Wye attacked the manor of Sir Thomas Fog near the city. Out on Thanet on 13 June, however, William Medmenham's house at

[21] See *Peasants' Revolt of 1381*, ed. Dobson, pp. 205 (but for Waltham read Weald), 139–40, 127–8.

[22] Flaherty, 'Great Rebellion in Kent of 1381', pp. 65–96; A. Réville and C. Petit-Dutaillis, *Le soulèvement des travailleurs d'Angleterre en 1381* (Paris, 1898); E. Powell and G. M. Trevelyan (eds.), *The Peasants' Rising and the Lollards* (London, 1899).

Manston was attacked by men from St Laurence and St John's, and the rolls found there of the Office of the Receiver of Green Wax were burned. Saturday 15 June saw a new stage of development. The continuator of the *Eulogium Historiarum* wrote that 'those who returned to Canterbury [from London] had their own ordinances proclaimed and killed a burgess there who contradicted them. They burned charters, records and writings in the house of justice.' The precise details of the presentments indicate, once again, the involvement of Henry Bongay the armourer, who made a proclamation on 15 June that John Tyece should be killed, and men from the local villages of Chartham, Petham, Elham and Harbledown carried out his instructions and probably also burned Tyece's muniments. On the same day Bongay led a mob to the house of William Watership and intimidated him into handing over cash and property, and also went with a certain assembly to Ospringe where they assaulted the Canterbury man Nicholas atte Crouch and forced him to pay a ransom of 100 shillings. Still on 15 June a Thanet man attacked the house of John Wynnepeny, the draper in the city, and extorted money from him. Though outbreaks of violent disruption continued in the Canterbury area at least until August and elsewhere as late as the early autumn, apart from an attack by Canterbury men on the house of Thomas Holbeame at Stalisfield on 16 June and an assault by a man from Ospringe on Hugh Hosier and Thomas Perot on 22 June, the involvement of the city is obscure, with the exception of the attempt by John Gyboun of Maidstone to make the bailiffs levy the whole community to resist the lords and justices assigned to keep the peace, and the continued evidence of clashes in the bailiffs' courts.[23]

The accounts of Froissart and the *Anonimalle Chronicle* seem far from the truth when they imply that Canterbury openly welcomed and co-operated with the rebels. What is so striking about the violent outbreaks in the city and its environs is that a detailed examination of the personnel reveals that the social divisions of the sixties and seventies, which emerged from the remnants of a society in which the authority of the élite was relatively secure, were clearly at the root of the conflict. John Tebbe, described in the poll-tax as 'cultor terre' (as was Edmund Horn, another member of the urban

23 *Peasants' Revolt of 1381*, ed. Dobson, p. 208; Flaherty, 'Great Rebellion in Kent of 1381'; Réville and Petit-Dutaillis, *Le soulèvement des travailleurs*; Powell and Trevelyan (eds.), *Peasants' Rising and the Lollards*.

élite), had held most high offices in the town, had been a member of parliament for the city, held land in an area to the south of Canterbury and was closely associated with Canterbury Cathedral Priory. In the immediate post-Black Death period he had acted as serjeant, beadle and rent-collector for the priory manor of Adisham during the time when severe depopulation caused disorder among tenants and tenancies, and he compiled a detailed description of conditions in his account for 1349–50. Later, his associate or appointee Roger Weddyng was to take on the lease of the same manor and himself become involved in a manorial dispute over tenancies and also in the revolt of 1381 when he fell victim to the menaces of Joan, wife of Henry Aleyn senior, at Petham. John Tyece, one of the very few survivors from pre-Black Death Canterbury and a member of an influential local family, had also been an important office-holder, possessed close connections with the cathedral priory, owned important properties in the town, had made substantial investments in rural property in the fifties, sixties and early seventies, and maintained strong trading contacts with London. And he it was who had, at least in part, been responsible for the imprisonment of Henry Bongay in 1375. William Medmenham added to his urban involvement the stewardship of the estates of St Augustine's Abbey and royal office in the county. William Makenade, similarly a local steward, was also involved in royal commissions. Nicholas atte Crouch, member of a well-established local family as well as being a major urban office-holder, had served as sheriff of Kent and on a variety of commissions and had acted as assessor and collector of taxes in the county. Thomas Oterington, described as 'squire' in the poll-tax, had held important office in the town and was also a rent-collector for the cathedral priory in the city. William Watership and his brother Laurence, as well as being urban officers, had acted as collectors and assessors of the poll-tax in the city. Sherman, Oterington and Wynnepeny were similarly members of the governing élite while Sir Thomas Fog and Sir Richard Hoo were members of a local gentry whose dealings tied them closely to the affairs of the ecclesiastical houses and the leading townsmen while they also served in the royal administration of the county. They were all, indeed, representatives of an authority in town and countryside against whom opposition had frequently flared into violence in the seventies. The town, a royal stronghold, provided a stage for the public display of hostility to what was seen as unjustifiable oppression by a social group to which the crown had traditionally looked for the maintenance of obedience but which could no longer be certain of the power which its economic strength and social status had once assured.[24]

When townsmen and villagers – family, friends, neighbours and kin, in this period often only recently separated – joined in attacks on the leading citizens, though their numbers might have been swollen by the poor, it is noticeable that they included in their number those such as John Lukke the carpenter, John Abel the sutor, John Dane the cobbler, Henry White the tailor and John Cogger the tiler, who were drawn from the middling and lower ranks of tradesmen and craftsmen in the city, who probably felt most keenly the injustices and frustrations of their position in relation to those more privileged, unable as they probably were to gain access to those institutional markets which offered protection against the fluctuations of demand. In this connection the figure of Henry Bongay the armourer is representative. His emergence as a local leader probably arose naturally from his failure to break into positions of authority in the town and from his conflicts with the officers of the town in the 1370s. His voice was doubtless one with a strong appeal to villagers, who resented this urban-based social group not only for its implementation of the oppressive policies of government and local landlords but for its invasion of the rural property market.[25]

The so-called alliance between townsmen and villagers in 1381 was not, in Canterbury's case, a temporary phenomenon but a natural expression of a regional social structure in which town and countryside were inextricably entwined. The extraordinary pressures of the fifties, sixties and seventies, and perhaps especially the sixties and seventies, when demographic, military and climatic forces combined, placed that social structure under such strain that its traditional bonds began to pull apart. At perhaps its most sensitive point, among the disaffected and underprivileged artisans and petty tradesmen, social tension began to resolve itself into open if sporadic conflict well before 1381. When their kinsmen, friends and neighbours in the villages turned to violent resistance they were

[24] P.R.O., E.179/240/308, 123/45, 123/47, 123/48, 123/59, 123/50, 123/51; C.C.A.L., Beadles' Rolls for Adisham, MA 20, 21; Flaherty, 'Great Rebellion in Kent of 1381', p. 95; Urry, *Chief Citizens of Canterbury*; C.C.A.L., OA/1 and 2, Register H, fo. 42, Misc. Bonds, Chartae Antiquae, JB/170–81, FA/3.

[25] P.R.O., E.179/123/50; Flaherty, 'Great Rebellion in Kent of 1381'.

already prepared and together took vengeance on the property and persons of those whom they identified as their oppressors in town and country, those whom they saw as betraying the trust which their status and office bestowed upon them.

# 5. The Risings in York, Beverley and Scarborough, 1380–1381

R. B. DOBSON

'From the uncertainty of good government, many insolences are committed among the inhabitants and commons of cities and towns, evils arise as well as scandals; and peaceful rule is badly hindered by the excitement of divers kind of dangers.'[1] Compared with the rulers of most other late medieval states, the kings of England rarely needed to be obsessively preoccupied with the dangers of widespread insurrection within their towns; but when the young Richard II sent this particular appeal for restraint to the burgesses of Beverley on 18 March 1382, he was expressing a sentiment that must have been shared by many. Certainly the potentially alarming implications of the recent 'malice et rebellion' displayed by so many English towns were much in the minds of the royal ministers and officials who had attended the king's sixth parliament at Westminster between November 1381 and February 1382. Quite apart from major upheavals in the city of London itself, as well as in the six boroughs (Canterbury, Bury St Edmunds, Beverley, Scarborough, Bridgwater and Cambridge) at first excluded from the general pardons proclaimed at that parliament, it is now well known that serious risings had occurred in more than a dozen other English towns as large as York and Norwich and as small as Rochester and Guildford.[2] Moreover, so dependent must any list of English provincial towns involved in the disturbances of 1381 be upon the vagaries of record survival that it could well be the case that few English boroughs of substantial size were entirely unaffected by the

[1] Beverley Corporation Archives (hereafter cited as B.C.A.), Town Cartulary, fo. 17. Other record repositories from which unpublished documents are cited in the following notes are abbreviated as follows: B.I.H.R. (Borthwick Institute of Historical Research, York); P.R.O. (Public Record Office); S.B.A. (Scarborough Borough Archives, deposited at County Record Office, Northallerton); Y.C.A. (York City Archives).

[2] *Rotuli Parliamentorum*, 6 vols. (Record Comm., London, 1783), iii, pp. 103, 118; *ibid.*, iii, p. 164 for the destruction of 'toutes les Chartres et Munimentz' of Guildford in one of the lesser known urban risings of 1381.

turbulence of the 'hurlyng time'. To an extent perhaps insufficiently acknowledged, most of the generalizations made about the geographical extent of the risings of 1381 are based on *ex silentio* assumptions that are dangerous in the extreme. Even the common belief that agrarian society in northern England was completely immune from the revolutionary enthusiasms of the year is hard to square with the revelation that in the autumn of 1382 hundreds of Yorkshiremen were summoned to York to appear before John of Gaunt and his fellow justices, then investigating unspecified (alas) 'treasons, felonies, uprisings and other misdeeds' in the county.[3]

Future investigation of such legal evidence may one day even come to suggest that some degree of urban as well as rural participation in 'les grands meschiefs deinz le roialme' during the early years of Richard II's reign was positively ubiquitous throughout much of England; but if ubiquitous it was certainly not uniform. It cannot of course be coincidental that the decade which followed the Good Parliament of 1376 seems to have been one of the most turbulent eras in the history of so many late medieval provincial towns as well as in the history of London itself; but in England, as in Western Europe as a whole during the years between 1378 and 1382, it has to be admitted that 'if there was a symphony, it was not at all played to time'.[4] The fact is that the study of urban conflict in this period presents the historian with a familiar but inescapable paradox. At one level, urban protest movements in late fourteenth-century England testify to one of the most intriguing features of medieval public life: the way in which small communities of men and women so much more localized in their needs and aspirations than ourselves were nevertheless even more likely than their modern counterparts to be stirred into violent demonstrations of feeling by national and international events. On the other hand, and much more frustratingly, the limitations and disparity of the surviving

---

[3] P.R.O., Just. 1/1138 is the now fragmentary assize roll (only three membranes survive) of proceedings heard at York in September 1382 before John of Gaunt and his fellow justices commissioned to investigate 'various treasons, insurrections and other evils' in Yorkshire. I am most grateful to Mr Andrew Prescott for lending me his transcripts of the even more interesting writ file of this commission (P.R.O., K.B.9/1069) which records the names, although unfortunately not the specific offences, of many of those summoned before Gaunt and his colleagues. Not surprisingly, inhabitants of Beverley and York figure prominently on this file but so too do men of Hull, Humberside, Whitby, south Yorkshire, Craven and even the vicars of Halifax and Doncaster (m. 9).

[4] M. Mollat and P. Wolff, *Ongles Bleus, Jacques et Ciompi* (Paris, 1970), p. 139.

written evidence are such that he who would identify the common characteristics of the towns of late medieval England is notoriously only too likely to conclude with an enhanced awareness of what made them different from, rather than similar to, one another. A hundred years of intermittent research on the history of the medieval English town has done sadly little to lessen the force of Bishop Stubbs's uncharacteristically cautious warning that 'the obscurity of the subject is not a mere result of our ignorance or the deficiency of the record, but of a confusion of usages which was felt at the time to be capable of no general treatment'.[5]

From such familiar dilemmas the study of the risings of 1381–2 in the three Yorkshire boroughs of Beverley, Scarborough and York itself is certainly not immune. To the late fourteenth-century as to the modern visitor these three towns, although located within only forty miles of one another, would readily have provided a classic object lesson in the distinctiveness of the 'urban place'. It is equally important to stress that they also afford a classic instance of the distinctiveness of the borough archive. By the second half of the fourteenth century the town governments of York, Scarborough and Beverley were all sufficiently sophisticated to employ the services of a common clerk, in some ways the only 'professional' civic officer in their administration. However, the records those three clerks compiled, and even more their chances of survival, could hardly have been more varied. The great Freemen's Register of York, the Great Guild Book of Beverley and the early records of the Scarborough Court of Pleas may all be invaluable documents in their own right but they hardly provide the basis for meaningful comparison between the three boroughs. As so often in the case of late fourteenth-century English towns, the surviving archives of York, Beverley and Scarborough are all abundant enough to provoke interesting questions but too fragmentary to provide much in the way of conclusive answers. Hardly surprising, it is not in any case among the official records of the borough that one is likely to discover revelations about serious disagreement and divisions with a community whose leaders were naturally intent on preserving at least the appearance of a unanimous *esprit de corps* within their ranks. Rather, as André Réville was the first to demonstrate, it is upon the central records of the English government that any serious

---

[5] W. Stubbs, *Constitutional History of England*, 3 vols. (Oxford, 1874–8), ii, p. 217.

analysis of the urban disturbances of late medieval England must ultimately rest. In particular, and to a positively alarming degree, almost all that can be known in detail about the course of events in York, Beverley and Scarborough between 1381 and 1382 derives from the indictments of local jurors as copied by the royal clerks of the King's Bench. Wherever those indictments can be tested, most fully at Beverley, they can be shown to be tendentious and at times fallacious in the extreme. No wonder indeed that the only detailed study to have been written on any one of the three Yorkshire urban risings of 1381 concluded with the observation that 'it is useless to attempt to build an elaborate superstructure of theory on slight and uncertain foundations of fact'.[6] Now however that the immeasurably better-documented urban uprisings of continental Europe in the later middle ages have themselves proved so increasingly resistant to over-schematic interpretation, such a verdict seems less gloomily defeatist than it did eighty years ago. On the premiss that what is currently needed is 'not more generalization but more investigation, investigation wherever possible based on identification of the participants'[7] the following summary and provisional account of the risings at Beverley, Scarborough and York may suggest that they are indeed explicable even if never capable of complete explanation.

In the first place it is an obvious comment on the endemic violence of all medieval England's largest towns that York, Scarborough and Beverley, dissimilar in many other ways, were alike in being regarded by Richard II's government as three of the five most potentially dangerous centres of urban unrest in northern England. Shortly after the young king reached Waltham in Essex on 22 June 1381 to begin the serious work of pacifying his realm seven days after Wat Tyler's death, York, Beverley and Scarborough as well as Kingston upon Hull and Newcastle-on-Tyne were the only five boroughs north of the Humber to be sent letters patent instructing them to proclaim the lamented deaths of Archbishop Sudbury, Treasurer Hales and Chief Justice Cavendish and to prohibit illegal

---

[6] C. T. Flower, 'The Beverley Town Riots, 1381–2', *Trans. Royal Hist. Soc.*, new ser., xix (1905), p. 90; similar reservations had previously been expressed in *Beverley Town Documents*, ed. A. F. Leach (Selden Society, xiv, 1900), p. xxix.
[7] R. A. Rotz, 'Investigating Urban Uprisings with Examples from Hanseatic Towns, 1374–1416', in W. C. Jordan, B. McNab and T. F. Ruiz (eds.), *Order and Innovation in the Middle Ages: Essays in Honor of Joseph R. Strayer* (Princeton, 1976), p. 233.

assemblies of any sort.[8] The king's advisers are hardly likely to have been mistaken in their selection; and by any of the familiar criteria, however individually suspect they may be, used to produce ranking lists of the principal towns of fourteenth-century England these five boroughs emerge as the most substantial urban communities in the north. Thus York, Newcastle, Beverley, Scarborough and Hull (in that order) are the only five northern towns to appear among the thirty-four English boroughs assessed at a wealth of more than £330 in the Lay Subsidy returns of 1334; similarly, these five towns were the only places in the north, with the exceptions of Carlisle and Doncaster, to have attracted the settlement of more than one community of mendicants in exactly the century (c. 1230 to c. 1330) when a distribution map of the English friaries is most likely to be a not unreliable guide to the relative size of the country's provincial towns.[9] More precisely still, and whatever the notorious problems of interpretation they present, the poll-tax returns of 1377 to 1381 can leave one in little doubt that these five towns were still the largest towns in the north on the eve of the Peasants' Revolt itself. That York, with its recorded tax-paying population of 7,248, stands revealed by the 1377 returns as the most populous provincial town in England is sufficiently well known. Less often emphasized is the fact that Beverley, where the first poll-tax was levied on a recorded 2,663 men and women, then ranks tenth in size among the leading English towns; and even Scarborough (which contained 1,480 taxpayers according to the obviously underestimated returns for 1381) was almost certainly as large or larger than the cathedral cities of Carlisle and Durham and must be considered a positively major town by the limited standards of fourteenth-century England.[10]

---

[8] *Cal. Pat. Rolls, 1381–5*, p. 69.

[9] *The Lay Subsidy of 1334*, ed. R. E. Glasscock (Records of Social and Economic History, new ser. ii, London, 1975), pp. 219, 357, 368–9, 370, 382; H. C. Darby (ed.), *A New Historical Geography of England* (Cambridge, 1973), p. 184; D. Knowles and R. N. Hadcock, *Medieval Religious Houses: England and Wales* (London, 1971), pp. 213–45. Of the seventy English towns compelled to contribute loans to Richard II in 1397, only six were located in Yorkshire, *viz.* York itself (£200), Hull (£100), Scarborough (£66 13s. 4d.), Beverley (£45), Pontefract (£26 13s. 4d.) and Whitby (£20): see W. Cunningham, *The Growth of English Industry and Commerce*, 5th edn, 2 vols. (Cambridge, 1910), i, p. 385, n. 3.

[10] P.R.O., E.359/8C, now most usefully tabulated by E. B. Fryde in C. Oman, *The Great Revolt of 1381*, new edn (Oxford, 1969), pp. 164–6. Detailed poll-tax returns survive, in an incomplete state, for York (1377 and 1381) and Beverley (1381). Scarborough, then taxed with the North Riding of Yorkshire, produced no separate return in 1377; and for 1381 there only survives a view of account (E.179/

Urban revolt in the north, it can accordingly be safely said, was at least in part a product of size and of a concentration of wealth as well as of population. For it would certainly be unwise to assume that, besides York, Beverley and Scarborough, the two other largest towns in the north were unaffected by the troubles of the early 1380s. In the case of Newcastle-on-Tyne, that most mysterious of medieval England's major boroughs, the evidence for its internal history is so deficient that even speculation seems pointless; but at the comparatively new town of Kingston upon Hull, on the evidence of its 1381 poll-tax return still a smaller community than Scarborough, there is indeed evidence of important constitutional debate and dissatisfaction at 'the great disease' resulting from an excessive concentration of authority in the hands of the mayor and only a few burgesses. By the terms of an ordinance proclaimed at Michaelmas 1379 with the assent of 'toute la commonalte' of Hull, the mayor, two bailiffs and two chamberlains of the borough were henceforward to be supervised by a council of eight annually elected burgesses whose special role it was to 'ordain all things for the common profit (*ordeigner toutes choses pur le commune profite*)'. As re-election to this council was only to be legitimate after a three-year interval, such a constitutional reform would have had the obvious effect of distributing power more widely among the burgesses of the town; and the short-term effect of this ordinance, not that it seems to have been properly observed by the fifteenth century, could possibly have been to defuse political tension and discontent at Hull in a way that was clearly not the case at York, Beverley and Scarborough. Nevertheless, there is evidence that Hull may not have been completely tranquil in 1381; and it was certainly a town which experienced several serious riots in protest at heavy taxation in the late fourteenth century.[11]

It is moreover fundamental to the understanding of the Yorkshire urban risings of 1380–1 to appreciate that they occurred not only in

211/40) certifying to the collection of tax from 1,190 unnamed lay persons by the Hilary term of 1381. The final returns for 1381, no doubt subject to heavy evasion, record 1,480 taxpayers at Scarborough but only 1,124 at Hull.

[11] Hull Corporation Archives, Bench Book 2, fo. 210; P.R.O., K.B.9/1069, m. 24 (requiring Walter Frost, Robert de Selby and many other Hull burgesses to answer for various trespasses before royal justices in the autumn of 1382); *Cal. Pat. Rolls, 1354–8*, p. 202; E. Gillett and K. A. MacMahon, *A History of Hull* (Oxford, 1980), pp. 35, 47, 63. I am indebted to Mr Jeremy Goldberg for first making me appreciate that civic conflict in late fourteenth-century Hull deserves further attention.

the largest towns of the region but also in those which enjoyed the greatest corporate privileges, exemption from shrieval authority and indeed, in the most common medieval sense of the word, the greatest 'liberty'. Nowhere is this more self-evidently obvious than in the case of York itself, from time out of mind the undisputed political and economic as well as ecclesiastical metropolis of York-shire and indeed the north of England as a whole. Nor can there be any doubt that the citizens of late fourteenth-century York were acutely aware of their exalted status. Only a few years after 1381 the inhabitants of York described themselves as living in 'une citee de graunde reputacion' and one which could be safely termed 'la secounde citee du Roialme'.[12] To the limited extent that there was ever a real possibility of the occasional transfer of the political capital of England from Westminster during the course of the fourteenth century, it has been said with some justice that 'York was the only conceivable choice.'[13] Although it was only in the period after the Peasants' Revolt that the city of York received the ultimate reward for its exceptional position by becoming, on 18 May 1396, only the third borough in the kingdom to attain county status in its own right, already by the 1370s the mayor and aldermen of the city could display a long line of royal charters providing them with franchises and immunities unrivalled by any other northern town.[14] The fourteenth century had witnessed an apparently steady development of their ability as well as their legal authority to manage the affairs of the city; and as recently as 1354 they had won perhaps their single most important jurisdictional conflict in the entire middle ages when the economic threat to their position presented by the suburban franchise of the monks of St Mary's Abbey in Bootham was finally removed.[15] Needless to say, no late fourteenth-century English town, not even London, was likely to defy an explicit assertion of royal will for long; but, as far as is

---

[12] York Freemen's Register (Y.C.A., D.1), fo. 348. Similarly, at the beginning of Richard II's reign the citizens of York had been at pains to point out that their contribution of three vessels to the royal navy had been greater than 'any other city in the realm except for the city of London' (P.R.O., S.C.8/10758).

[13] J. H. Harvey, 'Richard II and York', in F. R. H. Du Boulay and C. Barron (eds.), *The Reign of Richard II* (London, 1971), p. 203.

[14] Y.C.A., YC/Ch, A1–A8; E. Miller, 'Medieval York', *V.C.H. City of York* (1961), pp. 31–4, 69.

[15] *V.C.H. City of York*, pp. 68–9. The resolution, on terms favourable to the citizens, of this long and bitter conflict with St Mary's Abbey may help to explain why there was no recorded attack on the latter's liberties in June 1381.

known, in the aftermath of the great revolt of 1381 York seems to have been the only English borough prepared to defend itself from the judgements of royal justices by pleading the chartered immunity of its citizens from being impleaded outside the walls of their town for offences committed within York itself.[16]

But who actually exercised political authority within York in the years immediately before the great revolt? By the year 1376, when John de Rufforth, then common clerk, began to compile the city's famous *liber diversorum memorandorum*, it is abundantly clear that the government of late medieval York may have been magisterial in form but was oligarchic in substance. So to some extent it had no doubt always been since the first appearance of the mayoral office in 1213; but there is equally little doubt that in the middle of the fourteenth century the nature of that oligarchy had begun to change quite dramatically. At the risk of considerable over-simplification it can be said that at the beginning of the century the mayors and *probi homines* of York seem to have owed their wealth and predominance to their position as urban and rural *rentiers*; by the year of the Peasants' Revolt the overseas merchants resident in the town had already established a complete ascendancy over the internal and external affairs of the city.[17] The reasons for the remarkable efflorescence of mercantile activity in late fourteenth-century York still deserve further analysis; but that it had a profound effect on the nature and the personnel of the city's ruling élite there can be no doubt whatsoever. Nearly every mayor of York after the end of the forty-year long dominance of the office by the Langton family in 1364 can be proved to have been heavily involved in overseas trade from Hull. Equally evident is the determination on the part of the York mercers or merchants to share political power within the city amongst themselves. By the late 1370s it seems clear that most important political decisions within York were made with the assent of two councils, one of twelve (broadly to be identified with the aldermen) and one of twenty-four. How far these inner groups were

---

[16] This argument was deployed at length by the attorney of the mayor and bailiffs of York before the royal justices investigating the misdeeds of John de Gisburne in September 1382 (P.R.O., Just. 1/1138, m. 2).

[17] The classic account of these developments is provided by Miller, *V.C.H. City of York*, pp. 70–2, 100–5. For the possibility that mayors of York at the end of the thirteenth century had derived much of their wealth from money-lending see R. B. Dobson, 'The Decline and Expulsion of the Medieval Jews of York', *Trans. Jewish Hist. Soc. of England*, xxvi (1979), p. 41.

at all responsible to the mass of the York commons, to the *commonaltie* whose name they so often invoked, is another matter entirely. The disturbances at York in 1380 and 1381 can most plausibly be interpreted as a reflection of a double constitutional problem: a city oligarchy at serious odds with the aspirations of many of the town's freemen, and an oligarchy which had also not yet managed a harmonious transition towards complete cohesion within its own ranks. As the York jurors' indictments of 1381 testify in detail, the factionalism of that and the previous year was the product of tensions which went back to at least the early 1370s and the period when there was strident competition for the office of mayor between John Langton and John de Gisburne.[18]

Personal animosity towards John de Gisburne, from circles both within and without the mercantile élite, was in the event to prove the single most disruptive factor in the confused series of events that overtook the city of York at the beginning of the 1380s. An exceptionally wealthy merchant who traded extensively in most of the commodities of external and internal trade, Gisburne emerges from the records as a figure curiously isolated from the majority of his fellow York mercers. Already mayor for two consecutive years in the early 1370s, he attained the office again in November 1379 as a result of John of Acaster's death in mid-term. Some of Gisburne's ensuing unpopularity may have been due to his connections with court circles: in 1381 itself he was to gain the contract for providing William of Wykeham's recently founded New College, Oxford, with roofing lead.[19] More certainly, his regime as mayor of York in 1380 was associated with a number of scandals, not least the arbitrary imprisonment of John Savage, a prominent York citizen, and serious peculation on the part of the city's common clerk, John de Rufforth.[20] Whatever the precise reasons, it was on Monday 26 November 1380 that discontent with Gisburne's activities as mayor exploded into the 'horrible chose' reported almost immediately to Richard II's fifth parliament then sitting at Northampton. On that day a substantial section of the commons of the city had broken into the Guildhall by force, chased Gisburne out of the city and com-

---

[18] *Cal. Close Rolls, 1369–74*, pp. 59, 275. Many of the detailed charges brought against Gisburne by twelve York jurors on 29 August 1381 (P.R.O., K.B.27/482, m. 35) refer to his malpractices at the royal mint and his harbouring of felons and murderers over ten years earlier.

[19] Y.C.A., D.1, fos. 7–8; P.R.O. E.122/59/1, 2; *Cal. Pat. Rolls, 1381–5*, p. 50.

[20] P.R.O., S.C.8/10636, 10637; Just. I/1138, m. 2.

pelled Simon de Quixlay, allegedly against his will and that of the *bones gentz* of York, to become mayor in his stead. That this was no entirely spontaneous revolt is suggested by the rebels' subsequent decree that whenever the bells on Ouse Bridge should sound 'aukeward' all the commons of the city should rise again to defend the new dispensation.[21]

The York rising of 26 November 1380 not only made royal intervention a matter of urgency but unleashed a complicated series of disturbances at York only intermittently traceable in the surviving records. After twenty or so of the leading rioters had been imprisoned in the Tower of London and then released (on 4 January 1381) on bonds of good behaviour, the government must have hoped that violence in the city could be successfully contained.[22] Certainly the apparently quite peaceful election of Simon de Quixlay as mayor on 3 February, when accompanied by a subsequent series of investigative judicial commissions and bonds to keep the peace, might have been expected to lessen what the government interpreted (perhaps too simply) as strife and discord between John de Gisburne on the one side and the *communitas* of York on the other. The prospects of a reasonably harmonious resolution of prevailing animosities and tensions were however to be shattered by the arrival in York of rumours of the astonishing events in London between 13 and 15 June. It was on Monday 17 June, and therefore presumably before news can have reached the city of the débâcle at Smithfield two days earlier, that the walls and gates of the precinct of the York Dominican friars are reported to have been destroyed 'by the rebellious commons of the city'; and it seems highly likely that the other religious institutions of the city (St Leonard's Hospital, St George's Chapel and the Franciscan friary) known to have suffered at about this time were all attacked on the very same day.[23] More peacefully, but no less revealingly, it was on Monday 17 June 1381 too that Mayor Simon de Quixlay, the bailiffs and 'tut la commonalte' of York met in their Guildhall to make new

[21] *Rotuli Parliamentorum*, iii, pp. 96–7.

[22] *Cal. Pat. Rolls, 1377–81*, p. 580; *Cal. Close Rolls, 1377–81*, pp. 420, 421, 503, 524–5.

[23] *York Memorandum Book*, ed. M. Sellers, 2 vols. (Surtees Society, 1912–15), ii, pp. 69–70; *V.C.H. City of York*, p. 81. For the career of John Paris, the distinguished Dominican friar responsible for restoring harmonious relations between the city and Black Friars of York, see A. B. Emden, *A Biographical Register of the University of Oxford*, 3 vols. (Oxford, 1957–9), iii, p. 1425.

ordinances imposing the exceptionally severe penalties of a £40 fine and the loss of his freedom on any citizen who attempted to transfer to an external royal court any plea properly belonging to the jurisdiction of the city itself.[24] There is no clearer evidence, by its nature never likely to be abundant, that at York, as no doubt in Beverley and Scarborough, the intervention of the cumbersome judicial mechanisms of the central government in their internal disputes could be seen by the burgesses as positively unpalatable and objectionable.

Further governmental intervention in the affairs of the city was however now quite inevitable, not least because the political atmosphere in York continued to be highly inflammatory for the rest of the summer. According to indictments made by York jurors later in the year, John de Gisburne and a group of his servants and supporters, perhaps then in forced exile from the city, made an armed attack at Bootham Bar on Monday 1 July and then rode through the city distributing liveries in an attempt to enlarge their own confederacy, an activity in which they were indeed still involved as late as the beginning of August.[25] By this time the evidence suggests that the disputes at York had degenerated into something not too remote from gang warfare in which Mayor Simon de Quixlay and his party gradually found it possible to hold their own. Five of Gisburne's supporters were seized and imprisoned by Quixlay and his bailiffs even before the mayor was able to use his position on a special royal judicial commission to initiate proceedings against Gisburne himself. It was no doubt inevitable that the latter should in his turn make serious accusations of malpractice against his rival; but after a complicated series of claims and counter-claims both parties undertook to keep the peace on 28 February 1382. During the following months, while an inconclusive series of judicial proceedings continued, the city and its region continued to be the scene of several alarmingly violent episodes; and as late as 10 November 1382 the mayor, bailiffs and council of 24 were required to guarantee the security of St Leonard's Hospital against the dangers of a renewed assault.[26] Nevertheless, by the

[24] *York Memorandum Book*, i, p. 40.
[25] P.R.O., K.B.27/482, mm. 11, 35, briefly summarized in A. Réville and C. Petit-Dutaillis, *Le soulèvement des travailleurs d'Angleterre en 1381* (Paris, 1898), pp. 272–3.
[26] *Cal. Close Rolls, 1381–5*, pp. 31, 32, 115; *Cal. Pat. Rolls, 1381–5*, pp. 35, 81, 137, 187, 201; Réville and Petit-Dutaillis, *Le soulèvement des travailleurs*, pp. 273–4.

time the city received its formal letters of pardon, at a cost of 1,000 marks, on 18 October 1382 there can be no doubt that the dangers of violent disturbances had at last receded. Simon de Quixlay, re-elected mayor of York in both February 1382 and February 1383, continued to play a prominent role in the public life of a city he had managed to restore to acceptable tranquillity. Conversely, John de Gisburne never again held important civic office in the town and died in 1390, but not before he had taken steps to found one of the most lavishly endowed perpetual chantries ever established in late medieval York.[27]

Obviously enough, the correct interpretation of the risings at York in 1380 and 1381 is an exceptionally difficult and perhaps impossible task. That the troubles were exacerbated and probably precipitated by fierce personal antipathies between members of the mercantile élite of the late fourteenth-century city is certainly not in dispute: it is one of the ironies of the story that John de Gisburne and Simon de Quixlay must, as fellow aldermen and members of the council of twelve, have known each other only too well in the years before the risings.[28] Nor can there be much doubt that the wealthy but irresponsible John de Gisburne emerges as the most dangerous stormy petrel on the York scene. Apparently culpable of patronizing a criminal element on the fringes of York urban society, it was clearly profound distrust of his conduct of the mayor's office that not only broke the ranks of the governing élite but unleashed a genuine revolt of the commonalty. Of the twenty-one citizens of York imprisoned in the Tower of London for their role in expelling Gisburne from office in November 1380, one was a mercer and three were drapers; but the great majority were craftsmen, and especially websters and butchers, of the city.[29] Only a few months later the butchers of York also united in armed opposition to a city tax called 'Shameltoll' (Shambles Toll levied by the town's bailiffs) on the grounds that demands for this payment were extortionate.[30] From the viewpoint of both central and city government alike what made the turbulence at York a genuinely 'horrible chose' was that

---

[27] Y.C.A., D.1, fos. 8–9; B.I.H.R., Probate Register 1, fo. 15; R. B. Cooke, 'Some Early Civic Wills of York', *Assoc. Architectural Soc. Reports and Papers*, xxviii (1906), pp. 827–34.

[28] Both Gisburne and Quixlay attended many of the same council meetings before (and indeed after) 1381: *York Memorandum Book*, ed. J. W. Percy (Surtees Society, 1973), iii, pp. 7, 9, 15.

[29] *Cal. Close Rolls, 1377–81*, pp. 486–7.     [30] P.R.O. Just. 1/1138, m. 3.

on at least two occasions in these years, in late November 1380 and again in the summer of 1381, the craftsmen and commons of York had shown themselves ready to articulate their own grievances in their own way. Precisely what those grievances were must always be a matter for conjecture rather than certainty; but that they comprised not only their own economic self-interest (the most plausible explanation for their attack on the franchises of various religious establishments within the city) but also a profound dissatisfaction with the operations of a government system from which they were themselves largely excluded must certainly suffice to rescue the risings at York from being dismissed as no more than a 'squalid and obscure municipal quarrel, which had obviously no relation to the general causes of the rebellion of 1381'.[31]

The same conclusions must apply even more forcefully in the case of the disturbances of 1381 within the East Riding borough of Beverley, of particular interest because here as perhaps nowhere else in England at the time the control of civic office was actually captured for a substantial period by the *viri mediocres* of the town. Moreover, the very tenacity with which two quite sharply defined parties waged unrelenting legal as well as violent battle with one another from May 1381 until June 1382 may even make the Beverley of that year the most fully documented case of urban conflict in late medieval English history. Only a small proportion of the King's Bench and other records relating to this savage contest, themselves of course a reflection of the royal government's exceptional concern and indeed perplexity with the 'unwonted evils and dangers in the town of Beverley because of a grave lack of good government (*insolencia mala et pericula in villa de Beverlaco ob defectum maxime boni regiminis*)', have yet found their way into print.[32] No attempt can be made to do justice to the complications revealed by these records in the following pages; and even when the political and social struggles at Beverley in the 1380s receive the attention they deserve, it is still likely that parts of the story will seem to begin, as they seem to end, 'in mist and mystery'.[33] Not the

---

[31] Oman, *Great Revolt*, p. 146.

[32] Only a very small selection of the numerous relevant records now classified within P.R.O., S.C.8 (Ancient Petitions) are printed as the appendix to Flower, 'Beverley Town Riots, 1381–2', pp. 92–9. See also K.B.27/484, m. 25; K.B.146/3/5/1; C.49/9/14; C.255/1/3: Mr Andrew Prescott kindly drew my attention to the last three of these sources.

[33] *Beverley Town Documents*, ed. Leach, p. xxxii. Despite the assiduous labours of

least important reason for this obscurity and complexity was the distinctive and in many ways anomalous constitutional position of a borough most famous to economic historians for its woollen textile industry. Although for taxation and many other purposes fourteenth-century Beverley was assimilated into the general routines of royal administration, its immediate lord was the archbishop of York; accordingly in May 1388 Richard II had no hesitation in reminding the sheriff of Yorkshire that the archbishop's bailiff of the liberty of St Peter in Beverley enjoyed the franchise of return of royal writs.[34] To compound the complexities, both the provost and the canons of Beverley Minster, famous as the most important sanctuary church in Yorkshire, jealously retained their own liberties, thus creating a network of rival ecclesiastical jurisdictions extreme even by the standards of other late medieval English towns. By June 1381 Archbishop Alexander Neville of York had moreover already inflamed matters by his notorious attack on the privileges of the canons of Beverley Minster, one of the bitterest ecclesiastical disputes of the fourteenth century. Although Alexander Neville escaped the fate of the southern archbishop, Simon Sudbury, there is copious if cryptic evidence that his exceptional and probably deserved unpopularity provoked much violence in Yorkshire through the early 1380s. Why, one wonders, did the archbishop seek Richard II's licence (on 11 August 1381) to reside with his household and retainers in the royal castle of Scarborough?[35]

Such and similar tensions only do a little to explain the most remarkable feature of political struggles among the burgesses of

George Poulson and Arthur Leach, medieval Beverley still awaits its historian; but for a useful new topographical survey see *Beverley: An Archaeological and Architectural Study* (Royal Commission on Historical Monuments, London, 1982).

[34] B.C.A., Town Cartulary, fo. 2, wrongly dated in *Report on Manuscripts of the Corporation of Beverley* (Historical Manuscripts Commission, London, 1900), p. 8.

[35] *Cal. Pat. Rolls, 1381–5*, p. 35. Cf. A. F. Leach, 'A Clerical Strike at Beverley Minster in the Fourteenth Century', *Archaeologia*, lv (1896), pp. 1–20; S. W. Calkin, 'Alexander Neville, Archbishop of York: A Study of his Career with Emphasis on the Crisis at Beverley in 1381' (D.Phil. thesis, University of California, Berkeley, 1976), pp. 80–169. In May 1383 the mayor and bailiffs of Hull were accused by the archbishop of capturing one of his boats when it was lying in the Humber; and three years later the archbishop's palaces at Bishopthorpe, Cawood and even in York Minster Close were subjected to an armed assault (Hull Corporation Archives, Bench Book 2, fo. 281; *Cal. Pat. Rolls, 1385–9*, p. 172).

fourteenth-century Beverley, the fact that not only the personnel of the ruling body but the very forms and structures of urban government themselves were constantly in dispute. Whatever the origins of the alleged immemorial custom whereby the 'good men of the town of Beverley' assembled at their Guildhall on St Mark's Day (25 April) to elect twelve *custodes* to govern the town for the following year, it had already led to violent protest in 1356 when a group of five hundred men had broken into the Guildhall and prevented the holding of the election there.[36] Three years later the so-called Beverley 'Magna Carta', which prescribed that the twelve outgoing keepers should nominate eighteen candidates for election by the community as their successors, gives explicit confirmation of how self-perpetuating such a system could be.[37] But what was never seriously at dispute in Beverley during 1381 and 1382 was that in practice government by twelve keepers gave political power in the town to the wealthy, the *bones gentz*, of the borough at the expense of its *menes comunes*. As at York and Scarborough, it would be unwise to assume that the borough's oligarchy was a positively diminutive and isolated group within the town; but there is abundant evidence that it was dominated by a few rich merchant families, and in particular by those of Beverley and of Coppendale. Thomas Beverley's exceptional wealth and influence had made him steward of the Beverley chapter in the 1370s, a position which helps to explain why the rebels of 1381 appealed to Archbishop Alexander Neville, himself on such notoriously bad terms with the canons there. Among other leading members of the *bones gentz* were Thomas Jolyf, the vintner John Gervays, the goldsmith Thomas Gervays, William Dudhill, Peter le Catwyk and the outstandingly wealthy John de Ake, a draper and mercer: all these men appear in a surviving list of the twelve keepers of Beverley in April 1380 and all were to suffer at the hands of the rebels a year later.[38]

[36] *Beverley Town Documents*, pp. xxv–xxviii.

[37] *Ibid.*, pp. 1–5; B.C.A., Town Cartulary, fos. 15–16.

[38] B.C.A., Town Cartulary, fo. 19; 1366 Keepers' Account Roll; P.R.O., K.B.27/ 487, m. 21; K.B.146/3/5/1; C.49/9/14. A good impression of the unequal wealth of the *bones gentz* of Beverley in 1381 can be gained from the bonds extracted from them by the commons in June of that year; thus Thomas Beverley was obliged to pay £400, Adam Coppendale £200 and most of their fellows only 100 marks (P.R.O., S.C.8/11209, 11211, 11212, 11215, etc.). For John de Ake's munificent will of 1398 and his foundation of Trinity Hospital and Chapel, the most lavish charitable foundation ever made by a Beverley merchant, see B.C.A., Town Cartulary, fos. 84–6.

Curiously enough, and despite the abundance of the evidence, it proves exceptionally difficult to be certain precisely when the alleged oppressions of these men, many of them subsequently traced back for many years, precipitated a major revolution in Beverley's political regime. No attempt will be made here to recount in any detail a tortuous and prolonged struggle whose most important turning-points often remain partly conjectural. However it is unquestionable that by the end of May 1381 the commons of Beverley had not only wrested political power from 'the great and most sufficient burgesses of the town (*les grauntz et les plus suffisantz burgeis de la ville*)' but had also ('by a sudden change of custom') replaced the previous regime of twelve keepers by one consisting of a single alderman, two chamberlains, a recorder and a council of twenty-four wardens.[39] The alderman who assumed power as the result of what had been a genuinely populist movement was the draper Richard de Middleton while his chamberlains were Henry de Newark and Thomas White, a tiler, all three being assiduously supported by a clerk, Richard de Boston, who apparently acted as their common clerk and may have been the principal organizer of the movement. However, under closer examination the confederacy of so-called 'riotours et batettours' which had overturned the established constitution at Beverley emerges as a large and miscellaneous section of the borough's population, among whom the lesser craftsmen of the town, and especially its textile workers, were heavily represented.[40] By the time that news of the seriousness of the conflict between the *probi homines* and *communitas* of Beverley had reached Westminster on 25 May, the latter were already arraigning Adam Coppendale, Thomas Beverley and their colleagues for a variety of offences, including a raid earlier that month on the Guildhall itself, one of whose objectives had been to recapture possession of the borough's common seal.[41] Faced with the difficult problem of ensuring that their constitutional successes should remain permanent, Richard de Middleton and his fellow commons called an emergency meeting in

---

[39] B.C.A., Town Cartulary, fo. 17; *Beverley Town Documents*, pp. 6–7; cf. P.R.O., S.C.8/8356; Flower, 'Beverley Town Riots, 1381–2', pp. 82–5.

[40] P.R.O., S.C.8/4700 provides what seems the most reliable list of the names of the nine leading 'riotours et rebellours'; and for the names of 122 *rebelles de insurreccion* later at Tottenham see S.C.8/11233 (only partly printed by Flower, 'Beverley Town Riots, 1381–2', pp. 97–8).

[41] P.R.O., K.B.27/484, m. 25; cf. *Cal. Close Rolls, 1377–81*, pp. 523–4.

the Beverley Guildhall on 3 June; and during the following month, both before as well as after news of the revolt in south-eastern England must have reached them, bands of four hundred or more commons systematically extracted bonds from the *bones gentz* whereby the latter undertook to abide by the judgements to be made later that summer by Archbishop Alexander Neville.[42] Whether because they had no confidence in arbitration from such a source or because, as they later alleged, they were in genuine fear of their lives, many of these *bones gentz* then fled from Beverley to make their appeals to the royal courts from the comparative safety of London. According to one peculiarly enigmatic petition, probably misdated by C. T. Flower, they were followed there by sixty of their opponents, who had stolen horses from the Beverley's common pasture and came to lodge at Tottenham; from their base there these members of the Beverley commons allegedly not only threatened Coppendale and his colleagues with violence but went through the streets of London itself with pole-axes and swords.[43]

It had now of course become a matter of urgency for the royal government to pacify what showed signs of becoming an increasingly uncontrollable dispute. Nevertheless the legal complications of the conflict were such that it was only in the spring of 1382, and after a period of imprisonment in the Marshalsea, that Adam Coppendale and his fellows were finally exonerated not only from the previous adverse judgements but from the bonds they had made the previous summer. No doubt inevitably, the leaders of the commons in May 1381 were increasingly isolated and at last deprived of power, some probably taking refuge in sanctuary at Beverley Minster: in response to a royal writ of 16 April 1382 the bailiff of the liberty of St John of Beverley reported that he dared not arrest Henry de Newark, Thomas White and Richard de Boston for fear of his own life.[44] Only when Archbishop Neville of York, in the company of his brother John, Lord Neville of Raby, of the

---

[42] C. T. Flower was the first historian to make the 'fortunate discovery' that large numbers of copies of these bonds, with their defeasances, survive as P.R.O., S.C.8/11201–50; but much additional detail as to the duress under which they were extracted, and the eviction of the *bones gentz* and their families from their households, is provided by an enrolment of the latter's petitions which survives as C.49/9/14.

[43] P.R.O., S.C.8/11237 (Flower, 'Beverley Town Riots, 1381–2', pp. 96–7).

[44] P.R.O., S.C.8/11224; and cf. *ibid.*, 11221, 11223; C.67/29, m. 14; K.B.27/484, m. 25; *Rotuli Parliamentorum*, iii, p. 393; *Cal. Close Rolls, 1381–5*, p. 136; Réville and Petit-Dutaillis, *Le soulèvement des travailleurs*, pp. 268–70.

sheriff of Yorkshire and of many other Yorkshire knights, appeared in the town on 27 June 1382 to take pledges of good behaviour from four hundred or more of the townsmen, both *probi homines* and *communes*, did some form of political stability return to Beverley. At a cost of 1,100 marks (larger than the fines exacted from York and Scarborough) royal letters of pardon were granted to the town on 18 October 1382.[45] How far genuine tranquillity prevailed in the aftermath of the bitter feuds of the previous year and more is another matter. Accusations brought against one of Coppendale's supporters, John Erghom, in April 1385 leave no doubt that the latter had waged a veritable campaign of reprisals against the leaders of the rebellion, including an assault on the ex-alderman Richard de Middleton himself; moreover at least one 'of the chief captains of the late insurrection', Richard de Boston, was actually killed in a no doubt similar act of reprisal.[46] More ironically still, although the constitutional changes introduced in 1381 were to survive for a few years after the risings, these could not apparently prevent the re-establishment of traditional oligarchic power at Beverley: the surviving borough account roll for the year 1386 proves that the town was then still being governed by an alderman and two chamberlains rather than twelve keepers; but the alderman and at least one of the chamberlains in question (Thomas Gervays and John de Ake) had been prominent members of *les bones gentz* of 1381–2.[47]

No doubt Beverley in the later middle ages was never free from internal discord: in 1408 the traditional ambiguity of relations between the burgesses and the provost of Beverley Minster was again exposed when the latter accused the former of riot, murder and violence.[48] Nevertheless no later conflict in the town is at all as well documented as that of 1381; and at Beverley, as neither at York or Scarborough, a detailed impression may indeed be gained of how the commons of that year saw their adversaries. Arbitrary acts of violent aggression on the part of the ruling élite obviously lost

---

[45] B.C.A., Charter No. 35; *Rotuli Parliamentorum*, iii, pp. 133, 397; P.R.O., S.C.8/ 11242; Réville and Petit-Dutaillis, *Le soulèvement des travailleurs*, p. 270.

[46] Réville and Petit-Dutaillis, *Le soulèvement des travailleurs*, pp. 260–6; *V.C.H. Yorkshire* (1913), iii, p. 443.

[47] B.C.A., 1386 Account Roll. Both Gervays and Ake had been accused by the commons of assaulting the Beverley Guildhall in May 1381 (P.R.O., K.B.27/484, m. 25).

[48] Flower, 'Beverley Town Riots, 1381–2', pp. 89–90.

nothing in their relation before the royal justices, most melodramatically the murder (on 6 July 1381) of William Haldene: his body was thrown into 'le Bek in Walkerlane' after his brains had been literally knocked out by John Erghom and others with 'a pole-axe, two battle-axes, six swords, two forks and other weapons'. More generally revealing is the resentment displayed towards the two outstanding patricians of the town, Thomas Beverley and Adam Coppendale, for obstructing streets in the town by building a large tenter-yard and new house respectively. However it was the *potentiores*' responsibility for the financial exploitation of the community, partly by means of internal levies like *bustsilver* and *pundale* and partly by their supervision of national taxation, which seems to have produced the widest opposition in the town: Adam Coppendale and Thomas Beverley had indeed been collectors of the 1377 poll-tax there.[49] Such exploitation had the effect of uniting in opposition to the *probi homines* of Beverley drapers, mercers, tailors, butchers and indeed probably representatives of all the forty or more craft guilds known to have been in existence there by the late fourteenth century. So copiously are the names of the Beverley rebels of 1381 recorded that prosopographical research might one day make it possible to analyse their occupational structure in considerable detail; but the evidence already assembled leaves really no doubt that this was a communal movement which transcended all craft boundaries to create a formidable if temporary coalition of 'all craftsmen, sellers of victuals and workmen (*omnes artifices, victualium venditores et operarii*)' in the town.[50]

Although the rising of the commons at Scarborough in the last week of June 1381 also emerges, in Sir Charles Oman's phrase, as a 'clear instance of attacks on the local burgess oligarchy by the local democracy',[51] the detailed history of Yorkshire's most important medieval 'fischar toun' has received much less attention than have York and Beverley. For that reason alone it probably deserves a slightly fuller treatment in this essay even if it is still 'to be regretted

---

[49] P.R.O., E.359/8B, m. 19d; and 8C, m. 5d; cf. the allegation that Thomas of Beverley and his son Richard extorted £600 from the *communitas* on 30 June 1381 (K.B.27/487, m. 21).

[50] S.C.8/11233; Réville and Petit-Dutaillis, *Le soulèvement des travailleurs*, p. 263. B. Champion, 'The Gilds of Medieval Beverley', in P. Riden (ed.), *The Medieval Town in Britain* (Cardiff Papers in Local History, i, 1980), pp. 58–9, suggests some reasons why (and not at Beverley alone) the role of the craft guild as a political organization has often been exaggerated by medieval urban historians.

[51] Oman, *Great Revolt*, p. 142.

that the records of the Corporation should be unable to afford the collateral evidence and information necessary to confirm and establish that which the Government records eliminate'.[52] Such a verdict is in fact a little too pessimistic, for a few Scarborough records do survive from the later middle ages to throw considerable light on three of the most obvious themes of the borough's late medieval history: a continuously high level of crime and disorder, the concentration of political authority in the hands of a comparatively few local families, and the all-importance to the economic fortunes of the town of its fishing industry. Not for nothing did the self-styled 'povres burgeys' of Scarborough constantly remind the early parliaments of Richard II's reign that it was 'lour kay' which formed the 'salvacion de dite ville'.[53] More generally, the inhabitants of late fourteenth-century Scarborough seem often to have been well aware of the inescapable geographic paradox which made the development of their town so distinctive and erratic. This was a town which owed its fame, fortunes and very existence to that fact that 'theare is no other save Harboure betwixt Humber and Tyne but onelie Skarburghe'; on the other hand, here was a borough whose economic opportunities were always likely to be inhibited by its lack of good communications, especially by water, with the interior of Yorkshire as well as by the comparative poverty of its hinterland, 'for it joynethe to Yorke Woulde, Blakamore and Pykerying Lythe, beynge of no great ffertillitye'.[54] Similarly the fact that the inhabitants of medieval Scarborough lived in the shadow of the most impregnable royal castle on the east coast of medieval England, standing on that 'rock of wonderful height and bigness' so well known to William of Newburgh in the late twelfth century as well as to the modern holidaymaker, seems to have done more to expose them to military attack rather than to defend them from the attentions of external and internal enemy. On all the evidence available the political history of Scarborough in the

---

[52] J. B. Baker, *The History of Scarborough from the Earliest Date* (London, 1882), p. vi; cf. J. W. Rowntree, 'The Borough, 1163–1500', in A. Rowntree (ed.), *The History of Scarborough* (London, 1931), pp. 102–3.

[53] P.R.O., S.C.8/6944, 6956. For the 'chronic' decline of the Scarborough fishing industry in the 1420s and 1430s see P. Heath, 'North Sea Fishing in the Fifteenth Century: The Scarborough Fleet', *Northern History*, iii (1968), pp. 53–69; and for an account of repairs to the quay in 1365/6 see E.101/482/5.

[54] B. Waites, 'Scarborough 1366–1566: The Declining Years', in M. Edwards (ed.), *Scarborough 966–1066* (Scarborough and District Archaeological Society, 1966), pp. 52–3.

thirteenth and fourteenth centuries is largely a variation on the theme of exceptional truculence created by a sense of exceptional vulnerability and isolation.

Of Scarborough's vulnerability to foreign assault as well as to the much dreaded 'tempestes du meere' in the years immediately before 1381 there can be no doubt whatsoever: all allowances made for the inflated language of the town's own parliamentary petitions, its misfortunes at this period provide a neglected instance to support the now not unfamiliar case that in some ways 'the Peasants' Revolt was the fruit of the Hundred Years War'.[55] Long subjected to intermittent blockading and harassment of their own and visiting fishing vessels, the inhabitants and seamen of Scarborough suffered their greatest calamity in 1378 when they were the victims of an exceptionally audacious raid by Andrew Mercer, the son of John Mercer, a prominent Perth merchant and financial agent of the Scottish crown. According to Thomas Walsingham's apparently well-informed account, Andrew Mercer's assault on Scarborough was to some extent an act of reprisal against the town in whose castle his father had been imprisoned before his ransom: in any case it resulted in the deaths of several Scarborough seamen, the loss of their ships and the capture of many men who were later held to ransom at Boulogne.[56] Andrew Mercer's subsequent capture at the hands of a naval expedition prepared by John Philipot of London apparently did little to allay anxiety in Scarborough or indeed elsewhere on the coasts of England. Emergency measures on the part of the royal government, which included the requirement that the burgesses of the east coast ports should build balingers of forty to fifty oars for use as defensive warships, were themselves by no means popular in Scarborough itself. By 11 May 1378 a report had reached Westminster that many men of substantial landed property in the town had actually refused to contribute to the protection of their own port. When on 7 October in that year, Henry Percy, earl of Northumberland, was commissioned to supervise the defensive capabilities of both the town and castle of Scarborough, he was

[55] E. Searle and R. Burghart, 'The Defense of England and the Peasants' Revolt', *Viator*, iii (1972), p. 366.

[56] T. Walsingham, *Historia Anglicana*, ed. H. T. Riley, 2 vols. (Rolls Series, London, 1863–4), i, pp. 369–70; R. Nicholson, *Scotland: The Later Middle Ages* (Edinburgh, 1974), pp. 153, 166, 194–5. In Richard II's third parliament of April–May 1379 it was reported that Scarborough had lost £1,000 in ransoms and prizes during the two preceding years (*Rotuli Parliamentorum*, iii, p. 63).

informed that one of his additional responsibilities would be to appease the strife and discord in the town consequent on the lack of good justice there.[57] That this was an allegation which probably implied elements of criticism at the failure of the borough élite to protect the townsmen from enemy attack seems absolutely confirmed by the startling accusations subsequently brought against one member of that élite, Robert de Rillyngton. In November 1382 the latter had to pay no less than 100 marks for a pardon after being convicted before royal justices for his dealings with the king's enemies, dealings which included not only the purchase of ships and goods captured from his own compatriots but the conveying of victuals and money to hostile ships as well as 'leading them by night to inspect the town and castle of Scarborough'.[58]

Rillyngton's positively treasonable activities were no doubt exceptional; but no one who surveys the surviving records for the history of Scarborough in the later middle ages can fail to be impressed by the privateering and other excesses of the powerful ship-owning families who tended to dominate the official life of the town from the early fourteenth to the early fifteenth centuries. First fully revealed perhaps in the long list of 105 Scarborough burgesses assessed by the inquisition of nones in 1340,[59] it is tempting to suppose that these families owed their wealth to the new possibilities for commercial speculation introduced by such familiar features of the period as a developing coastal trade, the collapse of the Italian financial companies and the naval demands of a monarchy intent on war with Scotland and with France. These merchants were also the real beneficiaries of the great political conflicts between town and national government during the reigns of Edward I and Edward II which had won for the leading Scarborough burgesses a considerable degree of genuine independence from the crown's officials.[60] By the date (1356) of Edward III's confirmation of

---

[57] *Cal. Close Rolls, 1377–81*, pp. 32–3, 63; *Cal. Pat. Rolls, 1377–81*, p. 307. In the very same month Percy accused Robert Acclom and other Scarborough men of stealing goods in his custody at Hunmanby (*ibid.*, p. 308).

[58] *Cal. Pat. Rolls, 1381–5*, p. 190: this charge of treason presumably relates to Andrew Mercer's raid on Scarborough in 1378. Rillyngton continued to hold high office in Scarborough and still owned two ships, the *Seintmaryboite* and *le Kateryne* when he made his will in September 1391 (B.I.H.R., Probate Register 1, fo. 67). He also held much property in the town, including a plot of land on the 'Sandes' in front of the borough's Hall of Pleas (S.B.A., White Vellum Book, fo. 26).

[59] *Nonarum Inquisitiones* (Record Commission, London, 1807), pp. 243–4.

[60] No town in Yorkshire seems to have been so rebellious to royal authority as

Scarborough's constitutional ordinances, the town enjoyed the familiar accoutrements of sophisticated borough status, including chamberlains and a common clerk as well as two bailiffs annually elected by a wider body of 36.[61] Provided that these bailiffs duly accounted to the exchequer for the borough's fee farm of £91, responded to requests for parliamentary taxation, and maintained an acceptable level of law and order, they were largely free from interference by either the sheriff of Yorkshire or more significantly, the constable of the castle. Although the latter was partly maintained and repaired from rents and tolls derived from the borough itself, by the reign of Edward III the burgesses were more or less completely immune from the jurisdiction of the constable, himself a somewhat distant and probably often absentee royal sergeant-at-arms. The Ralph Standish, then king's knight, who was granted the constableship of Scarborough castle for life on 14 August 1381 does indeed deserve to be remembered – not of course for his role in Yorkshire but because, almost certainly, he was the esquire of Richard II who had dealt Wat Tyler his death blow two months earlier.[62]

More relevant in Scarborough, as the indictments produced after the riots of 1381 make abundantly clear, were the 'conspiracies, oppressions, extortions, damages, grievances and excesses to many of that town as elsewhere' committed by the borough's own *potentiores*. Despite some attempt in the constitutional settlement of the mid-1350s to ensure that the 'poor and middling people' should consent to the election of the town's bailiffs, the ascendancy in public office of a few remarkably long-lived family dynasties seems to have positively increased in the decades before the revolt of 1381. As Miss Jean Rowntree once pointed out, with pardonable exaggeration, 'The town bailiffs from 1344 to 1395 are largely

Scarborough in the early 1270s and again in the troubled decade after Bannockburn: for some reference to these conflicts see *V.C.H. North Riding of Yorkshire* (1923), ii, pp. 549–50.

[61] S.B.A., White Vellum Book, fos. 5–9; *Cal. Pat. Rolls, 1354–8*, pp. 453–4, 478. Some impression of the operations of town government at Scarborough can be obtained from a solitary surviving bailiffs' account roll of 1316–17 (P.R.O., E.101/506/22).

[62] *Cal. Pat. Rolls, 1381–5*, p. 32. Sir Ralph Standish (for whose role at Smithfield see *The Peasants' Revolt of 1381*, ed. R. B. Dobson (London, 1970), pp. 186, 196–7) died before 26 October 1382 when he was replaced as constable of Scarborough by Sir John de St. Quintin (*Cal. Pat. Rolls, 1381–5*, p. 212). For various accounts relating to Scarborough castle in the fourteenth century, see e.g. P.R.O., E.101/482/1–6.

Carters, Rustons and Accloms.'[63] As in the case of the much larger urban oligarchy at York, such concentration of power did not prevent bitter factional disputes within the ranks of the élite itself: according to a commission of oyer and terminer in February 1365, Adam Carter when bailiff of the town had been physically assaulted by William Sage, Robert Acclom and others when he tried to imprison the former 'for many enormities'.[64] Much better documented however are the accusations of illegal extortion at the expense of the inhabitants of Scarborough and its region brought against the very men (the Carters, the Rustons, the Accloms, the Shrophams, the Stockwiths and the Sages) whose responsibility it was to maintain law and order. Particularly instructive in this respect, not least because he was one of Scarborough's bailiffs in the year 1381 itself, is the career of Robert Acclom, profiteer as well as privateer for well over thirty years. Not untypical of the many charges brought against Acclom was the allegation that, only two years before the Peasants' Revolt, he had broken into the house of Matthew le Hosyer, a Scarborough burgess, carried off his goods and assaulted both him and his servants. What must have made the power of Acclom and his colleagues so much more formidable, and consequently so much more unpopular, was their close association with the royal administration itself. In 1376, the year of the Good Parliament, Henry de Ruston had been a deputy customs collector on behalf of the nefarious and ill-fated Richard Lyons; while Robert Acclom himself was appointed not only a commissioner to search towns and ports for gold, silver and letters of exchange but also a deputy to William Neville, Admiral of the North.[65] As early as February 1377 disorder and crime of all kinds at Scarborough was sufficiently notorious to elicit a special investigation on the part of royal justices;[66] and although the detailed incidence of pre-existing political and social conflict is much more mysterious here than at York and Beverley, it need occasion no surprise that violence erupted on the streets of Scarborough shortly after news of rebellion in Kent and Essex reached the town.

---

[63] Rowntree (ed.), *History of Scarborough*, p. 118.

[64] *Cal. Pat. Rolls, 1364–7*, p. 139.

[65] *Cal. Pat. Rolls, 1374–7*, pp. 149, 236–7, 321; *1377–81*, pp. 308, 363. Acclom may have been one of the Admiral's officials who tried to prevent the men of Scarborough from using the all-important 'Sandes' between town and quay as the customary site of their market and famous fair.

[66] *Cal. Pat. Rolls, 1374–7*, p. 486.

For our knowledge of what actually did happen at Scarborough in late June 1381 the only detailed sources are the three indictments (brought by jurors of Scarborough and the surrounding region) laid before Henry Percy, earl of Northumberland, and his fellow justices sitting in the town itself on the following 26 August.[67] As the nine named Scarborough jurors on this occasion included several individuals (John de Stockwith, Alan Waldyf, William Pereson) actually attacked by the commons of their town during the rising, such evidence is hardly likely to be impartial: in particular, the inquisitions of 26 August provide no information as to the grievances of the Scarborough rebels. However the rising which occurred on Sunday 23 June was undoubtedly a genuine mass movement, estimated as one of at least five hundred men by the Scarborough jurors and as a rising of 'all the commons of the said town (*omnes communes ville predicte*)' by others. Solidarity among the commons was achieved by those familiar features of England in the summer of 1381, a solemn oath of mutual self-support and a common livery, in Scarborough's case a white hood with a red liripipe or tail. More significant still, and the most obvious indication that the rebels at Scarborough had been stimulated by the then prevailing ethos of south-east England, were the oaths extracted by force from the town's élite to be faithful not only to the commons of Scarborough but to 'communibus tocius Anglie'. Moreover of the fourteen individuals named as victims in the indictments almost all can be proved to have been members of the town's ruling oligarchy, the most unpopular being John de Stockwith, one of the supervisors of the collection of the 1380–1 poll-tax in the borough.[68] Dragged through the streets of Scarborough to the accompaniment of a great shout called 'hountays', Stockwith might well have been beheaded or hanged had it not been for the support of his son-in-law, Henry de Ruston the younger. Although Robert Acclom, like many of his colleagues, escaped personal harm by taking sanctuary in the town's Franciscan priory, he was deposed from the office of bailiff as part of a complete replacement of all civic officials with candidates chosen by the commons. The rebel companies or *rowtes* continued to dominate the streets of Scarborough for at least

---

[67] P.R.O., K.B.27/500, m. 12, largely printed in Réville and Petit-Dutaillis, *Le soulèvement des travailleurs*, pp. 253–6. Rumours of unspecified robberies and destruction of houses at Scarborough had reached the king by 19 August (*Cal. Pat. Rolls, 1381–5*, p. 77).

[68] P.R.O., E.179/211/40.

another week, until Sunday 30 June when they besieged Robert Acclom's house 'for quarter of a day'. However it would probably be a mistake to assume that conditions in Scarborough were positively anarchic. Alice de Wakefield, the sister of Henry Wakefield, then bishop of Worcester, was admittedly dispossessed of her lands and rents in Scarborough by an allegedly 'great number of evil doers' during these tumultuous days;[69] but there appears to have been neither loss of life nor serious destruction of property to record before the royal government began the work of suppressing the revolt.

Although obviously a genuine mass movement, the rising at Scarborough in June 1381 is by no means easy to interpret in terms less vague than those of profound and widespread discontent with the borough's prevailing ruling élite. Of the many commons involved in the rising only seven are named in the indictments of August 1381; and the fact that one was a shoemaker and the other a *panyarman*, while a welcome reminder that even a fishing town like Scarborough was not devoid of a substantial body of craftsmen, hardly provides material for any sophisticated analysis.[70] More interestingly, two at least of the three main instigators of the rebellion (Robert Galoun, William Marche and Robert Hunter) were individuals of considerable substance. In the very year before the rising Robert Galoun had begun to endow what proved to be the wealthiest perpetual chantry ever established in the borough's parish church of St Mary's; and in December 1384 the draper William Marche, then a victim of violent reprisal by Robert Acclom, John de Stockwith and others, is known to have owned two ships and two hundred sheep as well as other goods.[71] Neither Galoun nor Marche ever seem to have held high office in Scarborough itself either before or after 1381; and to the extent that the rising there had been aimed at purging the personnel of local government it must be adjudged a complete failure. The 'forty persons drawn from the most substantial burgesses (*XL persones des mieultz vanez Burgeys*)' who contributed 500 of the 900 marks

---

[69] *Cal. Close Rolls, 1381–5*, p. 10.

[70] At least nineteen different crafts participated in the Corpus Christi festivities at Scarborough in 1467 (S.B.A., White Vellum Book, fo. lv); and there is copious evidence of a very active labour market at the beginning of the fifteenth century in S.B.A., Liber Placitorum 1 (1400–8), e.g. fos. 111, 132, 143–5.

[71] B.I.H.R., Probate Register 1, fo. 46; *Cal. Pat. Rolls, 1381–5*, p. 509; Rowntree (ed.), *History of Scarborough*, pp. 77, 129–33.

Scarborough was obliged to pay for its general pardon on 18 October 1382 were not only the richest inhabitants of the town but those who continued to dominate civic office in the years ahead.[72] Insecurity of course remained and according to an undated petition probably presented to Richard II's sixth parliament in the early months of 1382 a secret meeting of conspirators at a place two leagues from Scarborough the preceding Christmas had been called to foment yet another rising: the petitioners also predicted that the demoralization which had accompanied the collapse of the revolt might lead to a mass exodus of inhabitants of the town.[73] However the two Scarborough parliamentary burgesses who presented this petition were almost certainly Robert Acclom and Henry de Ruston themselves; their hopes that the dangers of a new popular rising in the borough might be defused by a general pardon seem to have been justified in the event. Although late fourteenth-century Scarborough continued to be a violent and at times murderous town, the Rustons, Accloms, Sages, Stockwiths and Shrophams were fully restored to their political control of the borough well before Robert Galoun and the other rebel leaders of June 1381 were finally pardoned nearly five years later, on 10 May 1386.[74]

Indeed of all the general conclusions to be drawn from the confused series of risings at York, Beverley and Scarborough, no doubt the least surprising is that the commons of 1380–1 all failed in their primary and common objective – the permanent limitation of the oppressive powers of a comparatively small circle of town rulers or *potentiores*. In all three towns too this objective had been associated with the determination to remove from civic office at least the most conspicuously unpopular members of the ruling circle. In these respects at least, one is reminded (and to compare small things with great) of that 'characteristic Florentine imbroglio' of three years earlier, 'neither very bloody, nor very destructive, and as strongly influenced by personal hatreds and loyalties as by any spirit or sense of class'.[75] By their very nature, English jurors'

---

[72] P.R.O., C.260/94/33; *Rotuli Parliamentorum*, iii, p. 136; *Cal. Pat. Rolls, 1381–5*, p. 209.

[73] P.R.O., S.C.8/6949, a petition which claims that six hundred of the 'communes' had risen in June 1381.

[74] P.R.O., K.B.27/500, m. 12 v (Réville and Petit-Dutaillis, *Le soulèvement des travailleurs*, p. 256).

[75] G. A. Brucker, 'The Ciompi Revolution', in N. Rubinstein (ed.), *Florentine Studies: Politics and Society in Renaissance Florence* (London, 1968), p. 270.

indictments are likely to be an unprofitable source for those who wish to unearth the ideological preconceptions of either the rebels or their adversaries; but it probably is genuinely the case that all three Yorkshire insurrections were more preoccupied with replacing old men than with introducing new measures. Even at Beverley the commons' decision to substitute government by aldermen and chamberlains for a regime of twelve keepers was based on past, if to us obscure, precedent. Further than this it can of course be difficult as well as dangerous to be certain. The evidence suggests that it would be wrong to suppose that the holders of civic office in the years before 1381 belonged to an exceptionally small and exclusive oligarchy; and, as has been seen, it would be equally a mistake to over-emphasize the internal cohesiveness of the *probi homines*. As in England as a whole in 1381, factions within the governing élite could have an important role to play in shaping the course of events; and in some ways Beverley, York and Scarborough can be seen as three different variations on the classic theme of oligarchical weakness – disaffection from those completely outside the ruling circles (Beverley), serious schism within that circle (York), and the dangers of an intermediate situation whereby men of considerable wealth and standing (like Robert Galoun and William Marche at Scarborough) were left isolated and could be induced to lend their support to a populist opposition. That said, not even at York are the risings of 1380 and 1381 solely attributable to personal animosity towards John de Gisburne and his henchmen. Similarly, although 'middle-rank merchants', currently so often held to be a crucial element in successful late medieval urban revolt, are indeed detectable among the York, Scarborough and Beverley rebels in the early 1380s, they only formed one element in a highly varied opposition to the prevailing élite. Nor, to touch on a more interesting negative feature of the three revolts, is there any evidence whatsoever that the craft guilds of the three towns (whose political as well as economic role has so often been exaggerated in the past) played any significant organizational role in the disturbances. In the last resort, and despite the notorious ambiguity of the terminology, it is hard to advance on the contemporary descriptions of these three conflicts as struggles between the *probi homines* and the *commonalte*. When placed in their respective contexts, the three Yorkshire revolts of 1381 can only enhance one's sense that this was indeed the greatest, most pervasive and perhaps even positively continuous political fissure within the late fourteenth-century English town.

Even if one were to concede (which not all would) that this antagonism was omnipresent if at times almost indefinable, what was consciously at issue was not resentment at inequality of wealth but at the misuse of authority by the *bones gentz* over the other citizens of the town. The grounds for such resentment in the case of all three Yorkshire towns have been documented at some length in this essay. Where the evidence is so partial, no historian can hope to be impartial; but it seems safe to suggest that an obvious lack of sympathy between the rulers and the ruled had been exacerbated in the late fourteenth century by two developments within the governing class itself. In York, Scarborough and Beverley an increased participation in overseas trade had not only created some substantial private fortunes but made many of the wealthy men of the three towns liable to a dangerous insensitivity towards the economic aspirations of their neighbouring craftsmen and retailers. Secondly, the involvement of this small minority of merchants in the operations of the Plantagenet government also made them vulnerable to the criticism increasingly brought against that government in the late 1370s and early 1380s. A position as a collector or controller of national taxation, a place on a royal commission of peace or even a seat as a parliamentary representative in the English commons was hardly guaranteed to win a burgess much popularity in the years before the Peasants' Revolt. At Beverley the 'workers, craftsmen, servants and others' were in fact specifically accused of violating the Statute of Labourers; and the indictments they themselves prepared leave no doubt of their hostility to what they regarded as extortionate and unjust taxation.[76] In these three Yorkshire towns as elsewhere it would not be excessively crude to suggest that the legal powers and sanctions of the late medieval civic officials were the product of an unofficial and no doubt largely unconscious contract between national and town government, whereby the authority of the latter over the citizens was increasingly strengthened in return for an appropriate display of loyalty and financial support to the crown. Not far below the surface at York, Beverley and Scarborough in 1381 was opposition to town councils which could give

---

[76] P.R.O., K.B.27/484, m. 25; Réville and Petit-Dutaillis, *Le soulèvement des travailleurs*, pp. 261–4, 268.

the impression to the commonalty of 'ruling in the same way, with the same goals, as nobles, princes and kings'.[77]

But this is only one way of making the obvious point that urban conflict in late fourteenth-century England cannot be interpreted in purely urban terms. In the first place, and although the strength of central government and their own comparatively small size and protectionist economic policies precluded formal town leagues on the continental model, English boroughs of the later middle ages were not at all unaware of each other's grievances and problems. Personal contacts, including migration and investment in property, between York, Beverley and (to a lesser extent) Scarborough are well documented in the years before and after 1400;[78] and although the risings in the Yorkshire towns were essentially self-generated, the participants must have been fully conscious that they were by no means acting in isolation from their counterparts elsewhere. Quite as much as the rebels in south-east England, those of York, Beverley and Scarborough reveal themselves as capable of considerable feats of organization and as adroit manipulators of complex legal procedures. Without denying the possibility (always open, never provable) of participation in the three revolts by the genuinely urban poor and destitute, all the evidence available bears witness to a remarkably self-confident and articulate commons, almost obsessively litigious and incapable of forgetting some private or public wrong however many years had elapsed since the event. Nor, despite their particularism, were the commons of York, Beverley and Scarborough isolated from the rural commons of England as a whole. Themselves so often first- or second-generation immigrants from the surrounding countryside, it is a final paradox that the problems they encountered as citizens of a chartered town were in many ways less fundamental to their lot than those, like bubonic plague and excessive taxation, which were faced by the English population as a whole.[79] The complete absence of relevant

---

[77] R. A. Rotz, 'The Lubeck Rising of 1408 and the Decline of the Hanseatic League', *Proceedings of American Philosophical Soc.*, no. 121 (1977), p. 42.

[78] E.g., S.B.A. White Vellum Book, fo. 17 v; *York Memorandum Book*, ii, pp. 67, 95, 98; and for some fifteenth-century examples of intermarriage between merchants of York, Beverley and Hull, see J. I. Kermode, 'The Merchants of Three Northern English Towns', in C. H. Clough (ed.), *Profession, Vocation and Culture in Later Medieval England* (Liverpool, 1982), p. 18.

[79] According to Thomas Walsingham (*Historia Anglicana*, i, p. 409), the outbreak of pestilence in the summer of 1379 was the most lethal the north of England had yet experienced.

manorial and other records will always make it impossible to place the late medieval Yorkshire towns of York, Beverley and Scarborough at all firmly within the rural society from which they derived their wealth; but that their own problems were expressions of, rather than contradictions to, the tensions of that society seems beyond doubt. It is easy to forget that, as in the case of London itself in June 1381, towns can often seem more important to those who visit them than those who live there. Why else, after all, did the East Riding rebel company of 1392 have publicly recited at Beverley and Hull that 'certain rhyme in English' whose message of solidarity had been so fundamental to the Peasants' Revolt in both town and country eleven years earlier: 'And on that purpos yet we stand, Who so dose us any wrang, in what place it falle / Yet he might als wele, Als have I hap and hele, do again us alle.'[80]

[80] The indictment which preserves the text of this famous poem is now best edited in *Select Cases in the Court of King's Bench*, ed. G. O. Sayles, 7 vols. (Selden Society, 1971), vii, pp. 83–5.

# 6. *Florentine Insurrections, 1342–1385, in Comparative Perspective**

SAMUEL COHN JR

For some time historians have noted the chronological clustering of urban and peasant insurrections across Europe during the second half of the fourteenth century.[1] Because of these chronological coincidences, historians have heeded the lessons drawn in Lucien Febvre's 'Une question mal posée?'[2] Instead of understanding these revolts in the contexts of local developments, they have studied them in recent years primarily in the context of general European patterns and causes. While Mollat and Wolff have seen these movements against the backdrop of the Black Death and the demographic crises of the second half of the fourteenth century,[3] other historians have examined them as manifestations of the crisis of feudalism,[4] or in some cases as the first proletarian struggles.[5] While these studies have brought a new analytical rigour to our understanding of late medieval social movements, the individual and local character of these revolts needs further investigation.

This essay will consider a region where the character of social protest was far different from that of England. The most striking difference is the complete absence of mass peasant movements in Tuscany and Umbria in the quarter century following the Black Death. It is true that large numbers of peasants in the wake of the

---

* For discussion of some of the points in this essay, see more generally Samuel Cohn Jr., *The Laboring Classes in Renaissance Florence* (New York, 1980).
[1] See Edward Cheyney, *The Dawn of the New Era, 1250–1453* (New York, 1936), pp. 110–41; and Henri Pirenne, *Economic and Social History of Medieval Europe*, trans. I. E. Clegg (London, 1936).
[2] Lucien Febvre, 'The Origins of the French Reformation: A Badly Put Question?', in Peter Burke (ed.), *A New Kind of History* (New York, 1973), pp. 44–107.
[3] Michel Mollat and Philippe Wolff, *Ongles bleus, Jacques et Ciompi: les révolutions populaires en Europe au XIVᵉ et XVᵉ siècles* (Paris, 1970).
[4] See R. H. Hilton, *Bond Men Made Free: Medieval Peasant Movements and the English Rising of 1381* (London, 1973).
[5] Victor Rutenburg, *Popolo e movimenti popolari nell'Italia del '300 e '400*, trans. Gianpiero Borghini (Moscow, 1958; Bologna, 1971).

plague immigrated to the cities and large towns (similar to most areas in Europe) and were able to enter the urban work-force as industrial artisans. The chemistry of this newly arrived 'peasant muscle' and the indigenous urban artisan consciousness may have formed (as Niccolò Rodolico has suggested) the politicized forces which toppled the Florentine oligarchy in July 1378.[6] None the less, the facts remain: (i) the urban protests of the late Trecento did not spread to the countryside or in any way provoke independent peasant insurrections; and (ii) different from the urban/rural mix which characterized the English uprisings of the 1370s and 1381 as well as the French Jacquerie of 1358,[7] there seems to have been little peasant participation in the urban insurrections of the second half of the fourteenth century. In the Florentine riots, from the earliest surviving criminal ledgers (1342) to the Revolt of the Ciompi (1378), few insurgents can be identified from the Florentine countryside. The food riot of 1368 stands out as the exception. Of the five arrested as ringleaders of a crowd estimated at five hundred, two were residents of the Florentine *contado* (countryside). But of these two, neither was identified as a tiller of the soil (*laborator terrae*) and one resided in the built-up suburb of S. Piero Monticello, which lay just beyond Florence's city walls.[8]

The chroniclers and later historians have commented on the role of men from the countryside in the ranks of the counter-insurgents, who besieged the city during the period of artisan and worker rule, the government of the Arti Minori (minor guilds) (1378–82), and who ultimately restored the old oligarchic regime. Historians have yet to study, however, the precise impact of peasant participation in the counter-revolutionary forces of the early 1380s. In the long lists of counter-insurgents prosecuted during the rule of the Arti Minori, only a handful of *contadini* (peasants) appear. From this evidence, the composition of the counter-revolutionary crowds was similar to the forces which overthrew the Florentine oligarchy in 1378, at least in one regard; they contained consistently urban and not rural rebels. Of the 105 insurgents who were sentenced for attempting to topple the new regime of artisans and workers, only nine were

[6] Niccolò Rodolico, *La democrazia fiorentina nel suo tramonto, 1378–1382* (Bologna, 1905), p. 44.

[7] See the essays in this volume by A. F. Butcher, Rosamond Faith and Raymond Cazelles.

[8] Niccolò Rodolico, *Il popolo minuto: note di storia fiorentina (1343–1378)*, 2nd edn (Florence, 1968), doc. 11, pp. 97–8.

residents of the countryside, and of these none was identified as a farm labourer.

How do we then explain the inertness of the Tuscan peasant in comparison with his confrères in northern Europe? Perhaps the answer lies in the different relationships of city and countryside between the two areas. Unlike towns in England, which must be seen in the larger context of the social relations of power and production in the countryside,[9] Florence by the second half of the fourteenth century exercised unquestioned political and economic domination over its *contado*.[10] Florence had embarked on the 'non-revolutionary way' to capitalism.[11] Mercantile capital dominated industrial capital, and the old patrician families after the Black Death began to amass for commercial purposes large tracts of rural properties throughout the Florentine territory.[12] Secondly, one can point to another obvious difference between England and Tuscany. In Tuscany the clash between new economic and social realities and juridical status was not a problem for the peasantry and their landlords. Serfdom had disappeared from northern Italy at least a century and a half before the social turmoil of the mid- and late Trecento.[13]

This essay, however, will not dwell on this history of silence; nor will its comparative perspective span Mediterranean and Atlantic economies and societies. Instead, it will concentrate on the patterns of social protest in mid-Trecento Florence, and then to a lesser

---

[9] See R. H. Hilton, 'Popular Movements in England at the End of the Fourteenth Century', in *Il tumulto dei Ciompi: un momento di storia fiorentina ed europea*, (Florence, 1981), pp. 223–40; and *idem*, 'Towns in English Feudal Society', *Review*, no. 3 (1979), pp. 3–20.

[10] See Marvin Becker, 'The Florentine Territorial State and Civic Humanism in the Early Renaissance', in N. Rubinstein (ed.), *Florentine Studies: Politics and Society in Renaissance Florence* (London, 1968), pp. 109–39; David Herlihy, 'Santa Maria Impruneta: A Rural Commune in the Late Middle Ages', in Rubinstein (ed.), *Florentine Studies*, pp. 242–76; *idem*, 'The Distribution of Wealth in a Renaissance Community: Florence 1427', in P. Abrams and E. A. Wrigley (eds.), *Towns in Societies* (Cambridge, 1978), pp. 131–57; and David Herlihy and Christiane Klapisch, *Les Toscans et leurs familles: une étude du catasto florentin de 1427* (Paris, 1978), pp. 267–300.

[11] For the distinction between the 'really revolutionary way' and the 'non-revolutionary way' see K. Marx, *Capital*, 3 vols. (New York, 1967), iii, p. 334.

[12] Herlihy, 'Santa Maria Impruneta', pp. 274–5; and Herlihy and Klapisch, *Les Toscans et leurs familles*, pp. 249–59.

[13] P. J. Jones, 'From Manor to Mezzadria: A Tuscan Case-Study in the Medieval Origins of Modern Agrarian Society', in Rubinstein (ed.), *Florentine Studies*, pp. 193–241.

extent urban unrest in other mercantile and industrial centres in Tuscany and Umbria. In these urban centres, insurrections staffed largely by artisans and workers contributed to changes in at least seven separate oligarchical regimes between 1355 and 1385.[14] By 1389 the rule of the old regimes had been restored throughout the region, never again to be seriously challenged by artisan and worker movements. Because of the vagaries of documentary survival, this essay will concentrate on the documentary-rich history of insurrections in Florence. I will argue that the waves of insurrections that threatened the stability of this city between 1342 and 1385 do not carve out a simple, unitary history which can be understood merely in terms of general European patterns and causes. Across the European canvas of the crisis of feudalism and the demographic transformations of the second half of the fourteenth century it is possible to demarcate three periods of insurrectionary activity in Florence; the character of each was dependent not on global changes in European society but instead on changes in the Florentine state.

The final section of this essay will reach beyond the history of Florence. As best the documentation will permit, I will compare the patterns of insurrection found in Florence with those of her neighbouring city-states. I will argue that beneath the chronological coincidences in the region lay crucial differences between Florence and her neighbours. In Florence social protest was distinctively more 'modern'. For this investigation, we must begin by setting out models for evaluating and distinguishing the forms and character of insurrectionary activity.

At the present state of historical research, the richest literature concerning typologies of popular protest exists in French historiography and turns in large part around the French Revolution. In the last twenty-two years, George Rudé and Charles Tilly have been its principal contributors. From this literature, one can generally identify two sets of tendencies in the forms, types and composition of popular protest, from the *ancien régime* through to the end of the nineteenth century. Tilly distinguishes between *communal* and *associational* forms of protest:

---

[14] See C. R. B. d'Ajano, 'Tumulti e scioperi a Siena nel secolo XIV', *Vierteljahrschrift für Social- und Wirtschaftgeschichte*, v (1907), pp. 458–66; *idem*, 'Lotte sociali a Perugia nel secolo XIV', *Vierteljahrschrift für Social- und Wirtschaftgeschichte*, viii (1910), pp. 337–49.

Communal: To the extent that contenders are communal, their collective actions – and hence the collective violence in which they engage – will tend to be localized, uncoordinated, dependent on normal rhythms of congregation like those of marketing, church-going, or harvesting, hard for the participants themselves to keep within bounds. To the extent that contenders are associational, their collective action will tend to be disciplined, large in scale, deliberately scheduled, and organized in advance.[15]

Tilly sees the fundamental shift in French history occurring in the 1850s: 'Almost all these changes involved in a shift away from casual congregation, communal organization, and uncoordinated protest toward the deliberate collective action typified by the demonstration or the strike.'[16] How do the waves of Florentine revolts fit into Tilly's typology? Certainly, we do not find all the forms of the associational model: industrial firms and trade unions, for example. On the other hand, there is evidence of the existence of strikes and secret societies. Moreover, the revolt of the Ciompi was not a village riot defined by lineages, religious congregation, or local markets. Rutenburg has even shown the regional interrelationships among Ciompi in Perugia, Siena and Florence. The Ciompi uprising of 1378 had a remarkable city-wide organization and participation that is particularly striking in comparison to the more localized participation revealed by the Bastille list of 1789.[17] But to understand the Ciompi further, we need to break down these large ideal types into more detailed categories.

In his studies on the French Revolution, George Rudé offers six characteristics of the *preindustrial crowd*: (i) the prevalence of the rural food riot; (ii) the resort to direct action, and violence to property; (iii) spontaneity; (iv) its leadership by those outside the crowd; (v) mixed composition, dominated by small shopkeepers and craftsmen in the towns, and by weavers, miners and labourers in the villages; and (vi) concern for the restoration of 'lost' rights.[18] From other articles by Rudé, one could add to this list the critical relationship between the price of bread and the frequency of

---

[15] Charles Tilly, 'How Protest Modernized in France, 1845–1855', in W. O. Aydelotte, A. G. Bogue and R. W. Fogel (eds.), *The Dimensions of Quantitative Research in History* (Princeton, 1972), p. 199.

[16] *Ibid.*, pp. 215–16.

[17] Cohn, *The Laboring Classes*, pp. 170–6.

[18] George Rudé, *Paris and London in the Eighteenth Century: Studies in Popular Protest* (London, 1974), p. 23.

rioting. During the French Revolution, Rudé distinguishes several periods or 'motions' of popular insurrection, 1789–94. Briefly, the Champs de Mars, July 1791, was a watershed. Before, there was a high percentage of food riots that bore a close relationship to the price of bread; afterwards, bread riots declined, and protest in general was less sensitive to fluctuations in bread or food prices. Strikes became more important, and the composition of the crowds included fewer women, shopkeepers and artisans, and a higher proportion of wage labourers of the manufactories.[19]

Let us now turn to the uprising of the Ciompi and those riots and insurrections that survive in the criminal archives – those of the Podestà, the Capitano and the Esecutore – from the beginning of the records in 1343 to the restoration of the oligarchy and the trials of the Ciompi insurrectionists. During this period, from 1343 to 1385, forty-three riots and insurrections which must have involved thousands of men and women have been found within the confines of the city alone. From these we can observe over three hundred and fifty persons who were fined or sentenced to death. These riots ranged from small attacks on individual *berrovarii* (police officers of the courts) or on officials of the Commune – from *nunptii* (messengers) to the *gonfalonieri* (heads of the political wards) – to the larger insurrections of the Otto di S. Maria Novella, and the mass counter-revolutionary conspiracies which were adjudicated throughout the rule of the Arti Minori.

Given the accepted models of insurrectionary activity in a preindustrial period, the most striking characteristic of these Ciompi insurrections is the insignificance of the grain and food riot. The criminal archives reveal evidence of only one grain riot. On 19 August 1368, five men, two from the rural suburbs and three then living in the city, were sentenced for congregating in front of a certain loggia where wheat and flour were sold.[20] These five men, along with the crowd which the officials of the Podestà estimated at more than five hundred,[21] then took 'a certain quantity of grain beyond twenty *starii*' and marched to the Palazzo de 'Signoria, where they slammed the grain to the ground, yelled 'Viva il

[19] *Ibid.*, pp. 131ff.
[20] The flood of November 1966 damaged the records of the criminal inquisition and sentences in both the Capitano del Popolo and the Podestà which pertain to this case: only Rodolico's published transcription of the sentence found in the Acts of the Podestà is now accessible: Rodolico, *Popolo minuto*, doc. 11, pp. 97–9.
[21] *Ibid.*, p. 98; Rodolico, *Democrazia fiorentina*, p. 124.

popolo', and began stoning the officials of the Podestà. It is curious that, from the little one can detect about causes and political expressions, even this riot was no explicit protest against prices and hunger, but rather a more general political protest against the Signoria itself and the government of Florence.

Secondly, within the rank and file of Trecento Florentine insurrectionists we do not find any women mentioned in the records. Unlike the riots of the *ancien régime* leading up to the march on Versailles, where women played a predominant role, the composition of the crowds on the eve of the Ciompi (at least, of those apprehended by the courts) was almost completely masculine. Certainly, they must have been part of the larger crowds of insurrectionists, in the crowd of five hundred in 1368 and among those thousands outside the Palazzo Vecchio who brought a change in the Communal government on 23 July 1378. But they do not appear to have been the ringleaders, or at least among those sought out by the *berrovarii* of the Capitano, the Podestà and the Esecutore. From these facts – the almost complete absence of grain and food riots and the absence of women – it seems that the motivation for collective political unrest did not spring from dire material conditions and problems of immediate necessity to the hearth.

Moreover, when the most recent research on price trends and wages during the period of the Ciompi is studied, the data do not exactly support the strong correlation drawn by Professor Brucker between rising grain prices and immiseration on the one hand, and the incidence of political unrest on the other. Charles de la Roncière charts a sharp rise in the prices of general necessities around 1335, which continued until several years after the Black Death, to around 1352. From the middle 1350s to the end of the 1360s prices fell; then, during the first half of the 1370s (a period of quiescence, according to Brucker) prices rose again, slightly surpassing the levels of the period of the Black Death. In the years immediately preceding the revolt of the Ciompi, however, prices fell.[22] From information compiled by Richard Goldthwaite on grain prices, 1375 and not 1378 should have been the critical year of the Ciompi uprising, had dire necessity been its principal underpinning.[23]

[22] Charles de la Roncière, *Florence: centre économique régional au XIVe siècle* (Aix-en-Provence, 1977), pp. 118, 260–2.

[23] Richard A. Goldthwaite, 'I prezzi del grano a Firenze del XIV al XVI secolo', *Quaderni storici*, xxviii (1975), table B, 'Medie annuali, 1359–1477', p. 33.

Instead, 1375, according to Brucker's periodization of social unrest, falls within the trough separating the turbulent years at the beginning of the decade from the Ciompi uprising itself.[24] Moreover, throughout the period 1340–78 (which was characterized by only a slight overall rise in prices), urban wages (especially for the more menial forms of labour) increased sharply and the purchasing power of workers rose.[25] It might, however, be argued that general wages do not adequately reflect the well-being of the major portion of the Florentine urban work-force – wage-earners of the Arte della Lana. There is evidence that this industry was experiencing a recession in the years 1366–78, and that workers were being laid off.[26] None the less, the point remains. The problems of the hearth, hunger and high bread prices (from which wool workers and the poor in general may have been suffering on the eve of the Ciompi), were not the triggers of this insurrection which led to their temporary control of the Florentine Commune. Rather, the causes are to be located in the principal industry of Florence, wool production, which drew its workers from the city at large. Its setting was associational – the firm; and the problems arising from the firm and the emerging capitalist structure of the Florentine economy were confronted squarely by the demands of the Ciompi in the petitions of July and the decrees of the Balìa of 32: the arbitrary jurisdiction of the guild court, the abolition of the *forestiere*, production quotas, and the right of working men to organize themselves into self-governing bodies which would have a voice in guild and Communal affairs.

Besides the revolt of the Ciompi, moreover, we find in the criminal archives other examples of insurrections organized among workers (*discipuli et operarii*) in the wool industry. On 9 October 1343 Aldobrandino di Ciecharino da Siena, called Trolquelio, who

[24] Gene A. Brucker, *Florentine Politics and Society, 1343–1378* (Princeton, 1962), p. 378. Similar to the English uprisings of 1377 and 1381 and to the Jacquerie of 1358, the weight of dire material conditions (rising bread prices and famine) cannot explain the outbreak of Ciompi insurrections. We will see later in this essay, however, that there were other insurrections during this period in the regions of Tuscany and Umbria whose incidence does bear a close relationship with rising grain prices.

[25] De la Roncière, *Florence: centre économique régional*, pp. 344, 371, 1302.

[26] Brucker, *Florentine Politics and Society*, p. 15; Richard Trexler, *Economic, Political and Religious Effects of the Papal Interdict on Florence* (Frankfurt-on-Main, 1964), pp. 100–2; none the less, according to de la Roncière, *Florence: centre économique régional*, pp. 387 (table 64), 1302, the wages of weavers rose during the period of the War of the Eight Saints, and their general conditions were certainly improving during the two years preceding the revolt of the Ciompi.

resided in the parish of S. Lorenzo in the city of Florence, led an armed insurrection of wool workers who worked in the shops of Salvi di Messer Lotto and Matteo di Parigio de'Albizzi.[27] Less than two years later, the skinner Ciuto Brandini of S. Pier Maggiore was captured and then hanged for organizing carders and skinners into *quedam fraternitas* (certain clubs) with *consules* (officials) and *capitudines* (ordinances) in many places throughout the city. These organizations collected dues and held regular meetings.[28] Following the night of Ciuto's capture the wool skinners and carders went on strike to demand his release.[29] The appearance of these workers, Aldobrandino di Ciecharino da Siena and Ciuto Brandini, as leaders of industrial insurrections leads us to the question of leadership in the popular insurrections during the period of the Ciompi. In the models of Tilly and Rudé, insurrections of the *ancien régime*, or even the entire pre-modern, preindustrial period (for Tilly, before 1850), relied on leadership from the outside, from the bourgeoisie or the aristocracy. No matter how large a Luca da Panzano or Salviato dei Medici, or the knighting of Vieri dei Medici may loom in the accounts and interpretations of the Ciompi revolt of 1378, when the mass of insurrections from 1342 to 1378 is considered, not only does one find the presence of leaders emerging from the working and artisan population, as in the cases above, but in fact it is rare to find in these documents the presence of leaders coming from above.

Only one clear exception survives in the criminal archives. In March of 1343 an inquisition was drawn up by the Capitano del Popolo against Pagnotto degli Strozzi, who led an insurrection against the city to protest the condemnation of his brother.[30] In this inquisition, the notary of the Capitano transcribed the words allegedly spoken by Pagnotto to arouse sedition: 'You wretched fools, who starve to death, who scrape for what should cost ten *soldi a staio*; even I could make a handful from this wretched bunch.'[31] Thus, Pagnotto was able to manipulate the crowd of impoverished urban dwellers for his own purposes – the overthrow of the Commune in a time of high grain prices.

---

[27] Atti del Podestà (hereafter A.P.), no. 23, fo. 87 r–v.

[28] The criminal documents pertaining to this case are again inaccessible because of the flood of 1966; Rodolico, *Popolo minuto*, doc. 14, pp. 102–3. See also Rodolico, *Democrazia fiorentina*, pp. 119–20.

[29] *Ibid.*, p. 39.

[30] Rodolico, *Popolo minuto*, doc. 9, pp. 93–4.     [31] *Ibid.*, p. 94.

But in the fifteen other insurrections preceding 1378 which come down to us in the criminal archives, we do not find a single participant bearing a prominent Florentine family name.[32] Indeed, 81 per cent of the rank and file found in the condemnation lists were disenfranchised workers of the wool industry. After the fall of the government of the Arti Minori, the percentages found in the condemnation lists dropped radically. Before analysing these later revolts, let us turn briefly to the much-studied tumult of 1378.

The revolt of the Ciompi, the overthrow of the oligarchy on 20–22 July 1378, was successful. Afterwards there were no arrests; nor did the Ciompi government or the government of the Arti Minori later grant titles, similar to the *vainqueurs de la Bastille*, to the insurgents of July 1378. Thus, we are not left with a Bastille list to aid in analysing its leadership and motivation in detail.[33] From the chronicle of Alamanno Acciaioli, a member of the overthrown Signoria of 1378, we learn that on the night of 19 July a certain Simincino, called Bugigatto, was captured, tortured and interrogated. Far from being spasmodic, it becomes evident from Simincino's testimony that the Ciompi uprising of 20 July relied on an organized leadership and secret meetings held in various parts of the city:

> Yesterday, during that day, I [Simoncino] and Pagolo del Bodda, Lioncino di Biagino, Lorenzo Ricomanni, Nardo di Camaldoli, Luca di Melano, Meo del Grasso, Zoccola and Guido Bandiera, Salvestrino from San Giorgia, il Guanda di Gualfonda and Galasso, we twelve in all, went into the Hospital of the Priests in San Gallo street; and when we were there, others came from a place called de 'Belletrani' and others of San Gallo; and there it was decided to begin the insurrection at three o'clock; and thus

---

[32] Atti del Capitano del Popolo (hereafter A.C.P.), no. 3, fo. 29 r, no. 11, fos. 23 r, 42 r, no. 19, fos. 5 v, 13 v, 25 r–v, no. 42, fo. 11 r, no. 63, fos. 11 r–12 r; Atti dell'Esecutore degli Ordinamenti di Giustizia (hereafter A.E.O.G.), no. 17, fo. 17 r–v; A.P., no. 23, fo. 87 r–v, no. 116, fo. 3 v, no. 127, fo. 336 v; Rodolico, *Popolo minuto*, doc. 11, pp. 97–9, and doc. 15, pp. 104–5. Outside the city, on the other hand, we find numerous examples in the criminal sentences of *magnates et potentes* arousing villagers to join their riots and pillaging. Usually these offences were directed against other *magnati* or villagers, but rarely against the institutions of the Commune or its officers.

[33] See Jacques Godechot, *The Taking of the Bastille, July 14th, 1789*, trans. Jean Stewart (London, 1970), pp. 221–6; Rudé, *Paris and London in the Eighteenth Century*, pp. 256–88.

the order was given by certain officers, which we made at the Ronco outside and beyond the gate of San Piero Gattolino.[34]

Despite the connections of the twelve men with certain *ammoniti* (those whose names had been struck from the lists of eligible office holders) and the patrician Salvestro de' Medici, the organization and manipulation of the masses was quite different from Andrea or Pagnotto Strozzi's leadership of the hungry in 1342, or the later conspiracies against the government of the Arti Minori, organized, led and staffed in large part by citizens of Florence bearing notable family names. Among the twelve revealed by Simincino, those who organized the secret meetings and planned the strategies for insurrections – the leadership in the streets – we do not find any patricians, but rather men who clearly appear to have been common artisans, petty shopkeepers and *sottoposti* (salaried artisans).

After the ousting of the old oligarchy, the *popolo minuto* elected their own Balìa of 32, which effectively ran the government of the Commune until the insurrection of the Otto di S. Maria Novella. Because of discontent with the justice rendered by the Podestà and the Capitano, moreover, the government of the Ciompi on 25 and 29 July nominated their own judges and officials of the courts. Of the twelve elected (three from each quarter), we again do not find the presence of notable men; they were men without family names.[35] Among them there were a certain Magister Christofanus Gensi (perhaps a grammar school teacher or a stone-worker), a notary and a son of a notary. In addition, we find a *riveditore* ('cloth finisher'), and a baker. Finally, despite his later co-optation (which has been carefully documented by Niccolò Rodolico), the *gonfaloniere* of justice, Michele di Lando, came from humble origins. And notwithstanding his later social success, during the summer of 1378 he was found among the ranks of the *Popolo di Dio* (People of God).[36]

The petitions of 21 and 22 July, the changes in the officials of the Podestà and Capitano on 25 and 27 July, and the changes instituted during the brief tenure in office of the Balìa of 32, moreover, do not reflect the heavy hand of a faction within the patriciate operating surreptitiously behind the scenes. The revolt of the Ciompi was

[34] *Cronache e memorie sul tumulto dei Ciompi*, ed. Gino Scaramella (Rerum intalicarum scriptores, xviii, pt. 3, Bologna, 1917), pp. 20–1.

[35] Carlo Falleti-Fossati, *Il tumulto dei Ciompi: cronache e memorie* (Florence, 1873), doc. 10, p. 119.

[36] Rodolico, *Democrazia fiorentina*, pp. 200–6.

indeed an amalgam of struggles; its success depended on their alliance with the Arti Minori, *ammoniti*, and even individuals such as Salvestro de' Medici, well ensconced in the oligarchy of Florence. From this amalgam should we be so cynical as always to expect the force and direction to have come from above, and conversely assume the passivity of the labouring classes? We find similar alliances and divisions of conflict in the French, Russian and Chinese revolutions.

Gene Brucker, Mollat, Wolff and de Roover, on the other hand, have argued that the demands of 21 to 22 July were modest, and even reflected a deep-seated conservatism.[37] Brucker has argued that the creation of the three revolutionary guilds was a throwback to former times – the restoration of the guild-world of Dino Compagni. The Florentine Ciompi did not simply copy the corporate forms and structures of their masters.[38] But the three guilds of 1378, which interlocked the whole of the *popolo minuto* (labouring classes), had only the name *arte* in common with the seventy-two or more guilds that structured the medieval economy of Dino Compagni. They differ, moreover, from the radical journeymen's societies which sprang up in London and other English towns after the Black Death.[39] Instead of a plethora of brotherhoods isolated and organized around various steps of production and crafts, and outside the political world of the Commune, the three guilds of 1378 unified the wage-earners of Florence in such a way that they could for the first time make demands which would alter the political and economic policy of the Commune. The other side of the Ciompi's 'acceptance of the constitutional structure' was their participation in it, which radically changed that structure from representing less than 20 per cent of the population to almost all of the adult male population. The creation of the three revolutionary guilds, moreover, which gave wage-earners in the wool industry the right freely to buy and sell raw materials and finished goods, and which gave them the opportunity to participate in the decisions of production, fundamentally altered the relations of production in the dominant

---

[37] Gene A. Brucker, 'The Ciompi Revolution', in Rubinstein (ed.), *Florentine Studies*, p. 352; Mollat and Wolff, *Ongles bleus, Jacques et Ciompi*, p. 161; Raymond de Roover, 'Labour Conditions in Florence around 1400: Theory, Policy and Reality', in Rubinstein (ed.), *Florentine Studies*, p. 309.

[38] For a different opinion, see John Najemy, ' "Audiant omnes artes": Corporate Origins of he Ciompi Revolution', in *Il tumulto dei Ciompi*, pp. 59–93.

[39] See Hilton, 'Popular Movements in England', pp. 237–8.

industry of Trecento Florence. Indeed, during the brief tenure of the Signoria under the direction of the Balìa of 32 the government made decisions which very certainly cut into the ancient prerogatives of the wool merchants and the merchant-banking class. First, the interest rates on forced loans – the principal means of taxation which in effect redistributed the incomes from direct taxation (the *gabelles*) back to the rich – were cut from 15 per cent to 5 per cent. Secondly, fluctuations in the ratio between gold and silver (before and after the revolt of the Ciompi a means of lowering the real wages of artisans and workers) was stabilized at 3.5 lire per florin. Thirdly, the wool workers imposed production quotas on the wool manufacturers in order to reduce unemployment and underemployment. Fourthly, by abolishing the *forestiere* and by placing members from the three new guilds in the courts of the Arte della Lana, the wool merchants could no longer exercise complete and arbitrary freedom of action over the personal and economic behaviour of their workers.[40]

The government of the Balìa of 32 lasted only six weeks. At the end of August, the radical wing of the *popolo minuto* – the Otto di S. Maria Novella – tried to push the revolution further. They failed, and as a result the Ciompi then in power formed a broader coalition government with the minor guildsmen. With the condemnations of the Otto di S. Maria Novella in September 1378 we begin to find again, for the first time since the early 1340s, members of the patriciate among the indicted *popolo minuto*. Among the *cardatori*, *pettinatori*, *scardassieri* and *revitori*, the patrician da Panzano and a member of the Strozzi family were among those condemned to death by the government of Michele di Lando.[41] It is, however, after the government of the Arti Minori had secured power that the crucial shift in the character of Florentine insurrection occurred. In the early 1380s the Commune of Florence was besieged by a series of assaults. These insurrections clearly originated from the 'outside', both geographically and in terms of social class. In sharp contrast to the insurrections leading up to the Ciompi uprising, the tumults during the last two years of the regime of the Arti Minori possessed all the characteristics which an Edmund Burke, Hip-

[40] Rodolico, *Democrazia fiorentina*, pp. 136ff.
[41] Marchionne di Coppo Stefani, *Cronica fiorentina*, ed. Niccolò Rodolico (Rerum italicarum scriptores, xxx, pt. 1, Città di Castello, 1903), pp. 336–7; and *Diario d'anomino fiorentino dall'anno 1358 al 1389*, ed. A. Gherardi (Florence, 1876), pp. 384–5.

polyte Taine or a Pierre Gaxotte[42] would have wished of a popular insurrection. In the criminal archives, for the first time, there were substantial numbers of the patriciate intermingled with Ciompi. In a list of conspirators condemned by the Esecutore degli Ordinamenti di Giustizia, twelve were prominent figures of the old ruling class and only one of twenty-nine condemned practised an occupation in the wool industry. This group of conspirators allegedly ran through the *contado* and district of Florence capturing men and women, carrying off movable goods and animals, murdering people, burning fields, buildings and homes, and kidnapping virgins, women and men.[43]

On 2 January 1380 eleven patricians were condemned as rebels for congregating outside the city walls of Siena and conspiring to besiege the Commune's fortress at Figline. Among the eighteen *rebelles*, only two bore Ciompi occupations.[44] The Capitano del Popolo condemned to death on 1 January 1380 nineteen members of the Florentine patriciate from among the fifty-one *rebelles* arrested. They conspired in Bologna during November 1379, and besieged Florence at six o'clock at night sometime in December. Among the fifty-one, only five were clearly of Ciompi status: two weavers, two combers and a skinner. The conspirators entered the city of Florence raising the cry of 'Viva el populo et Parte Guelfa'; they bore the insignia and banners of the Parte Guelfa (the traditional aristocratic faction of Florence).[45]

The motivation, moreover, for insurrection expressed in these sentences again seems to fit the Taine–Burke model. A utopian image of power, vainglory and even cash impelled some of the desperate *popoli minuti*, then in exile or out of favour with the government of the Arti Minori, to ally and conspire with members of the patriciate. In a conspiracy condemned by the Esecutore in October 1381, a certain Ricco cajoled Tommaso Buzaffi of the parish of S. Lorenzo to join the armed insurrection against the present regime of Arti Minori with the following words: 'If you are not one of the *priores*, here, within six months, you'll never be; because there will be another new scrutiny, you will be made rich and you will never have to have any more to do with poor men.'[46] In

[42] See Rudé, *Paris and London in the Eighteenth Century*, pp. 125–6.
[43] A.E.O.G., no. 870, fos. 37 r–38 v.
[44] A.C.P., no. 1198, fos. 47 v–49 v.
[45] *Ibid.*, fos. 54 v–59 r.
[46] Rodolico, *Democrazia fiorentina*, doc. 7, p. 477.

addition, on 16 September 1380 the forces of the Capitano apprehended three men from Laterina, one man from Monte Longo and
another conspirator from the Florentine parish of S. Felicità for an
attempted seizure of the castle of Laterina. In the inquisition it is
made clear that these men were paid 200 florins each by the
nobleman, Nannino di Messer Canagni da Arezzo, to subvert and
rebel against the castle. And if successful, Nannino promised his
*amici* a part of the new regime.[47]

But not all of the insurrections following the defeat of the Otto di
S. Maria Novella in September 1378 had the same composition or
motivation. By 1382, after the fall of the coalition government of
the Arti Minori and the restoration of the oligarchy, we enter a third
period of Florentine insurrections: these counter-revolutionary
movements, organized outside the city of Florence and staffed, in
large part, by members of the patriciate, disappear from the
criminal archives. On 13 March 1382 the Podestà condemned three
men to death and condemned their property to be destroyed
because of rioting and the destruction of property along the streets
running into the piazza of S. Michele Berteldi.[48] In the 'conspiracy'
the influence of the patriciate is again not apparent. Less than two
weeks later, the Podestà condemned twelve men to be beheaded for
congregating and inciting to riot. Of the twelve, only one bore a
family name – nine were identified by profession. Of these, eight
were clearly members of the Ciompi, and all nine could be considered members of the *popolo minuto*. Moreover, instead of the
cry of 'Viva la Parte Guelfa e il popolo' – the slogan of the *popolani
grassi* – these insurrectionists raised the cry of the Ciompi, 'Vivano
vinti e quattro arti.'[49] A month before these sentences, the oligarchy
had been restored to power and had completely obliterated the
remaining accomplishments of the revolt of the Ciompi, 1378 – the
revolutionary guilds of wool workers (the Arti dei Farsettai and
Arti dei Tintori) had been abolished.

In 1383 the oligarchy began its efforts in earnest to round up and
purge from the Commune those remaining parties which might
threaten the stability of the restored regime. On 11 and 12 September 1383 the Esecutore condemned eighty-two men to death. Of
this crowd, only four possessed family names. Of the remaining

[47] A.C.P., no. 1313, fos. 26 r–27 r.
[48] A.P., no. 3053, fos. 102 v–103 v.
[49] *Ibid., passim.*

seventy-eight, seventeen were identified by profession. There was perhaps only one major guildsman, and six minor guildsmen – a belt-maker, two cobblers, a grocer, a maker of armour and a tavern-keeper. The remaining ten were outside the Florentine guild structure.[50] The slogans and actions of this crowd, despite the participation of at least three persons of notable family backgrounds, again distinguishes this insurrection from those conspiracies against the regime of the Arti Minori. Instead of hailing the arch-patrician club – the Parte Guelfa – these rebels marched through various parts of the city, carrying the three banners corresponding to the three revolutionary guilds of *sottoposti* and raising the insignia of the lamb against the field of the city, the sign of two of the new guilds. According to two sets of sentences in the Esecutore, the rebels chanted, 'Long live the twenty-four guilds and death to the traitors who make us starve.'[51]

In conclusion, the insurrections following the suppression of the Otto di S. Maria Novella on 31 August 1378 fall into two categories separated by a single local event – the defeat of the Ciompi and the end of the government of the Arti Minori. In the period from 1378 to 2 January 1382 the broadly based government of the Arti Minori, which retained a representation of a large portion of the labouring population, was under siege from conspiracies organized outside the city and comprised in large part by exiled members of notable families: the Alberti, de Castiglionchio, Albizzi, Medici and others. In marked contrast to those lists of condemned insurrectionists in the period preceding the Ciompi, 1343–78, where we find only two participants with notable family names, one-third of the conspirators in these riots of 1379–81 bore prominent family names. Moreover, those identified by the professions of the Ciompi are rare; they do not dominate the insurrectional crowds as they did in the thirty years preceding the Ciompi. Of eighty-one persons condemned to death in the years 1379–81 and who can be identified either by a family name or an occupation, only eight were *sottoposti* – a spinner, four combers, two weavers and a skinner – while forty-five bore prominent Florentine family names. Second, the ideology or motivation for action was clearly different from the riots of the preceding period. Personal vainglory, money and opportunism dominated the designs of the leadership and were the means for manipulating their following. The chants raised by these groups

---

[50] A.E.O.G., no. 950, fos. 25 r–27 v, 29 r–30 v.    [51] *Ibid.*, fos. 27 v, 29 v.

were in support of the *ancien régime* symbolized by the Parte Guelfa.

In the period 1382–3, the insurrections described in the criminal sentences reflect a different crowd. With the restoration of the oligarchy, the target of insurrection had changed: the counter-revolutionary groups of exiled noblemen disappear, and in their place we find, once again, crowds dominated by the rank and file of the Ciompi. They banded together to protest against the cancellation of their advances of 1378: political recognition and the right to bind together in working men's guilds. Their slogans, moreover, did not represent the designs of the patriciate – 'Viva la Parte Guelfa' – but instead, the interests of working men and women – 'Vivano li vinti et quattro arti.'

Once we move beyond the territory of Florence, the possibilities for examining the composition of insurrectionary crowds, the character of their leadership and the relationship of the occurrence of riots to bread prices became more difficult. Of the three industrial cities in the region – Lucca, Siena and Perugia – criminal archives survive intact only at Lucca, and here popular protest was far less prevalent than in the other two cities. From the chronicle of Giovanni Sercambi and a survey of the criminal archives, only one insurrection staffed by workers and artisans appears during the second half of the Trecento. During the period of transformation of the Lucchese government from an aristocratic Commune to the government of the 'Popolo' (dominated by bankers and international merchants), the Podestà charged eight artisans, including two silk weavers, with plotting to overthrow the newly formed 'Popolo'. This abortive insurrection of 1370 appears to have had a character quite unlike the series of popular revolts which threatened the Florentine state in the period 1342–78. Instead of revolting for their own collective interest or for the formation of workers' organizations, these artisans protested against the ousting of certain noble families from Communal offices. Their rallying cries were in defence of the arch-aristocratic party – the Parte Guelfa. The chronicler Sercambi characterizes these artisans as 'di parte guelfa amici', and asserts that the degli Obizi (one of the families banned from participating in the government of the 'Popolo') were behind the artisans' plot.[52]

---

[52] Christine Meek, *Lucca, 1369–1400: Politics and Society in an Early Renaissance City-State* (Oxford, 1978), p. 183; *Le croniche di Giovanni Sercambi Lucchese*, ed. Salvatore Bongi, 2 vols. (Lucca, 1892), i, p. 204.

In Siena and Perugia popular insurrections certainly played a more important role than they did in the history of Lucca. In 1355 an uprising of the Sienese *popolo minuto* contributed to the fall of the government of the Nine after sixty-eight years of rule. The *popolo minuto* of Siena, however, was a social group considerably wider than the *popolo minuto* (disenfranchised wool workers) of Florence. At Siena it included not only independent artisans, but shopkeepers, some merchants, and even the professional class of notaries.[53] In the Sienese revolt of 1355, moreover, we do not find secret organizations of workers or independent petitions expressing workers' demands. Instead, the slogans of this *popolo minuto* fit a particular characteristic of Rudé's 'preindustrial crowds' and Tilly's 'communal forms of protest' which never appears in the insurrectional history of Trecento Florence. The Sienese movement appealed to a force beyond themselves, the Holy Roman Emperor, to intervene and to restore the ancient order: 'Long live the Emperor and death to the Nine.' In addition, this social movement not only attacked the symbols and objects of their oppression. After burning documents in the Merchants' court, they invaded the impoverished district of S. Pietro d'Ovile, attacking wool workers and burning down their homes.[54] Again, these Sienese actions bear 'preindustrial' characteristics. The relatively spontaneous and 'direct' action, which spread even to the burning of workers' homes, contrasts sharply with the much better enforced and limited violence inflicted by the Florentine Ciompi.

In 1369 and again in 1371 riots by the *popolo minuto* of Siena contributed to changes in the composition of the ruling oligarchy. In these insurrections we do not find the clear reactionary impulses of 1355. Indeed, Victor Rutenburg has described the Sienese revolt of 1371 as the predecessor of the Florentine revolt of 1378. It was, according to Rutenburg, a revolt primarily of wool workers from the quarter of Ovile who demanded higher wages and equality with the bosses.[55] But we do not find any evidence of petitions expressing concrete and specific demands. Moreover, the organization of wool workers which *might* have been behind the planning of the tumult of 1371 – the Company of the Bruco – appears to have been categori-

---

[53] Victor Rutenburg, 'La vie et la lutte des Ciompi de Sienne', *Annales, E.S.C.*, xx (1965), p. 103.

[54] *Cronaca senese di Donato di Neri e di suo figlio Neri* (Rerum italicarum scriptores, xv, pt. 6, Bologna, 1936), pp. 577–8.

[55] Rutenburg, 'La vie et la lutte des Ciompi de Sienne', p. 104.

cally different from the revolutionary guilds of the Ciompi and their city-wide organizations which plotted the overthrow of the Florentine Commune seven years later. The Bruco was a neighbourhood association, named after the *contrada* (neighbourhood) where the mass of Sienese wool workers were concentrated. More importantly, there was a distinct difference in the timing of both of these Sienese revolts (1368, 1371) and the waves of popular insurrection which preceded and included the revolt of the Ciompi of 1378. Unlike the Florentine revolts which were not precipitated by sharp rises in the price of bread, these two tumults similar to the Sienese revolt of 1355 followed immediately periods of famine and soaring grain prices.[56]

In fact, if there were a regional conjuncture between high bread prices and popular revolt, it occurred in the period 1369–71. Similar to Lucca and Siena, a major insurrection which contributed to the fall of an oligarchic regime followed a severe economic crisis and rising grain prices in Perugia in May 1371.[57] Again, similar to Lucca and Siena, we do not find in Perugia evidence of secret workers' organizations plotting the strategies behind this revolt nor petitions expressing the independent demands of wool workers and other disenfranchised workers. The geography of this tumult, moreover, appears different from the city-wide networks of the Florentine Ciompi. The revolt in Perugia was 'communal' in character; it arose and seems to have been confined largely to the depressed wool workers' neighbourhood of Sant'Angelo.[58]

It is important here to distinguish the conjuncture of events in Lucca, Siena and Perugia from those occurring at the same time in Florence. Although grain prices rose in Florence during 1370–1,[59] the period remained one of social calm. The timing of insurrection in Trecento Florence was different. As we have seen, revolution in the Arno city followed falling and not soaring grain prices and arose from wholly different causes. While the forms of revolt in Florence in the periods 1342–78 and 1382–5 were 'associational' in character, arising out of organizations and problems of the industrial workplace, those of her neighbours fit well the models of preindustrial crowds – communal in geographic scope, organized apparently by

[56] *Cronaca senese*, pp. 616, 633, 636.
[57] D'Ajano, 'Lotte sociali a Perugia', pp. 343, 345.
[58] *Ibid.*, pp. 345–6.
[59] Goldthwaite, 'I prezzi del grano a Firenze', p. 33.

forces outside the labouring classes and correlated directly with economic crises and problems bearing on the immediate needs of the hearth. Thus, against the backdrop of demographic crisis and the crisis of feudalism which characterized most of Western Europe during the latter half of the fourteenth century, we find a clustering of insurrections in the regions of Tuscany and Umbria. But an investigation into the forms and composition of insurrections reveals (i) that the history of social movements in Florence during the period 1342–85 was not a unitary period which can be entirely explained by general patterns and conjunctures, and (ii) that the social movements in Florence were categorically different from those of her neighbours during the same period.

If the remarkable 'modernity' of Florentine revolt in 1342–78 and 1382–5 cannot be explained solely by general European demo-graphic and economic conjunctures of the late fourteenth century, can we point to local causes, forces within the political economy of Trecento Florence, which might lead to a better understanding of this social history? In fact, in late fourteenth-century Florence there was a curious disequilibrium between the development of the forces of production and the organization of the state. From a third to a half of the work-force were disenfranchised wage-earners in the wool industry – about the same percentage of wage-earners one finds in Paris in 1789.[60] The Florentine Ciompi, brought together by new capitalist relations of production that cut across old *communal* networks of association, challenged the domination of a state which was still medieval. The courts and the organization of social control were distributed among three overlapping institutions – the Podestà, the Capitano del Popolo and the Esecutore degli Ordinamenti di Giustizia. A different foreign dignitary directed each of these judicial and executive bodies. There were no precise divisions in the functions of the three bodies, nor a clear hierarchy of control. In short, there was no sovereign body in the modern sense. The actual positions of social control, moreover, were decentralized. The most important organizations of police surveil-lance and law enforcement were the 'hue and cry' of the inhabitants.[61] Because of this uneven development between the organization of production and state formation, the Florentine

[60] Giovanni Villani, *Cronica*, ed. F. G. Dragomanni, 4 vols. (Florence, 1844–5), iii, pp. 323–6; Cohn, *The Laboring Classes*, p. 11.
[61] Cohn, *The Laboring Classes*, pp. 198–201.

Ciompi could assume modern *associational* forms of protest as opposed to the *communal* ones which characterized her neighbours as well as the history of insurrections in France until the late 1840s.

On the other hand there is some evidence to suggest that the state apparatuses of Florence's smaller neighbours during the late fourteenth century might have been more developed and more centralized than those of Florence – supposedly the birthplace of the modern state.[62] At least in regard to the forces of social control and repression, the courts of Perugia and Lucca were not entirely fragmented between jurisdictions headed by foreign dignitaries. The Commune centralized and controlled the final process of sentencing in the criminal tribunals in these cities.[63]

The comparison with Siena is more striking. The government of the Nine, an oligarchy composed largely of merchants and bankers[64] which ruled Siena without serious threat to its hegemony for nearly seven decades (1287–1355), transformed fundamentally old medieval judicial and political institutions. It whittled down the authority and police power of the Podestà and the Captain of the People and created three new judicial and executive bodies. Instead of a foreign dignitary with short periods of office, the Nine presided over two of these new bodies – the court and police force of the Nine and an organization for the daytime surveillance of urban neighbourhoods called the Quattrini. In addition, a new official, the Captain of War, entered the Sienese constitution. Although a foreigner, the tenure of office for his dignitary and his police force was not as ephemeral as the six-month periods usually enjoyed by the Captain of the People and the Podestà. The most famous of the war captains – Guidoriccio, who was immortalized by Simone Martini's fresco in the Palazzo Comunale – served the Sienese state for six and a half years.[65] Thus, through this mix of power and the creation of courts directly under the aegis of the highest Sienese councils, the Nine anticipated by the 1330s developments in political sovereignty and the centralization of power which the Florentine

---

[62] Jacob Burckhardt, *The Civilization of the Renaissance in Italy*, trans. S. G. C. Middlemore (New York, 1954), p. 61.

[63] D'Ajano, 'Lotte sociali a Perugia', p. 345; Salvatore Bongi, *Inventario del Regio Archivio di Stato in Lucca*, 4 vols. (Lucca, 1872–88), ii, p. 303.

[64] William Bowsky, 'The *Buon Governo* of Siena (1287–1355): A Medieval Italian Oligarchy', *Speculum*, no. 37 (1962), p. 369.

[65] William Bowsky, *A Medieval Italian Commune: Siena under the Nine, 1287–1355* (Berkeley, 1981), pp. 23–84.

state did not realize until well into the fifteenth century. Besides these qualitative differences in the state structure of the two communes, there was a quantitative difference during the period of insurrections which must have weighed heavily on the attempts of Sienese artisans and workers to organize themselves and to develop traditions of insurgency. While in late Trecento Florence the ratio of police to inhabitants was 1 to 800, in Siena there was a policeman for every 145th person.[66]

But even if the state structures found in Lucca, Siena and Perugia were no more advanced than those of Florence, one thing is certain: industrial production and capital formation were not nearly as developed or as extensive in these cities as they were in Florence. The wool industry in the hilltop towns of Siena and Perugia, always plagued by problems of water supply, never dominated artisan and industrial production as it did in Trecento Florence. And in Lucca its major industrial sector – silk production – employed only 285 people in 1372.[67] In summary, one wonders what forms (if any) the protests of the Florentine Ciompi would have assumed had the Florentine state resembled in its structure the monarchy of absolutist France or even the oligarchy of Trecento Venice.[68] With the defeat of the Ciompi, and the consequent development and centralization of the police, the courts and other bureaucratic structures, which culminated first in the rise of the Medicean Republic and ultimately in the Principality of the sixteenth century, all vestiges of Ciompi organization and insurrection disappear from Florentine history.

[66] William Bowsky, 'The Medieval Commune and Internal Violence: Police, Power and Public Safety in Siena, 1287–1355', *American Historical Review*, no. 73 (1967), p. 7.

[67] Meek, *Lucca, 1369–1400*, p. 35.

[68] See the examples of class antagonism collected in Guido Ruggiero, *Violence in Early Renaissance Venice* (New Brunswick, 1980), pp. 96–7.

# 7. *The Revolt against the Justices*

ALAN HARDING

The discontent which came to a head in 1381 may have been largely economic in origin, but a revolt which culminated in two meetings between the king and the rebels, who are described by the chroniclers as claiming to be the 'true commons of England' and demanding far-reaching changes in the law and the way it was made, can hardly be denied the adjective 'political'.[1] This essay will argue that the political aspects of the revolt, and the very possibility of the first political revolt of the lower orders, can best be explained in terms of the development of justice and policing over the previous hundred years.

Although the chief impression to be gained from an analysis of the judicial records of the attacks on lawyers in London is naturally that the confusion of the revolt was used to pay off individual scores, sometimes by 'rebels' of respectability who took no further part in events,[2] the aims which the chroniclers attribute to Wat Tyler are evidence of a general hatred of lawyers as such. According to Walsingham, Tyler wanted a commission from the king 'to behead all lawyers (*juridicos*), escheators and others who had been trained in the law or dealt in the law by reason of their office. He believed that once all those learned in the law had been killed, all things would henceforward be regulated by the decrees of the common people.'[3] The *Anonimalle Chronicle* takes further the suggestion that the people had their own vision of the proper working of the law: Tyler is said to have put at the head of his demands at

---

[1] Thomas Walsingham, *Historia Anglicana*, ed. H. T. Riley, 2 vols. (Rolls ser., London, 1863–4), i, p. 464; *The Anonimalle Chronicle, 1333–1381*, ed. V. H. Galbraith (Manchester, 1927), pp. 139, 147. The latter source relates that 'les ditz comunes avoient entre eux une wache worde en Engleys, "With whom haldes yow?" et le respouns fuist, "Wyth kynge Richarde and wyth the trew communes": et ceux qe ne savoient ne vodroient respondre, furount decolles.'

[2] A. J. Prescott, 'London in the Peasants' Revolt: A Portrait Gallery', *The London Journal*, vii, no. 2 (Winter 1981).

[3] *Historia Anglicana*, i, p. 464.

Smithfield, that there should be 'no law but the law of Winchester and that henceforward there should be no outlawry in any process of law, and that no lord should have lordship in future, but that it should be divided among all men, except for the king's own lordship'.[4] In the context of the process of law, rather than of legal status, the reference must be to Edward I's Statute of Winchester, which laid down regulations for policing, and not to Domesday Book (very occasionally called 'the book of Winchester') as used to support the claims to privileged status of villeins on ancient demesne.[5]

The core provision of the statute of 1285 was

that every man have in his house arms for keeping the peace in accordance with the ancient assize; . . . that every man between fifteen years and sixty be assessed and sworn to arms according to the amount of his lands and chattels . . . And in each hundred and liberty let two constables be chosen to make the view of arms: and the aforesaid constables shall, when the justices assigned to this come to the district, present before them the defaults they have found in arms, in watch-keeping and in highways . . . And the justices assigned shall present again to the king in each parliament and the king will provide a remedy therefor.[6]

It is easy to see how the Statute of Winchester might have come to represent an ideal of communal self-policing, which gave the people the right as well as the duty (as the Chartists were to say) 'to possess the arms of free Englishmen'.[7] Their duties and rights under the statute were kept before the people's eyes in the years preceding the revolt by further ordinances such as one of 1354 which reinforced the obligation of the country to pursue robbers 'according to the form contained in the Statute late made at Winchester', in order to

[4] *Anonimalle Chronicle*, ed. Galbraith, p. 147.
[5] For the rarity of this way of referring to Domesday Book, see above, Rosamond Faith, 'The "Great Rumour" of 1377 and Peasant Ideology', note 21. V. H. Galbraith's suggestion in his notes to the *Anonimalle Chronicle* (p. 196) that the reference is to a 'coveted privilege' of the town of Winchester which 'substituted the mutilation and blinding of felons for common hanging' is not convincing (cf. *V.C.H. Hampshire*, v, p. 144).
[6] *Statutes of the Realm (1101–1713)*, ed. A. Luders *et al.*, 11 vols. (Record Commission, London, 1810–28), i, p. 96. The intention of the statute to reinforce the traditional peace-keeping obligations of the local community is emphasized by Edward's declaration that he would delay its implementation until he saw 'how the country behaved (*coment le pais se portera*)'.
[7] Eileen Yeo, 'Christianity in Chartist Struggle 1838–42', *Past and Present*, no. 91 (May 1981), pp. 124–5.

give 'greater will and courage' to alien merchants to trade in England.[8] The charge of the justices of the peace to presenting juries would also have reminded the local community of such obligations.[9] Finally, judicial commissions regularly juxtaposed the Statute of Winchester with the Statutes of Northampton and Westminster. General commissions of the peace 'pursuant to the statutes of Winchester, Northampton and Westminster' had thus been issued for all counties on 2 July 1377; and on 5 December 1380 the order went out to the mayor and bailiffs of Cambridge, on information that there were various evildoers in the town, to cause to be proclaimed and kept therein the articles in the Statutes of Winchester, Northampton and Westminster against 'roberdesmen', 'wastours' and 'draghlatches'.[10]

To the community policing of the Statute of Winchester, there had been added by the Statute of Northampton in 1328 and the Statute of Westminster in 1361 enforcement of the peace-keeping laws and punishment of 'rebels' against them, by justices drawn from the great lords (the *grantz*) and the leading gentry and burgesses. In 1285, England might have seemed to be moving towards the exclusive lordship of the king, who was confining the privileges of the magnates within narrow limits by the process of *quo warranto*, and dealing out justice to an increasingly wide range of his subjects directly through the eyres of a small number of professional justices sent from Westminster.[11] In his courts, of

[8] *Statutes of the Realm*, i, p. 347.

[9] *Proceedings before the Justices of the Peace in the Fourteenth and Fifteenth Centuries*, ed. B. H. Putnam (London, 1938), p. 11 (ch. 1 of the charge). Cf. the complaint of the chief pledges of a Hertfordshire township in 1377 that the watch was not summoned there 'according to the statute of Winchester' (Christopher Dyer, 'The Social and Economic Background to the Rural Revolt of 1381', above, p. 41).

[10] *Cal. Pat. Rolls, 1377–81*, pp. 44, 578.

[11] On *quo warranto* and the king's close supervision of the lords' exercise of their franchisal powers, see *Statutes of the Realm*, i, pp. 45–50 (for the Statute of Gloucester of 1278); Helen M. Cam, *The Hundred and the Hundred Rolls* (London, 1930); and A. Harding, 'Political Liberty in the Middle Ages', *Speculum*, lv (1980), pp. 430–1, 439–41. 'Wilful lordship', the unrestrained exercise of baronial liberties, could be seen as the opponent of 'common justice' and 'common right' a century before the Peasants' Revolt. In 1329, Chief Justice Scrope maintained that the purpose of eyres was to see how the barons governed the people, since 'franchise is to have jurisdiction and rule over the people of the king'. For the way in which bills, presented first of all in the eyre, and then before special commissions of oyer and terminer and (from at latest 1278) in parliament, provided a means of direct political communication between the king and the people, see A. Harding, 'Plaints and Bills in the History of English Law', in D.

which the highest was parliament, he received the written complaints or bills of individuals and local communities. But a few central justices could not bear the weight put upon them, especially when the Scottish wars began to bring them new tasks and simultaneously threw English society into turmoil by their demands for men and supplies. Already in 1287, between two and six landowners in each county had been commissioned to attend to the execution of the Statute of Winchester, not yet two years old, because the justices 'appointed to take assizes in divers parts of the realm' did not 'go every year as often as was ordained'.[12] In fact, it was two sets of events which fragmented any common interest in the enforcement of justice which seemed to be emerging in the 1280s: the wars which began in the second half of Edward I's reign, with all the strains they imposed on local society, and the Black Death and the subsequent labour crisis. The strains of war made the king resort to special criminal commissions, almost punitive expeditions, in the hands of magnates, and the labour crisis caused criminal justice to be turned over to the gentry for use in controlling the servant classes. The effect of the extension to new types of justices of power to enforce the Winchester peace-keeping measures changed the social groups in whose interests the law worked. At the same time, the definition of new offences against the peace for the justices to punish changed the social groups against whom the law was directed. The peace-keeping statutes and commissions of the century preceding the revolt register the shifts of power in the countryside, and explain why the social lines were drawn as they were in the conflicts of 1381.

This was so in particular because the statutes and commissions were usually responses to parliamentary petitions. The county community grew in definition in the fourteenth century through its regular meetings during the visits of the assize judges and the sessions of the keepers, soon justices, of the peace – and through its regular petitioning of the king, by means of its representatives in

Jenkins (ed.), *Legal History Studies 1972* (Cardiff, 1975). Bills provided a means by which villeins could demand justice from the king against their lords and in particular claim ancient demesne status: see Harding, 'Plaints and Bills', pp. 75, 78–9; *Rotuli Parliamentorum*, 6 vols. (Record Comm., London, 1783), i, pp. 4 (no. 14) and 10–11 (no. 49) for the petitions of tenants of the abbots of St Augustine's Canterbury and of Hales for ancient demesne rights in the autumn parliament of 1278.

[12] *Cal. Pat. Rolls, 1281–92*, pp. 264–5.

parliament, for more frequent visits of the judges and above all for more powers for the justices.[13] We may guess that petitions like this prompted the original Statute of Winchester: no petitions survive from the parliament of October 1285, but an ordinance of 1305 about the challenging of jurymen which is generally taken for a statute actually seems to have been inspired by the petition of a prisoner in Canterbury jail.[14] 'The community of the county of Cumberland' petitioned in Edward II's reign to have indictments in the county 'at common law and according to the Statute of Winchester' and not attachment by bailiffs on mere suspicion.[15] Alongside the petitions and complaints about secular justice there were continual appeals to king and council from 'the people (*plures de populo*)' for the curbing of the officials and ministers of the church courts, 'whose vexations, citations and exactions' were said to be more oppressive than 'all the lay courts (*omnes Curiae laycales*)'.[16] Wat Tyler's demand in 1381 for 'no bishop but one' in England (the counterpart of no lordship but the king's) would have evoked a response at any time in the previous hundred years.[17]

If the series of parliamentary petitions, statutes and judicial commissions are taken together, local justice and not taxation is seen to be the first great subject of political discussion between the king and the people at large. (Poll-taxes provoked an outburst in 1381 only when they were backed by judicial commissions.) But the strains of war had soon revealed conflicts of interest in the administration of lay justice between the *potentes*, *mediocres* and *pauperes* (the powerful, the middling people and the poor), to use the petitioners' imprecise but suggestive language. No doubt the self-styled 'poor' were far above the common people in status; and

[13] J. R. Maddicott, 'The County Community and the Making of Public Opinion in Fourteenth-Century England', *Trans. Roy. Hist. Soc.*, 5th ser., xxviii (1978); *idem*, 'Parliament and the Constituencies, 1272–1377', in R. G. Davies and J. H. Denton (eds.), *The English Parliament in the Middle Ages* (Manchester, 1981), pp. 71–2.

[14] *Memoranda de Parliamento*, ed. F. W. Maitland (Rolls ser., London, 1893), p. 11 (no. 10). See *Rotuli Parliamentorum*, i, pp. 47 (no. 28) and 48 (no. 32) for petitions associated with ordinances: the Statute of Consultation of 1290 and the Ordinance of Conspirators attributed to 1293.

[15] *Select Cases in the Court of King's Bench*, ed. G. O. Sayles, 7 vols. (Selden Society, London, 1936–71), iii, p. cxvii; cf. *Rotuli Parliamentorum*, i, pp. 46 (no. 6), 51 (no. 67).

[16] *Rotuli Parliamentorum*, i, pp. 28, 60 (nos. 180–3).

[17] *Anonimalle Chronicle*, ed. Galbraith, p. 147: 'et nulle evesque serroit en Engleterre fors une'.

it is not suggested that justice only now became a means by which one class oppressed another. The argument of the following pages is rather that the administration of justice now emerged as a political issue between different levels of society, which would eventually allow the common people also to enter consciously into the political struggles of the nation.[18]

Shire communities began to petition urgently in parliament for 'special justices', if the regular judges from Westminster were to be so long in coming;[19] and special commissions of 'oyer and terminer' were used with increasing frequency to deal with offences of particular kinds in individual counties, or committed by particular persons, or against particular complainants.[20] These special criminal commissions were given their most general form in 1305 by the 'ordinance of trailbastons', which empowered justices organized in five circuits covering the whole country to hear and determine accusations of specific types of offence against the peace committed since the onset of war in 1297. This was an acknowledgement of the breakdown of the eyre system, though it was still hoped that general eyres would resume after the emergency.[21] That they never did (despite a brave try to relaunch them in 1329) was due to the 'enormous trespasses' which the justices of trailbaston discovered, and which are a persistent theme of English history for the rest of the middle ages: the use of 'power and lordship' to retain gangs of thugs (the 'trailbastons'), conduct protection rackets, and (by the newly defined crimes of maintenance and conspiracy) contrive lawsuits and false indictments, bribing corruptible jurors and browbeating honest ones in the process.[22] But the trailbaston commis-

---

[18] For examples of these terms, see *Rotuli Parliamentorum*, i, pp. 52 (no. 83), 117 (the king grants, in answer to the 'public and frequent complaint of his middling people (*pupplicam et frequentem querimoniam mediocris populi sui*)', that no one with less than 100*s*.-worth of land shall be made to serve on a jury outside his county).

[19] J. Parker, *A Calendar of the Lancashire Assize Rolls* (Lancashire and Cheshire Record Society, xlvii and xlix, 1904–5), pp. x and xv–xix; *Memoranda de Parliamento*, ed. Maitland, pp. 19 (no. 20), 21 (no. 26); *Rotuli Parliamentorum*, i, p. 292.

[20] A. Harding, *The Law Courts of Medieval England* (London, 1973), p. 89.

[21] A. Harding, 'Early Trailbaston Proceedings from the Lincoln Roll of 1305', in R. F. Hunnisett and J. B. Post (eds.), *Medieval Legal Records Edited in Memory of C. A. F. Meekings* (London, 1978), pp. 144–5. The most up to date account of the decline of the general eyre is David Crook, 'The Later Eyres', *Eng. Hist. Rev.*, xcvii (1982), pp. 241ff.

[22] Harding, 'Early Trailbaston Proceedings', pp. 148–50.

sions simply helped to convert judicial powers into weapons for use in local struggles. They were a form of the commission of oyer and terminer, and as 'the community of the people of his realm' complained to Edward II in the parliament of January 1315, 'when a great lord, or man of power' wished to ruin an enemy he alleged an enormous trespass by him or maintained someone else to do so, and then purchased commissions of oyer and terminer to justices favourable to his side. The sheriff and his bailiffs would be brought into the plot (*covigne*), to make sure that the defendant was summoned too late, or summoned to appear in his opponent's territory where he dared not go for peril of his life, with the consequence that enormous damages were awarded against him. In this way, many were condemned to perpetual imprisonment unless they sold up their inheritances, or they were outlawed and driven into exile.[23] The Statute of Northampton of 1328 linked together, as encouragements to offenders, the too easy granting of pardons and the procuring of commissions of gaol delivery and oyer and terminer by great men, and ordained that oyers and terminers should 'not be granted but before justices of the one bench or the other, or the Justices in Eyre, and that for great hurt or horrible trespasses'.[24] The Statute of Westminster of 1361 tried the other solution of assigning the hearing and determining of felonies and trespasses to keepers of the peace, and ordering that all general inquiries which had been granted within lordships should cease because of the mischiefs and oppressions they had caused to the people.[25]

In 1380, the Commons were still asking that no writ of oyer and terminer should be granted unless three men of good repute swore to the honesty of the complainant.[26] Such petitions were part of a wider stream of complaints against the magnates' oppression of the commons by livery, maintenance and simple force.[27] The 'quest-

---

[23] *Rotuli Parliamentorum*, i, p. 290 (no. 8). Cf. Richard W. Kaeuper, 'Law and Order in Fourteenth-Century England: The Evidence of Special Commissions of Oyer and Terminer', *Speculum*, liv (1979), pp. 734–84. The continued granting of special oyer and terminer commissions might be justified in terms of the remoteness of the counties from which cases arose, so that the bench justices could not deal with them speedily (see, for instance, *Rotuli Parliamentorum*, i, p. 292).

[24] *Statutes of the Realm*, i, p. 257.

[25] *Statutes of the Realm*, i, pp. 364–5.

[26] *Rotuli Parliamentorum*, iii, p. 94 (no. 35).

[27] *Rotuli Parliamentorum*, i, p. 290 (no. 8); iii, pp. 21 (no. 83), 23 (no. 92).

mongers' who were a target of the rebels in 1381 were those who corruptly procured special commissions for the men of power. The revenge taken on London lawyers and Wat Tyler's perhaps ironical solicitation of a commission to punish the lawyers as a class were linked to his demand for the total abolition of seigneurial power by this long tradition of resistance to seigneurial oppression by judicial means.[28]

Special commissions of oyer and terminer were used by the powerful against each other's retinues, and maintenance linked men of different ranks in hierarchical alliances.[29] The general commissions of trailbaston were more decisive in making a whole stratum of the commons wary of justice in the hands of the great lords and the Westminster judges. In the 'song of trailbaston' an old soldier who has served the king in Flanders, Scotland and Edward's own land of Gascony, rails against the ordinance of 1305 and complains that a mere box on the ears to correct his boy will get him arrested and cost him a large bribe to the sheriff to escape a deep dungeon. He promises to take a cruel revenge on the trailbaston justices and the jurors who indict out of spite: it is better to take refuge in the green forest of Belregard, for 'the common law is too uncertain'.[30] But the jurymen, browbeaten as 'rustics' or prosecuted for corruption, were also victims. The 'poor men of the land of England' petitioned the king against jurors 'who were so commonly corrupted by the gifts of the rich that no truth could be known by them', and against the 'conspirators' who suborned them; but the 'middle people' who actually 'served the king before the justices of trailbaston' complained rather that they were scared to tell the truth by threat of indictment for conspiracy by juries composed of the very men they had 'faithfully indicted'.[31]

[28] Walsingham, *Historia Anglicana*, i, p. 464: Tyler wished 'before anything else, to obtain a commission for himself and his followers to behead all the lawyers (*ante alia, commissionem pro se et suis obtinuisse, ad decollandum omnes juridicos*)'. For the hunting down of Leggett, the questmonger, see *Anonimalle Chronicle*, ed. Galbraith, p. 142, and Prescott, 'London in the Peasants' Revolt', pp. 134–5: a questmonger was surely one who obtained commissions rather than just sat on juries. For the lords' use of the judicial system for their own ends, see J. R. Maddicott, *Law and Lordship: Royal Justices as Retainers in Thirteenth- and Fourteenth-Century England* (Past and Present Supplement no. 4, Oxford, 1978), especially p. 25.

[29] Prescott, 'London in the Peasants' Revolt', p. 136.

[30] *Anglo-Norman Political Songs*, ed. I. S. T. Aspin (Anglo-Norman Text Society, 1953), pp. 67–78.

[31] Harding, 'Early Trailbaston Proceedings', p. 151.

So, the commons wavered in their attitude to the further use of trailbaston commissions. The knights and burgesses repeatedly asked a remedy for enormous trespasses, conspiracies and confederacies, as they had been listed in the trailbaston ordinance; and sometimes it was proposed that the *plus grantz* of the land, 'earls and barons each in his march, and men learned in the law' should be chosen in parliament by the advice of Lords and Commons to hear and determine bills of complaint and supervise the keeping of the peace.[32] Such justices on the model of 1305 were used particularly in the early part of Edward III's reign; and the Statute of Northampton gave standing authority for the appointment of justices to deal with 'oppressors of the people . . . as it was done in the time of the king's grandfather, of great men of the land, which be of great power, with some of the justices of the one bench or the other, with other learned men in the law'.[33] Yet in 1344 the Commons asked that the 'new enquiries' they themselves had asked for in the previous year should be abandoned because the outrageous fines and ransoms imposed in them were more to the destruction than the amendment of the people: the king should remember that fines and amercements profited the lords of franchises rather than the royal treasury, and appoint half a dozen keepers of the peace in each county to punish offences reasonably according to their gravity.[34] In 1378, the Commons asked for a remedy for the affrays and routs made throughout the land, especially by companies from the counties palatine of Chester and Lancaster and other 'franchised places'; and were given the Statute of Gloucester confirming Northampton 'in all points' and providing for the assignment of 'valiant persons' to arrest the rioters as soon as they had credible report of them 'without waiting for indictment or other process of law'.[35] In the next parliament, however, this ordinance 'seemed to

[32] *Rotuli Parliamentorum*, i, p. 371 (no. 5: 1320); ii, pp. 64–5 (1332), 136–7 (1343), 238 (no. 13: 1351–2); iii, pp. 42–3 (1378).

[33] *Rotuli Parliamentorum*, i, p. 371 (no. 5); *Statutes of the Realm*, i, p. 259: justices are to be assigned 'as was done in the time of his grandfather, from the magnates of the land who are of great power, with some justices from one bench or the other, or others learned in the law (*come estoit faite en temps de son dit ael, des grantz de la terre qi sont de grant poair, ovesqes ascuns des justices de lun Baunk ou de lautre, ou autres sages de la lei*)'; for the trailbaston commissions of 1328, and King's Bench's part in them, see *Select Cases in the Court of King's Bench*, iv, p. lxiv.

[34] *Rotuli Parliamentorum*, ii, pp. 148–9 (no. 1).

[35] *Rotuli Parliamentorum*, iii, pp. 42–3 (no. 44) and 81 (no. 30); *Statutes of the Realm*, ii, pp. 9–10.

the Commons very horrible and perilous to the good and loyal people', many of whom would be imprisoned by the false accusations of their enemies and the malice of the commissioners, so that every freeman in the realm would be a serf (*en servage*) to the said lords commissioners and their retinues. Since it was clearly against the provisions of the Great Charter and several statutes that no free man should be taken or imprisoned without the due process of law, the king agreed that the ordinance should be repealed, and those imprisoned without indictment released, and the normal process of indictment restored 'as the ancient law requires (*come l'aunciene Loy le voet*)'.[36]

Wat Tyler's demands for a return to the law of Winchester, with its arrangements for presentment by properly elected constables, and for no outlawry in any process of law and no lordship, thus stand in a long tradition of debate between the king and the people of England on the proper administration of justice – a debate which had reached a climax in parliament eighteen months before the revolt. A recurrent theme in the debate had been how to get the real offenders indicted in the face of the conspiracies and patronage of the lords.[37] The king tried suspending the normal processes of indictment altogether, as in 1306 and 1378;[38] enacting that indictments should be authenticated by indentures between sheriffs and indictors, as in 1327;[39] and prohibiting, as in 1354 and 1370, the inclusion of sheriffs in commissions of inquiry in their own counties which they might use to procure indictments merely to increase the fines they obtained for bailing the indicted.[40] The severity of these royal measures to prevent judicial corruption evoked other petitions in support of the community-based procedures of indictment and presentment, answered by statutes confirming these as constituting the 'due process of law' in chapter 39 of Magna Carta,[41] and ordering that sheriffs, bailiffs and hundredors should possess lands in their bailiwicks.[42]

[36] *Rotuli Parliamentorum*, iii, p. 65 (no. 46); *Statutes of the Realm*, ii, p. 12.
[37] *Rotuli Parliamentorum*, i, pp. 293–4 (no. 24: 1314); Dorothy Hughes, *A Study of Social and Constitutional Tendencies in the Early Years of Edward III* (London, 1915), pp. 214ff.
[38] Harding, 'Early Trailbaston Proceedings', p. 151; *Cal. Close Rolls, 1302–7*, p. 397; *Statutes of the Realm*, ii, pp. 9–10.
[39] Hughes, *Social and Constitutional Tendencies*, p. 214.
[40] *Statutes of the Realm*, i, p. 347 (c. 9); *Rotuli Parliamentorum*, iii, p. 64 (no. 41).
[41] *Rotuli Parliamentorum*, ii, p. 239 (no. 19); *Statutes of the Realm*, i, p. 347 (c. 4).
[42] *Statutes of the Realm*, i, p. 257.

There were in fact two themes to the politics of justice – the corruption of local justice by landed power, and the rights of the county community (great lords and commons together) over against the royal judges in the matter of peace-keeping – and both are prominent in the parliament immediately preceding the revolt. The Commons complained of the livery and maintenance of the lords,[43] of the sheriffs' habit of outlawing several people of the same name as the offender so as to confiscate all their property,[44] and of the way the keeper of the Fleet prison allowed debtors to come and go as they liked.[45] But it was the arbitrary exercise of royal justice from the centre which roused the people of London and the neighbouring counties to united action in 1381 against the London lawyers.

In 1305 the king used his own immediate court of King's Bench as the trailbaston justices for the city of London, Middlesex, Kent, Surrey and Sussex; and he gave it another trailbaston commission, with additional articles like 'inquire of those who took ransoms from people at will after the destruction of Sir Adam Banastre', to restore order in the north after the battle of Boroughbridge in 1322. From this time onwards, the court enjoyed regular commissions of trailbaston, and in consequence developed its own forms of prosecution by bill, so that by 1381 'trailbaston' had come to mean primarily the use of King's Bench to punish serious outbreaks of crime.[46] The deployment of King's Bench was the government's alternative to the use of the *plus grantz*. The court made a number of excursions away from London in the 1320s and 1330s, and in reply to a Commons' petition for justices of oyer and terminer in 1352, the king said that 'he would send his Bench where he saw there was most need'.[47] It could be significant that it was in this same parliament that the king was asked to 'declare the points of treason' since the king's justices were condemning people as traitors 'for divers causes not known to the Commons to be treason'.[48] There was an increasing wariness of visitations of royal justice, which was manifested in the grant of taxation in the April parliament of 1348 only on condition that there should be neither eyres nor 'general

[43] *Rotuli Parliamentorum*, iii, pp. 21 (no. 83), 23 (no. 92).
[44] *Rotuli Parliamentorum*, iii, p. 94 (no. 36).
[45] *Rotuli Parliamentorum*, iii, p. 25 (no. 107).
[46] *Select Cases in the Court of King's Bench*, ed. Sayles, iv, pp. lv–lxvi; v, pp. 47–9.
[47] *Statutes of the Realm*, i, p. 257; *Select Cases in the Court of King's Bench*, ed. Sayles, iv, pp. cii–cv; *Rotuli Parliamentorum*, ii, p. 238 (no. 13).
[48] *Rotuli Parliamentorum*, ii, p. 239 (no. 17).

inquiries throughout the land'.[49] In 1354, there was an attack on abuses in sessions of the King's Bench when sitting in a 'foreign' county and a request for evidence to be given openly at the bar and no interference with juries in reaching their verdicts.[50] The similarity between fourteenth-century 'eyres' and trailbaston visitations was their direction at individual counties, in a way which conflicted with the county communities' growing sense of their rights. Five eyre sessions were summoned in Kent and two in Durham in the fourteenth century, the last in 1374, to enable the king to exploit his rights during vacancies in the sees of Canterbury and Durham.[51] The eyres held in London in 1321 and begun on a wider scale in the east midland counties in 1329, only to be abandoned in favour of trailbaston-type inquiries, were more clearly policing measures which were given eyre jurisdiction probably because it was essential to supervise the exercise of franchises.[52] Ultimately, both eyre and trailbaston could be used as threats which county communities would pay to have removed: 'in 1341 the citizens of London protested against a general oyer and terminer commission only to have it replaced by an eyre, while in 1353 the prince of Wales reversed this process by allowing an eyre in his earldom of Chester to be bought off for 5,000 marks and then replacing it by a trailbaston commission'.[53]

By the end of Edward III's reign, King's Bench no longer travelled far from London, but in the 'home counties' its weight was felt all the more. ('Home counties' is, of course, a nineteenth-century term, perhaps originally for the area covered by the south-eastern assize circuit. But it is reasonable to think that by 1381 the activities of the bench justices had already given a unity, if only a unity of resentment, to the counties neighbouring London, which dictated the course of the revolt.[54]) In London itself the king used an

---

[49] *Rotuli Parliamentorum*, ii, pp. 200–1; Crook, 'The Later Eyres', p. 267.
[50] *Rotuli Parliamentorum*, ii, p. 259 (no. 30), and cf. p. 266 (no. 26).
[51] Crook, 'The Later Eyres', pp. 256, 264.
[52] Crook, 'The Later Eyres', pp. 259–61, 266; it was at the beginning of the eyre of 1329 that Chief Justice Scrope made the statement of the responsibility of franchise-holders quoted in note 11 above.
[53] Crook, 'The Later Eyres', pp. 259–60.
[54] On the term 'the Home Counties', see Alan Everitt, 'Country, County and Town: Patterns of Regional Evolution in England', *Trans. Roy. Hist. Soc.*, 5th ser., xxix (1979), p. 79; on the restriction of King's Bench to London and its neighbourhood, see *Select Cases in the Court of King's Bench*, ed. Sayles, vi, pp. ix–xii; vii, p. liii; the *Anonimalle Chronicle*, ed. Galbraith, speaks of a sudden

additional means to impose his justice at the expense of the city's franchises, but one closely related to King's Bench in origin. This was the court held by the steward and the marshal of the household, and commonly known as the Marshalsea court. Its jurisdiction was supposed to be limited to civil pleas concerning people in the king's household, prosecutions for resistance to purveyance (the compulsory purchase of supplies for the king's use, at preferential rates) and other trespasses within 'the verge', which extended for a radius of twelve miles round the king's person. The court seems on occasion to have attracted a wider business and justified Commons' petitions that it trespassed on the jurisdiction of the common law courts, but in any event its jurisdiction extended over London during the lengthy periods when the king was at Westminster, and in the city purveyance was a major concern. The Marshalsea court also drew hostility from its association (indeed, confusion) with the Marshalsea prison at Southwark. Though this Marshalsea was in the charge of the separate marshal of King's Bench and was important principally as the King's Bench prison, the Marshalsea court sat within its precincts when the king was in London, and the city complained with particular force against the consequent withdrawal of Southwark from ordinary municipal authority. Commons' petitions of 1376 asked that the limitations earlier imposed on the Marshalsea court's jurisdiction be strictly observed and complained of the punishment of villages which had sheltered escapees from the Marshalsea prison who had never been formally indicted of crimes. In 1377, amongst the large number of petitions for the confirmation of franchises predictable in the first parliament of a new reign, there was a complaint by the clergy of the exactions of the Marshalsea and petitions from the Commons of England in conjunction with the Mayor, Aldermen and Commons of London, that the Marshalsea should not make attachments or enforce judgements within the city.[55] And there was another petition that 'no manner of Eyre, nor

---

rising of 'the commons of the south country of England . . . in two parties, one in Essex and the other in Kent (*les comunes del southpais Dengleterre . . . en deux parties, une partie en Excesse et une autre en Kent*)' (p. 133).

[55] *Select Cases in the Court of King's Bench*, ed. Sayles, vii, pp. xliii–lii; W. R. Jones, 'The Court of the Verge: The Jurisdiction of the Steward and Marshal of the Household in Later Medieval England', *Journal of British Studies*, x (1970); Marjorie K. McIntosh, 'Immediate Royal Justice: The Marshalsea Court in Havering, 1358', *Speculum*, liv (1979); David J. Johnson, *Southwark and the City* (Oxford, 1969), pp. 68–75; *Statutes of the Realm*, i, p. 347; *Rotuli Parliamentorum*, iii, pp. 18 (no. 65), 19 (no. 71), 26–7.

Trailbaston, travel the Realm during the War, or for the space of 20 years'.[56]

These petitions received evasive replies, and in 1380 the Commons followed their grant of the third poll-tax with a renewed prayer that 'during the war, neither eyre justice nor trailbaston should have course among the said poor commons'.[57] The taxes themselves were granted 'lightly', says the chronicler.[58] The commons of Essex and Kent rose up because the money was collected 'extortionately amongst the poor people', and then only because the government sent commissions of inquiry into evasion of the tax, backed in turn, when these were violently resisted, by the king's judges exercising that trailbaston jurisdiction in 'the home counties' which the Commons in parliament had petitioned against. The commissions of inquiry were solicited, according to the chroniclers, by John Legge and others, archetypal 'questmongers'.[59] They were issued on 16 March 1381 to people like John of Bampton, 'a lord's steward who was taken for a king or great lord in that country because of his great bearing', whose actions provoked the first clash at Brentwood in Essex on 30 May.[60] Bampton fled to inform the king's council in London, and in his place appeared almost instantly Robert Bealknap, Chief Justice of Common Pleas, holding sessions of 'traylbastunerie'. He collected so many indictments that the people thought of abandoning their tenements and hiding, but instead they forced him to swear on the Book that he would never again take part in such hearings, or be 'a justice of inquiries'.[61] It is in fact surprising to find the lead in trailbaston work being taken by the chief justice of Common Pleas rather than of King's Bench. Sir John Cavendish C.J.K.B. seems to have been preoccupied with his duties as a leading justice of the peace in his home county further north, and his name does not appear in the list of lords, ministers

[56] *Rotuli Parliamentorum*, iii, p. 24 (no. 101). There are other petitions concerning the judicial process, against the use of royal protections to avoid legal suits, for example, and the hearing of civil cases by the king's council: pp. 21 (no. 87) and 23 (no. 97).

[57] *Rotuli Parliamentorum*, iii, p. 90.

[58] *Anonimalle Chronicle*, ed. Galbraith, p. 133.

[59] Henry Knighton, *Chronicon*, ed. J. R. Lumby, 2 vols. (Rolls ser., London, 1889–95), ii, p. 129.

[60] See *The Peasants' Revolt of 1381*, ed. R. B. Dobson (London, 1970), pp. 119–22; *Anonimalle Chronicle*, ed. Galbraith, p. 134; J. A. Sparvel-Bayly, 'Essex in Insurrection, in 1381', *Essex Archaeol. Trans.*, new ser., i (1878), pp. 218–19.

[61] *Anonimalle Chronicle*, ed. Galbraith, p. 135; no commission or record survives of these trailbaston hearings.

and lawyers, beginning with the duke of Lancaster and including Bealknap, Legge and Bampton, whose heads the rebels were soon to demand of the king.[62] Almost simultaneously with the Essex visitation a session of trailbaston had begun in Kent, held by an unnamed justice and attended by John Legge serjeant-at-arms, bearing a great number of indictments 'to make the king rich'. This was enough to bring together the commons of Kent in great numbers, though as yet they had no captain.[63]

Having roused the men of Essex and Kent, the judicial proceedings, combined with a wish to meet the king, drew the rebels towards London. On the evening of Wednesday 12 June or the morning of Thursday they dragged down the walls of the Marshalsea prison at Southwark, released all the prisoners and destroyed the houses of the marshal of King's Bench and of the jurors and questmongers. They then moved through the city, doing no harm till they reached Fleet Street, where they broke down the Fleet prison and the chambers of the apprentices of law in the Temple. Further west still, the sacking of the duke of Lancaster's palace of Savoy was a diversion between an attack on the lodgings of the keeper of the king's privy seal and the burning of the house of Sir John Butterwick, under-sheriff of Middlesex, at Westminster. From there, after releasing the prisoners 'condemned (*foriugez*)' by the law at Westminster, the rebels returned by way of Holborn and the Newgate prison to St Martin-le-Grand, where they dragged out of the church and beheaded Roger Legett, a lawyer well known as a *cisour* (assize juryman) and questmonger. On the Friday morning the first meeting between the rebels and the king took place at Mile End, which was the signal for the killing at the Tower of Archbishop Sudbury, the chancellor, Robert Hales, the treasurer, Brother William Appleton, the duke of Lancaster's physician and adviser, John Legge, serjeant-at-arms, 'and of a juror'. Early on Saturday, another party of rebels was back at Westminster Abbey to complete their task (their single-mindedness in pursuing legal officials is remarkable) by wrenching Sir Richard Imworth, marshal of King's Bench and 'a tormentor without pity' from the shrine of St Edward and carrying him to Cheapside for execution. Later on Saturday the

---

[62] *Anonimalle Chronicle*, ed. Galbraith, p. 139; see below, p. 183, for Cavendish as a J.P. in Cambridgeshire and Norfolk, whereas Bealknap was in commissions of the peace for Essex and 'the home counties'.
[63] *Anonimalle Chronicle*, ed. Galbraith, p. 136.

fifteenth the second meeting with the king at Smithfield took place, at which Wat Tyler demanded the law of Winchester and no lordship but the king's, but which ended in Tyler's death and Richard's persuasion of the true commons to disperse by himself assuming the role of their captain.[64] In the country, meanwhile, other groups of rebels were on the march, and on that same Friday the fourteenth, when Sudbury, Hales and Legge died at the Tower, a party discovered Sir John Cavendish, chief justice of King's Bench, at Bury St Edmunds, cut off his head and set it on a pillory. Uniquely, there is no plea-roll for the Trinity term of King's Bench which should have begun on 16 June.[65]

In June 1381, hatred of an oppressive law administered from London briefly united different ranks of the commons, from peasants to quite prosperous burgesses.[66] Yet the peasantry had no real interest in defending the rights of London citizens, and the insistence of the rebels that they were the 'true commons' suggests the divide between them and the Commons in parliament who granted the poll-taxes 'lightly' and, even when they petitioned against eyre and trailbaston, did so in favour of increased powers for the J.P.s who enforced the labour laws. The politics of justice had by 1381 opened two horizontal divides in society, not one; and when the gentry who protested against the maintenance of the great lords and the punitive exercise of royal justice were given jurisdiction of their own, they used it to mark themselves off from the common people by a line far more enduring and difficult to cross than that between gentry and *grantz*. The major fact of the development of fourteenth-century society was the growth of an aristocratic county community embracing both magnates and gentry, which formed in the indictments brought before sessions of oyer and terminer and of the peace its own image of a rebellious servant class. By means of this image, the frightening events of early June 1381 could at least be made comprehensible.

The age-old public power of the landlord, apparently challenged by Edward I's *quo warranto* proceedings, was confirmed for many centuries to come by the transference to gentry *custodes pacis* (keepers of the peace) of the duty of enforcing the Winchester

---

[64] *Anonimalle Chronicle*, ed. Galbraith, pp. 136–49; R. B. Dobson provides a useful chronological table in *The Peasants' Revolt of 1381*, pp. 39–40.

[65] *Anonimalle Chronicle*, ed. Galbraith, pp. 150–1; *Select Cases in the Court of King's Bench*, ed. Sayles, vii, p. xxii.

[66] Prescott, 'London in the Peasants' Revolt', pp. 131, 134.

peace-keeping measures.[67] The indictment and arrest of *contrarios aut rebelles* (opponents or rebels) against the Statute of Winchester was the root of the commission of the peace.[68] Yet in the social crisis caused by the Scottish and French wars, the king relied on the great lords and the judges of King's Bench to maintain order, and the *custodes pacis* had a subordinate role.[69] Judicial powers, as distinct from supervision of the statutory policing measures, were given to them only reluctantly. Even in 1338, when the punishment of 'delinquents' under the Statute of Northampton (this had confirmed Winchester 'in all points' and added a duty to arrest those who made affrays in fairs, markets and courts of law) and the power to determine as well as hear accusations of felony and trespass were included in the commission of the peace, the keepers were to act under seven circuits of magnate overseers.[70] The king gave a

[67] In conquered Wales the old conservators of the peace called 'keys', much like the lords' serjeants of the peace in the English marcher counties, were swept away because of the burden of their subsistence on the community; but during Edward III's reign the provisions of the Statute of Winchester were introduced and keepers of the peace appointed in each commote, apparently at the instance of the inhabitants. See R. Stewart-Brown, *The Serjeants of the Peace in Medieval England and Wales* (Manchester, 1936), pp. 36–7; *The Record of Caernarvon* (Record Commission, London, 1838), p. 131; Llinos Beverley Smith, 'The Statute of Wales, 1284', *Welsh History Review*, x (1980), p. 152.

[68] *Proceedings before the Justices of the Peace*, ed. Putnam, pp. xxi–xxii; *Cal. Pat. Rolls, 1281–92*, pp. 264–5; *Select Cases in the Court of King's Bench*, ed. Sayles, iii, p. cxvi (the king 'explains' the clauses of the Statute of Winchester on the array of arms for the benefit of 'hesitant' *custodes pacis* in Wiltshire), and iv, pp. 35, 47, 147; *English Constitutional Documents, 1307–1485*, eds. Eleanor C. Lodge and Gladys A. Thornton (Cambridge, 1935), pp. 327–8. The continued importance of the Statute is shown by an argument in King's Bench, Chancery and parliament in 1328 about the responsibility it imposed on a hundred for the losses of the victims of robbers whom it failed to arrest (*Select Cases in the Court of King's Bench*, ed. Sayles, v, p. lxxviii); and by the complaint of the Commons in 1379 that churchmen were claiming as mortuary dues arms and equipment kept by deceased persons in accordance with the Statute, to the peril of the realm (*Rotuli Parliamentorum*, iii, p. 82 (no. 36)).

[69] *Select Cases in the Court of King's Bench*, ed. Sayles, iv, p. lvi; *Proceedings before the Justices of the Peace*, ed. Putnam, pp. xxxviii–xxxix; Hughes, *Social and Constitutional Tendencies*, p. 229.

[70] *Statutes of the Realm*, i, p. 257; *Proceedings before the Justices of the Peace*, ed. Putnam, pp. xxxix–xl, 7, 149–52. Nevertheless, the commission did represent a considerable shift to the *custodes pacis* of judicial powers which the Statute of Northampton had given to the justices of assize. The relevant clause of the Statute ran: 'this is added to the said statute of Winchester, where it is contained at the end that justices of assize shall have power to inquire concerning failures [to execute the statute] and report them to the king (which no one ever saw happen), that the said justices of assize shall have power to punish the disobedient and contrary (*ajoustè au dit estatut de Wyncestre, la ou contenuz est en la fin, qe*

guarded reply to a Commons' petition in 1344 that the trailbaston-type inquiries by *grantz* set on foot the previous year should be replaced by sessions of half a dozen *custodes pacis* in each county: he agreed only that there should be commissions of the peace of two or three of the most worthy, who when need arose might be given extra powers to hear and determine felonies and trespasses along with 'autres sages et apris de la leye'.[71] On the eve of the plague in 1348, the Commons were still petitioning against 'eyres and inquiries, except of oyer and terminer by justices of the peace in each part of the country chosen from that country'.[72]

Yet by 1351 the watershed between the Statute of Northampton and the Statute of Westminster had been passed. A commission of that year gave the *custodes pacis* comprehensive judicial powers which were never again omitted: this, as a by-product of the Statute of Labourers compelling the service and regulating the wages of all sorts of workmen, which the justices were to enforce in four sessions a year, at specified dates.[73] Only truly local justices could regulate local society in this detail. From 1352 to 1359, the government experimented with separate commissions to justices of labourers (though often to men who were also *custodes pacis*), and these justices were given jurisdiction over other economic matters, such as weights and measures, the activities of victuallers and hostlers, and the price of iron. Perhaps some of the justices of labourers were of too low a rank and identified too much with the labourers themselves for in 1359 these commissions were amalgamated with the commissions of the peace. Since at the same time the array of arms was separated from the peace commission, the process of transforming the keepers of the peace into true justices was complete, and had only to be ratified in 1361 by the Statute of Westminster.[74] After the middle of the fourteenth century, the cases from the lower criminal courts working through to the court of

---

*Justices assignez eient poair denquere des defautes et des reporter au Roi en parlement dont home nad pas veu issue, qe les ditz Justices assignez eient poair de punir les desobeissantz et contrevenantz)' (Statutes of the Realm, i, p. 259).*

[71] Note 34 above; *Statutes of the Realm*, i, pp. 300–1.

[72] *Rotuli Parliamentorum*, ii, p. 202.

[73] Bertha H. Putnam, *The Enforcement of the Statutes of Labourers* (New York, 1908), appendix, pp. 12–17, 21–4; *Proceedings before the Justices of the Peace*, ed. Putnam, p. xliv.

[74] Bertha H. Putnam, 'The Transformation of the Keepers of the Peace into the Justices of the Peace, 1327–80', *Trans. Roy. Hist. Soc.*, 4th ser., xii (1929), pp. 19–48; *Statutes of the Realm*, i, p. 364.

King's Bench, which in the early part of Edward III's reign had come almost exclusively from trailbaston or special oyer and terminer justices, were increasingly from the sessions of the justices of the peace, and at the beginning of the fifteenth century cases from this source made up nine-tenths of the *rex* rolls of King's Bench.[75] As they won their battle against the routine use of trailbaston-type commissions to preserve the peace, the Commons went on to petition that they and the lords should choose justices of labourers and keepers of the peace in parliament and that these should 'not be removed at the suggestion of evil-wishers to make way for men of lesser means'.[76] By the time of the commissions of 1380, which added 'all manner of extortions' and livery and maintenance to their jurisdiction, the justices of the peace 'had apparently outdistanced their various rivals'.[77]

From the point of view of the aristocratic county communities, it must also have seemed that the inclusion of the magnates and bench justices in the commissions of the peace for groups of counties had tamed the trailbaston visitations by absorbing them. In 1380, the duke of Lancaster appeared first in the commissions for Hertfordshire, Warwickshire, Leicestershire, Derbyshire and Norfolk; Robert Bealknap, chief justice of Common Pleas, who fanned the first sparks of the Essex rising into a conflagration by his trailbaston session, and appeared behind Lancaster in the rebels' 'hit list', was behind him too in the commission for Hertfordshire, and was also a justice of the peace in Essex, Middlesex, Kent, Surrey and Sussex; and Sir John Cavendish C.J.K.B. was in the commission for Bedfordshire, Buckinghamshire, Cambridgeshire and Norfolk, and stood first in the commissions for Huntingdonshire and the towns of Cambridge, King's Lynn and Norwich.[78] From below, from the point of view of the true commons, there must have seemed little difference in their oppressiveness between the commissions of trailbaston and the peace, as they had developed by 1380.

As justices rather than simple peace-keepers, the country gentry became the moral arbiters of society, enforcing their values in the

---

[75] *Proceedings before the Justices of the Peace*, ed. Putnam, pp. lxiii–lxiv.

[76] N. Saul, *Knights and Esquires: The Gloucestershire Gentry in the Fourteenth Century* (Oxford, 1981), p. 130.

[77] *Rotuli Parliamentorum*, iii, pp. 84–5; *English Constitutional Documents*, eds. Lodge and Thornton, pp. 333–5; *Proceedings before the Justices of the Peace*, ed. Putnam, p. xlviii.

[78] *Cal. Pat. Rolls, 1377–81*, pp. 512–14.

courts. From the first, the extortion of royal and ecclesiastical officials was one of their targets, and again the labour legislation gave them jurisdiction over it. By the Statute of Labourers, the justices were to hear and determine complaints against sheriffs, stewards and bailiffs who arrested labourers under colour of these statutes and released them 'for fines and ransoms appropriated to their own use'.[79] This was of particular interest to the gentry communities, since they had impressed upon the king that the excess wages extracted from them by labourers had reduced their ability to pay royal taxes, and that any excess recovered and fines imposed should therefore be counted towards the subsidy due from that shire. Under this inducement, indictments were brought even against justices for turning the labour laws to their personal advantage but to the detriment of the community.[80] The legitimate diversion of many of the fines to the lords of liberties, especially to ecclesiastical lords, must have hardened the attitude of the justices of the peace to the extortion practised by seigneurial officials and the officers of the church courts.[81] In 1380, the king and the lay peers had to override bitter opposition from the prelates to the inclusion of 'all manner of extortions' in the jurisdiction of the justices.[82] In fact, juries had long been indicting extortionate clergy as 'common thieves', if we are to believe a statute of 1352 forbidding so vague a charge.[83] The practice points to a factor more important than royal ordinances in giving the values of the gentry communities legal force: that is, the way in which indictments were made before the justices. The fourteenth century was a crucial period in the definition of crime in English law, and the defining was done by the

[79] Putnam, *Enforcement of the Statutes of Labourers*, appendix, pp. 25–6; *Proceedings before the Justices of the Peace*, ed. Putnam, pp. 14–15, 365.

[80] Putnam, *Enforcement of the Statutes of Labourers*, pp. 99ff, and appendix, pp. 212–13, 264ff, 291. On the use of the profits of justice as a substitute for direct taxation, see Crook, 'The Later Eyres', p. 267, and P. W. Booth, 'Taxation and Public Order: Cheshire in 1353', *Northern History*, xii (1976).

[81] Revenue from fines, which was vastly increased by the labour legislation, often belonged by right to the lords of the liberties in which the offenders lived. The reason for the amalgamation of the commissions of labourers and the peace after 1359 may have been the administrative difficulty of getting the fines from two sets of jurisdictions to the proper recipients. Churchmen relied heavily on such fines, and new grants of penalties under the Statute of Labourers were sometimes made to them. (Putnam, *Enforcement of the Statutes of Labourers*, pp. 138ff, and appendix, pp. 373–5.)

[82] *Proceedings before the Justices of the Peace*, ed. Putnam, pp. xlvi, 14 (c. 12); *Rotuli Parliamentorum*, iii, pp. 83–4.

[83] *Proceedings before the Justices of the Peace*, ed. Putnam, p. cxxxiv.

framers of the bills of accusation, and by the jurors who found them true bills under the guidance of the justices. Since these were all concerned to describe crimes in such serious terms that the accused would not be pardoned (talking of burglary as breaking in by night to the dread of the inhabitants, and murder as homicide with malice aforethought), the descriptions of crimes as they appear in the rolls are a good indication of the social values of the gentry and yeomen who staffed the courts.[84]

Royal ordinances set out the duty of labourers and servants to work for their masters at specified wage-rates, but precisely who were to be regarded as members of the servant class might often depend on the subjective judgement of the court, as two hundred years previously, in a more exclusively agrarian context, had the drawing of the line between villeins and free peasants.[85] The Ordinance and the Statute of Labourers were concerned to fix the wages of farm-labourers, carpenters, masons and tilers, and other workmen of houses; and the prices charged by 'those who carry by land or by water' and by all sellers of victuals. But they also stipulated that

each and every man and woman in our realm of England, of whatever condition, free or servile, who are strong in body and under sixty years of age; if they are not living by trade or exercising a specific craft, do not have property to live from or land to cultivate, and are not already in the service of others; shall be bound to serve anyone who requires their services in work suitable to their status.

Any servant who wandered away from his master before the end of the agreed term of service (perhaps in search of a better deal) rendered himself liable to imprisonment, and no other master was to take him on. Nor was anyone to encourage the mass of able-

[84] T. F. T. Plucknett, 'A Commentary on the Indictments', in *Proceedings before the Justices of the Peace*, ed. Putnam; Thomas A. Green, 'Societal Concepts of Criminal Liability for Homicide in Medieval England', *Speculum*, xlvii (1972), and 'The Jury and the English Law of Homicide, 1200–1600', *Michigan Law Review*, lxxiv (1976). The requirement of the Statute of Gloucester of 1378 (*Statutes of the Realm*, ii, p. 10) that local men should arrest delinquents without indictment 'and send them to the next Gaol, with the Cause of their Arrest clearly and distinctly put in Writing' would also have been a stimulus to the communal definition of crimes.

[85] For the methods and difficulties of proving villein status at an earlier period, see Paul R. Hyams, *King, Lords, and Peasants in Medieval England* (Oxford, 1980), ch. 10.

bodied beggars in their idleness under pretence of charity.[86] No
document or witness was necessary for an obligation to serve to be
assumed – and it was a much more general social obligation than
villeinage. There was much debate as to whether the parish clergy
came within the meaning of the act. It was argued in a case at
Westminster that:

> He who is a parochial chaplain can be sooner judged a labourer
> than another chaplain who only has to serve a parson in a private
> capacity, for the parson of a parish has many things to do besides
> chanting his mass and other divine services. It is his business to
> visit the sick in his parish in their homes, and see that they have
> the rights of Holy Church, and it is also necessary that the parsons
> of Holy Church should have their necessary services, for they
> cannot do [everything] for themselves.[87]

Though the judges decided that a parochial chaplain did not 'lie
within the statute like another person', local juries sometimes took
the opposite view and can be found presenting even the vicar of an
Essex parish who was 'unwilling to administer the sacrament of the
apostles to anyone, unless he has 5s. or 6s. from each householder',
and in this way had 'taken by extortion . . . sums amounting to 20s. in
oppression of the people'.[88] Except in the case of chaplains, there
was no challenge in the central courts to the applicability of the
contract clause of the Statute of Labourers to men who were clearly
not manual labourers. Routine actions for leaving a master without
good reason, or of retaining the servant of another, involved a
*senescallus* (steward), an *armiger et camerarius* (esquire and
chamberlain), *camerarii et sagittarii* (chamberlains and archers),
bailiffs and schoolmasters.[89] It could very well have been the
application to them of the Statute of Labourers that roused some of
the more substantial rebels in 1381, particularly to attacks on
J.P.s.[90]

---

[86] Putnam, *Enforcement of the Statutes of Labourers*, appendix, pp. 8–11.

[87] *Ibid.*, pp. 187–9, 213, and appendix, pp. 11–12, 432–3.

[88] *Ibid.*, appendix, pp. 141, 171.

[89] *Ibid.*, pp. 186–7.

[90] John Ball, 'an evilly disposed chaplain (*une chaplein de male part*)', may have had
good personal reasons for becoming a leader of the revolt, and even urging the
commons to kill all churchmen down to parsons and vicars (*Anonimalle
Chronicle*, ed. Galbraith, pp. 137, 140). But it was a vicar of Ware in Hertfordshire who was indicted along with a hermit for preaching in the town against the
Statute of Labourers in 1356, and a later vicar who led the town in rebellion in
1381. The men of Ware and Thaxted in Essex who joined together to attack the

The way the courts had developed between the Statute of Winchester and the commissions of the peace of 1380 had created a new serfdom, to which Wat Tyler pointed when he demanded that 'no man should serve another except at his own will and by a proper covenant'.[91] The main struggle in 1381 was for civic, not tenurial, freedom, because the landlords had got a new public jurisdiction which allowed them to enforce service far more general than the obligations of villein tenure: everyone 'physically capable (*suffisantz de corps*)' should serve or be imprisoned. The most effective defence to a charge of refusing to serve was indeed that you were someone else's villein – and even then the statute allowed landlords to keep back from the labour market only so many of their villein tenants as were absolutely necessary.[92]

'Entrenched lordly power' had certainly preserved itself through the crises of the fourteenth century, but only by taking on a more political form.[93] The resistance of the lower orders correspondingly assumed a more political image in the indictments brought before the gentry justices. The rebellion of 1381 was seen as a coherent movement, so that outbreaks as far away as York were described as happening at the time of 'the diabolical insurrection of the counties of Kent and Essex'.[94] The standard terms for the disturbances were *conventicula illicita*; *horrible rumur et insurreccion*; *insurrecciones, levaciones et congregaciones contra pacem nostram* and *contra ligeanciam suam*.[95] 'Congregations and unlawful gatherings' go back to the early days of the commission of the peace in Edward II's reign;[96] but 'rumour' (meaning din or tumult) came into vogue to

duke of Lancaster's castle at Hertford and then marched to London to join the sack of his palace of the Savoy were amongst those whose economic condition seems to have been improving, and who may therefore have resented the labour legislation all the more (*Select Cases in the Court of King's Bench*, ed. Sayles, vi, pp. 110–11; Prescott, 'London in the Peasants' Revolt', pp. 129–31).

[91] ['E]t qe nulle ne deveroit servire ascune homme mes a sa volunte de mesme et par covenant taille' (*Anonimalle Chronicle*, ed. Galbraith, pp. 144–5).

[92] Putnam, *Enforcement of the Statutes of Labourers*, pp. 201–2, and appendix, p. 9.

[93] Cf. Christopher Dyer, above, p. 41.

[94] A. Réville and C. Petit-Dutaillis, *Le soulèvement des travailleurs d'Angleterre en 1381* (Paris, 1898), p. 273.

[95] 'Illicit conventicles', 'horrible rumour and insurrection', 'insurrections, risings and congregations against our peace', 'against their allegiance'. *Ibid.*, pp. 176, 183–4, 205, 234, 236–7, 238, 243, 244, 246, 251, 252, 253, 257, 276, 279, 280, 281, 285, 291, 292, 293.

[96] *Proceedings before the Justices of the Peace*, ed. Putnam, pp. 1–2: *congregaciones et conventicula illicita*; and see R. E. Latham, *Revised Medieval Latin Word-List* (London, 1965), pp. 106, 113.

describe the peasant movement for rights as ancient demesne villeins in 1377;[97] and the nouns 'insurrection', 'rising (*levacio*)' and 'common insurgent' were new in the indictments of the rebels of 1381.[98] These words seem intended to suggest spontaneous riot. More interesting are the implications of organized subversion which creep in as the courts attempt to comprehend the phenomenon of political revolt. The rebels are said in the indictments to have 'bound themselves together (*interligaverunt*)'[99] in 'a great society (*in magna societate malefactorum insurgencium de Kent*)',[100] and to have revolted out of 'their false and traitorous allegiance (*ex sua falsa et prodiciosa allegancia*)' to some rebel captain in whose 'band' or 'covin (*comitiva, covina, coniva*)' they march.[101] None of this second set of terms was quite new (the most recent were those attributing to the rebel groups an alternative allegiance).[102] What is striking about them is that they are often words which came into general use during the first of the two social crises – that caused by the war emergency which began at the end of the thirteenth century – and as descriptions of the activities of the lords, rather than of the servant class on which they are now projected.

Accusations that captains had gone about collecting bands of rebels 'falsely, feloniously and traitorously (*proditorie*), against their faith and allegiance, in denial (*adnullacionem*) of the king's state and perversion of the king and realm', and had then led them off 'with banners displayed', assimilated the fomenting of revolt to high treason.[103] There had been the same implication in a petition of the Commons in 1380 concerning rioters at York, who drove out the mayor and installed another of their own choosing, 'accroaching to themselves royal power, by false confederacy and alliance made between them'.[104] Much more frequent however was the language of livery and maintenance, as it had first appeared in the articles of trailbaston in 1305, and been included, along with extortion, rioting and riding in routs, in the jurisdiction of the justices of the peace in

---

[97] See above, Rosamond Faith, 'The "Great Rumour" of 1377 and Peasant Ideology'.

[98] Latham, *Revised Medieval Latin Word-List*, pp. 254, 274.

[99] Réville and Petit-Dutaillis, *Le soulèvement des travailleurs*, pp. 221, 254, 256–7.

[100] *Ibid.*, p. 199.

[101] *Ibid.*, pp. 177, 180, 184, 186, 192, 206.

[102] Latham, *Revised Medieval Latin Word-List*, p. 15.

[103] Réville and Petit-Dutaillis, *Le soulèvement des travailleurs*, pp. 178, 183–4, 186, 194, 209, 212, 222, 238, 246, 258, 276.

[104] *Rotuli Parliamentorum*, iii, p. 96 (no. 50).

1380.[105] At Scarborough in 1381 a band of malefactors had donned a livery or uniform of 'white caps with red liripipes, so that each of them might sustain and maintain the others' in their evil deeds.[106] Thomas atte Raven of Southwark, who led the attack on Imworth's 'mansions' at the Marshalsea, was a 'principal and chief malefactor and maintainer'; others are called 'leaders and maintainers of wicked bands' or simply 'maintainers, malefactors and disturbers of the king's peace'.[107] Maintainers were strictly speaking 'maintainers of quarrels': those who received 'men of the country to their liveries and fees, to maintain their wicked enterprises and stifle truth' in the lawcourts; particularly 'stewards and bailiffs of great lords who, by lordship, office or power, undertake to maintain and further the pleas and litigations of parties, other than those which touch their lords' estate or their own'.[108] But as it was applied to lower levels of society, the concept of maintenance widened out to embrace all sorts of concerted action.

This was even more strikingly true of conspiracy, defined along with maintenance in the Ordinance of Conspirators of 1305. When the party of trailbaston justices reached York in that year, they found that all 'great matters' were being concealed from the commission 'by the procurement and alliances of the people of that

---

[105] *Proceedings before the Justices of the Peace*, ed. Putnam, pp. 12–13; *Rotuli Parliamentorum*, iii, pp. 84–5: 'And also concerning those who wear hoods or other uniform livery to mark their confederacy or following (*Et etiam de hiis qui capiciis, et alia liberata de unica secta, per confederationem et pro manutenentia . . . usi fuerint)*'. Cf. Réville and Petit-Dutaillis, *Le soulèvement des travailleurs*, p. 268 (n. 1).

[106] *Ibid.*, p. 257: 'ac quandam liberatam de unica secta capiciorum alborum cum liripipiis rubiis, ut unusquisque eorum alterius factum in hac parte sustineret et manuteneret, liberando'. The sixty doublets that Froissart tells us were ordered by Wat Tyler for his followers, and one of which Tyler wore at Smithfield, were presumably a livery: see Jean Froissart, *Chroniques*, ed. Kervyn de Lettenhove, 25 vols. (Brussels, 1867–77), ix, p. 411.

[107] Réville and Petit-Dutaillis, *Le soulèvement des travailleurs*, pp. 186, 188, 254, 257; P.R.O., K.B.9/166/2, m. 2: 'leaders and maintainers of a wicked company (*ductores et manutentores comitive inique)*'.

[108] *Rotuli Parliamentorum*, i, p. 183, iii, p. 83 (no. 38); Réville and Petit-Dutaillis, *Le soulèvement des travailleurs*, pp. 254–5: the Scarborough band were 'with one assent sworn to maintain the quarrel of any of them as the quarrel of them all (*unanimi assensu jurati ad manutenendum quilibet eorum querelam alterius ut communes)*'; cf. Harding, 'Early Trailbaston Proceedings', pp. 148–9, 164 (nos. 44–5), for Ranulf Friskney, a *custos pacis* who was accused before the trailbaston justices in Lincolnshire in 1305 of being a 'common fomenter and maintainer of pleas and complaints (*communis sustentator et manutentor placitorum et querelarum)*', retaining known malefactors 'to his livery (*ad robas suas)*' to beat men in fairs and markets, and terrorizing juries over a period of six years or more.

country' and asked the king for more powers to deal with the situation. As a consequence of this report, 'conspirators' were formally defined in parliament as 'those who ally with each other by oath, covenant, or other bond, that each shall aid and sustain the other's undertaking to make indictments or cause indictments to be made falsely and maliciously, or to acquit people falsely'. In membranes headed 'de conspiratoribus', the trailbaston rolls contain a large number of cases of such corruption of the legal process, particularly by the organized manipulation of criminal juries.[109] The essential feature of conspiracy was, however, the sworn compact between several parties to carry through what might be a complicated scheme, and it was this which allowed the concept to be extended to political subversion at lower levels of society. Oaths such as those taken by jurymen to tell the truth and by the populace at large to keep the peace and maintain the arms required by the Statute of Winchester were part of the fabric of medieval society. But communal oaths of obedience to established authority had always been in danger of becoming oaths of communal solidarity against the authorities; especially when the ruling aristocracy included the peace-breakers against whom the community most needed to defend itself.[110]

Conspiracy continued to be strictly the corruption of legal procedures by the relatively powerful. In 1354, for instance, a group of Surrey men, headed by a knight and including a parson, a vicar and a notary, were accused in the King's Bench at Southwark of making a 'confederacy together by covenant' in the chapter of the Friars Preachers of Guildford and swearing 'by conspiracy' to support each other's felonies and wrongdoings – and to destroy John of Rowley who refused to join the confederacy. The conspirators

---

[109] Harding, 'Early Trailbaston Proceedings', pp. 148–9; *Rotuli Parliamentorum*, i, pp. 201, 289.

[110] Maintainers were often 'sworn' to aid each other in their manipulation of legal procedures (see note 108 above). Jurymen were vulnerable to accusations of conspiracy, so that Edward I ordered that civil writs of conspiracy were not to be granted against indicting jurors without his express approval (Harding, 'Early Trailbaston Proceedings', p. 151). Georges Duby remarks on the fear of popular conspiracy which grew along with the governmental use of mass oath-taking from Carolingian times (*The Three Orders: Feudal Society Imagined*, trans. Arthur Goldhammer (Chicago and London, 1980), p. 28). J. H. M. Salmon, 'Peasant Revolt in Vivarais, 1575–1580', *French Historical Studies*, xi (1979–80), depicts an uprising of peasants, formed into sworn combinations and conspiracies, against aristocratic garrisons whom they saw as criminals and breakers of royal peace edicts (pp. 9, 27).

succeeded in getting a commission of the peace issued to two of their number.[111] Yet, as the administration of justice passed more and more into the hands of the gentry, there was a perceptible extension of 'conspiracy' downwards in society to comprehend, for example, the banding together of the villeins of Great and Little Ogbourne in Wiltshire who contributed to a common purse in 1327 in order to fight for ancient demesne status.[112] In 1329, the villeins of Darnhall in Cheshire 'plotted maliciously against their lords', the abbot and convent of Vale Royal, assembling together at night and declaring 'against the liberty of the aforesaid house'; seven years later they again 'conspired against their lords . . . and endeavoured to obtain their liberty' – by laying a complaint before the justiciar of Chester, presenting a petition in parliament and, 'like mad dogs', sending a deputation to seek out the king in person at Windsor.[113] By 1381 there were regular commissions of oyer and terminer concerning bondmen who had 'rebelliously withdrawn the customary services due' from them to their lords, and had 'in divers assemblies mutually confederated and bound themselves by oath' to resist the lords' ministers.[114] Banding together to claim ancient demesne status in the courts was simply regarded as a variety of conspiracy to corrupt legal processes. Resistance to the labour laws on the part of 'workmen of houses', the masons and carpenters, seems to have needed different and more permanent forms of association, to go by a statute which annulled their 'alliances and covins . . . congregations, chapters and ordinances, and the oaths taken between them or to be taken in the future'.[115]

In the proceedings against the rebels of 1381, the most extended accounts of conspiracy still concern the townsmen of London and York, amongst whom the offence was first recognized at the end of the previous century. John Horn and four other London aldermen, sent by the mayor to talk with the Kentishmen, were alleged to have conspired with the rebel leaders to let them into the city, by Horn's

[111] *Select Cases in the Court of King's Bench*, ed. Sayles, vi, p. 95.
[112] R. H. Hilton, 'Peasant Movements in England before 1381', in E. M. Carus-Wilson (ed.), *Essays in Economic History*, 3 vols. (London, 1954–62), ii, p. 84.
[113] *The Ledger-Book of Vale Royal Abbey*, ed. John Brownbill (Lancs. and Ches. Rec. Soc., lxviii, 1914), pp. 31–2, 37–42.
[114] *Proceedings before the Justices of the Peace*, ed. Putnam, p. li: but these commissions were not part of the 'aftermath of the Great Revolt', for *Cal. Pat. Rolls., 1377–81*, p. 204, shows that they had a well-established form in 1378.
[115] *Statutes of the Realm*, i, pp. 342, 367; for masons in the revolt, see Prescott, 'London in the Peasants' Revolt', p. 130.

'premeditated covin, counsel and conspiracy'.[116] But rebels from outside London were also sworn together, and in Kent Robert Cave's band was said to have imprisoned several gentlemen until they would swear to be of their conventicles.[117] Allegations of secret councils in the woods and forced oaths were widespread. At Scarborough, the rioters were said to have bound themselves 'with one assent', by oaths as well as liveries, to support each other's quarrels, and to have forced people to swear loyalty to them and to the commons of all England.[118] There was another conspiracy at Beverley, 'to the destruction of the community', but here the *communes conspiratores* were the official collectors of a local customs duty who had plotted together to extort money for their own pockets.[119]

Since the quelling of the revolt required emergency measures, the indictments against the rebels of 1381 were brought before special trailbaston-type inquiries, and it was the business of such commissions to search out conspiracies. In later emergencies there was the same resort to special commissions of oyer and terminer, as they had developed in the war crisis at the beginning of the fourteenth century; but these progressively took on the appearance of temporary reinforcements of the powers of the justices of the peace, as they had been fashioned in the mid-century labour crisis.[120] For Thomas

---

[116] *Rotuli Parliamentorum*, i, p. 48; above, p. 189; Réville and Petit-Dutaillis, *Le soulèvement des travailleurs*, pp. 190–7, and cf. B. Wilkinson, 'The Peasants' Revolt of 1381', *Speculum*, xv (1940), pp. 12–35, where it is argued that the conspiracy charge was a calculated attempt to put all the blame for the admission of the rebels to London on a small group of aldermen.

[117] *Ibid.*, pp. 187, 206, 256: 'confederated, leagued and sworn together (*ad invicem confederati, interligati et jurati*)', 267: 'confederated and sworn together (*invicem confederati et conspirantes*)'.

[118] *Ibid.*, pp. 253–4. Cf. P.R.O., K.B.9/166/2, m. 4, where an Essex leader is indicted of assembling the men of a township and making them swear to rise (*et fecit eos jurare quod surgent*). In the summer of 1381 the villeins of the abbot of Chester were said to have 'gathered in secret confederacies within the woods and other hidden places' in the Wirral (E. Powell and G. M. Trevelyan (eds.), *The Peasants' Rising and the Lollards* (London, 1899), pp. 13–16).

[119] Réville and Petit-Dutaillis, *Le soulèvement des travailleurs*, pp. 260ff: 'by their confederacy and conspiracy (*per eorum confederacionem et conspiracionem*)'; 'common conspirators who banded together in the town of Beverley and conspired amongst themselves . . . to the total obstruction of the community of the said town (*communes conspiratores confederati in villa de Beverlaco et conspiraverunt inter se . . . in adnichilationem communitatis ville predicte*)'. This was also a conspiracy in the narrower sense in that false appeals were one of the means of extortion.

[120] *Proceedings before the Justices of the Peace*, ed. Putnam, p. xlix; Ancient

Marowe, when he gave his reading on the peace in 1503, the justices' ancient duty to suppress 'conventicles' covered not only riotous assemblies but also livery and maintenance, and conspiracies such as inciting another person to make false accusations or proclaim falsehoods in court – indeed, any conversation between two or more persons with a view to committing an unlawful act, even if all the parties were never together at the same time and never carried through their design.[121]

This was the beauty of the concept of conspiracy: that it could be used to outlaw organized political activity on the part of artisans and labourers which had no real chance of achieving its object and did not even result in violence. The terms of the indictments of the rebels in 1381 showed a perception on the part of the gentry of the stirrings of a new political force below them; and Wat Tyler's demands of the king, that a major factor in this incorporation of the common people into the political structure had been the way in which justice and policing had developed since the promulgation of 'the law of Winchester' towards the end of the previous century.

Indictments in King's Bench (K.B. 9) as listed in vol. cvi of the List and Index Society (1974).

[121] B. H. Putnam, *Early Treatises on the Practice of the Justices of the Peace in the Fifteenth and Sixteenth Centuries*, Oxford Studies in Social and Legal History, ed. P. Vinogradoff (Oxford, 1924), pp. 372–3; '*Item* the justices of the peace have power to inquire of conspiracies and confederacies . . . by this word "conventicles" (*Item lez Justicez de peas poient enquirer de conspiracies & confiderasies . . . par ceux parols "conventicles"*)'. Indictments of conspiracy were occasionally brought before the justices of the peace from the mid-fourteenth century: the misappropriation of fines 'by their confederacy and illicit agreement (*per eorum confederacionem et illicitam convencionem*)' (Devon, 1353); the forging of a charter 'by false and malicious conspiracy (*falso et maliciose conspiracione*)' (Devon, 1353); the forging of a notarial instrument, in which the accused 'were confederated and conspired together (*confederati fuerunt et inter se conspiraverunt*)', and the abduction of a married woman which the accused 'conspired with other confederates (*cum aliis sibi confederatis inter se conspiraverunt*)' (successive Wiltshire indictments, 1383–4) – all in *Proceedings before the Justices of the Peace*, ed. Putnam, pp. 69, 79, 386.

# 8. *Nobles, Commons and the Great Revolt of 1381*

J. A. TUCK

The reaction of the English governing class to the great revolt of 1381 is a subject that has received little attention from historians. The recent works on Richard II, even those which dwell specifically upon his relations with the nobility, devote little attention to it, and knowledge of the subject has scarcely progressed beyond generalizations based on chronicle accounts of the rebellion and on the legislative programme of the Cambridge parliament of 1388.[1] The prevailing view is expressed most vividly by Anthony Steel. When the rebels were in control in London, those around the king in the Tower were evidently one and all paralysed with fright. In East Anglia, Henry Despenser bishop of Norwich 'almost alone among the governing classes . . . kept his sense of proportion and his wits about him'. Their fear showed itself immediately in suspicion and resentment of the initiatives taken by the king at the height of the revolt, in a new determination to tackle the problem of heresy, and, later, in the labour legislation of the Cambridge parliament, which showed 'how deeply the revolt of 1381 had eaten into upper class consciousness'.[2]

This view of the reaction of the nobility and the commons in the face of the most widespread expression of peasant discontent in medieval England is firmly founded upon the contemporary chronicles. Walsingham stated that when the rebellion began, the lords 'remained inert, staying quiet and motionless in their homes until the men of Kent and Essex had attracted an army of about one hundred thousand commons and rustics'.[3] The same chronicle tells us that the earl of Suffolk

---

[1] A. Steel, *Richard II* (Cambridge, 1941); J. A. Tuck, *Richard II and the English Nobility* (London, 1973). But see also J. R. Maddicott, *Law and Lordship: Royal Justices as Retainers in Thirteenth- and Fourteenth-Century England* (Past and Present Supplement no. 4, Oxford, 1978), esp. pp. 61–71, for the beginning of a new approach to the problem.

[2] Steel, *Richard II*, pp. 87, 170.

[3] Thomas Walsingham, *Historia Anglicana*, ed. H. T. Riley, 2 vols. (Rolls ser.,

was warned of the approach of the rebels and immediately rose from the table at which he was having his meal; always avoiding the crowds of commons, he made his way circuitously and through lonely areas to St. Albans. And so he reached the king, disguising himself as a groom of Lord Roger de Boys and carrying a knapsack on his back.[4]

John Capgrave, in his biography of Bishop Despenser, made a much more sweeping allegation of cowardice amongst the nobility: 'The lords, knights and other nobles all fled because they were afraid (*Dominis, militibus et aliis nobilibus se propter timorem abscondentibus*)'. Only Bishop Despenser marched forth openly.[5] The *Anonimalle Chronicle* paints a vivid picture of the fear felt by those round the king in the Tower, and the monk of Evesham suggests that even the king was afraid and feared for his life when he rode to meet the rebels at Mile End.[6]

The essence of the received account is that the bishop of Norwich alone offered any resistance to the rebels until, with Tyler dead, the king was able to recapture the initiative, rally his forces, and put down the revolt in Kent and Essex. The tradition of aristocratic cowardice and pussillanimity in face of such a fundamental challenge to their authority requires investigation and explanation; but the problem of the governing class's reaction to the revolt does not end there. It is also necessary to investigate the attitude subsequently taken by the landowners, great and small, to the rebels themselves, to the grievances which they believed underlay the revolt, and to the threats of further social unrest in the 1380s.

The terms 'nobility' or 'governing class' do not admit of precise definition. All were landowners, though of course not all still cultivated their demesnes with servile labour. The interests of the smaller landowners, the knightly class represented in the house of commons, did not necessarily coincide with those of the great ecclesiastical landowners or the titled nobility, and the advice which the king received from those nobles who surrounded him at court

London, 1863–4), i, p. 456. This translation and others in the essay are taken from *The Peasants' Revolt of 1381*, ed. R. B. Dobson (London, 1970).

[4] Walsingham, *Historia Anglicana*, ii, p. 5.

[5] J. Capgrave, *Liber de Illustribus Henricis*, ed. F. C. Hingeston (Rolls ser., London, 1858), p. 170.

[6] *The Anonimalle Chronicle, 1333–1381*, ed. V. H. Galbraith (Manchester, 1927), p. 143; *Historia Vitae et Regni Ricardi Secundi*, ed. G. B. Stow (Philadelphia, 1977), pp. 64–5.

was very obviously not, in the 1380s, the advice which many of the titled nobles and a substantial body of opinion in the Commons thought he ought to receive.[7] It is wrong to suppose that the landowners formed a homogeneous group, or that the 'governing class' had a single view of the events of 1381 which it sought to express by military action, by legislation, or by private dealings with their tenants.

There were some amongst the lesser landowners who sought to profit for themselves from the rebellion; others joined the rebellion under duress, or so they subsequently claimed.[8] Such men, however, constituted a small minority amongst the landowners of East Anglia, Kent and Essex. There seems good foundation for the chroniclers' belief that most landowners offered no resistance to the rebels until the king was able to rally his forces in London and begin the suppression of the rebellion. The one exception, according to the chroniclers was Henry Despenser, bishop of Norwich. On hearing of the rebellion he set out, according to Walsingham, from his manor of Burleigh near Stamford, and made his way through Norfolk, attracting forces to his side as he went. At North Walsham, where the Norfolk rebels made a stand, the bishop and his forces routed them and executed their leader John Litster.[9] Henry Knighton suggests that the bishop put down the rebellion at Peterborough and at various places in Cambridgeshire and Huntingdonshire before moving into Norfolk.[10] Both chroniclers portray Despenser as the instrument of divine vengeance on the rebels, a leader of great vigour moving swiftly through East Anglia to suppress the rebellion, and attracting to his side many of the knights and gentlemen of the region who had gone into hiding when the rebellion broke out.

[7] Tuck, *Richard II and the English Nobility*, pp. 87–105.

[8] Walsingham, *Historia Anglicana*, ii, p. 6; R. H. Hilton, *Bond Men Made Free: Medieval Peasant Movements and the English Rising of 1381* (London, 1973), p. 184.

[9] Walsingham, *Historia Anglicana*, ii, pp. 6–8. Bishop Despenser's register suggests that he was in Norwich on 14 and 15 June. There is no further entry in the register relevant to his movements until 1 July, when he was again in Norwich. If he left Norwich on 15 June, perhaps to tackle the rebels elsewhere in Norfolk or further west, this may explain why Litster did not attempt to enter the city until 17 June. I hope to return to this problem on another occasion. (The register is in the Norfolk Record Office. I am grateful to the Librarian of the Seeley Historical Library, Cambridge, for lending me a microfilm of the register.)

[10] *Chronicon Henrici Knighton*, ed. J. R. Lumby, 2 vols. (Rolls ser., London, 1889–95), ii, pp. 140–1.

Walsingham's account of the bishop's part in the suppression of the rising should, however, be read in the context of his subsequent highly flattering account of Despenser's crusade in Flanders in 1383 and in the light of the fact that Walsingham was not only, of course, a member of the clerical order but also (presumably) a native of the diocese of Norwich and that he became prior of the St Albans cell at Wymondham in 1394.[11] It may be that in some respects the later and more sober account by Capgrave is to be preferred. According to Capgrave, the bishop proceeded first to Cambridge and thence via Thetford to Norwich with only a small number of armed men in his company. His main claim to distinction was his willingness to put rebels to death without formal royal warrant when other, lesser nobles who had captured some of the rebels did not dare do so.[12] It was this, rather than the size of the army he gathered on his progress across East Anglia, that put fear into the hearts of the rebels, and the final encounter at North Walsham was nothing like as bloody or spectacular as Walsingham made it seem.[13]

Approached from this point of view, Despenser's action represents an effective, if technically unlawful, approach to the problem of resisting the rebels. Lesser landowners, on the other hand, as Capgrave's account suggests, were unlikely to have the nerve to execute rebels out of hand, without the king's commission. Furthermore, rumours reaching East Anglia about the king's intentions towards the rebels could scarcely have encouraged landowners to take a harsh line.[14]

Of the secular nobles who had extensive lands in East Anglia, Essex or Kent, few were in any position to resist. It is clear from the Despenser story that the personal initiative of the lord was essential if resistance were to be offered. Of the lord's officials on his manors,

[11] V. H. Galbraith, 'Thomas Walsingham and the Saint Albans Chronicle, 1271–1422', *Eng. Hist. Rev.*, xlvii (1932), pp. 12–30.

[12] Capgrave, *Liber de Illustribus Henricis*, p. 171. Despenser was not amongst those authorized to resist and punish insurgents under letters patent issued on 23 June, two (or perhaps three) days before the 'battle' of North Walsham, nor was he named in the order of 30 June empowering certain individuals in areas affected by the revolt to 'arrest and imprison any found rebellious' after the proclamation ordering all tenants to perform customary works and services. In any case, this order merely authorized the arrest of rebels 'until *the king* shall take order for their punishment'. Despenser's name does not appear in any commission to deal with rebels until 22 July: *Cal. Close Rolls, 1381–5*, p. 74; *Cal. Pat. Rolls, 1381–5*, pp. 69, 74.

[13] E. Powell, *The Rising in East Anglia in 1381* (Cambridge, 1896), pp. 37–8.

[14] Walsingham, *Historia Anglicana*, ii, p. 6.

only the constables of his castles were in theory in a position to take some military initiative against the rebels, but in practice in East Anglia castle garrisons were likely in normal times to have been virtually non-existent, even if the castles had not fallen down and constables were still appointed. The lesser landowners for their part had little if any military force at their disposal and would in any case be reluctant to use what force they had without encouragement from a great lord such as Despenser, or without explicit instructions from the king or the sheriff. Furthermore, although many of the great nobles with land in East Anglia, Kent and Essex had substantial armed retinues, these retinues could not be rallied in an instant. The system of indentured retinues had developed in the fourteenth century in response to the demands of war overseas and in Scotland; it was not adapted to cope with the problem of unexpected and widespread social unrest. Although nobles such as Despenser or Gaunt usually travelled with a small military escort,[15] the mustering of a retinue took time and might well require the assembling of men from many different parts of the country. Furthermore, the lesser landowners would not necessarily welcome the use of a lord's armed retinue to put down rebels without due process of law. As complaints in parliament showed, not least in 1384 and 1388,[16] the lesser landowners represented in the Commons distrusted the military power wielded by the great magnates and wished to see legislation designed to curb it. The juxtaposition of the labour code and the complaints against liveried retainers in the proceedings of the Cambridge parliament of 1388 show with great clarity that the lesser landowners in no way saw the military power of the magnates as a means of protection against social disturbances.

Even had they wished to do so, the great landowners would have found difficulty in mobilizing their retinues to deal swiftly with the rebellion. Walsingham's account of Ufford's flight in disguise to London may well be substantially correct (there is nothing in the sources to contradict it) but the whereabouts of most of the other great lords with lands in East Anglia, Essex and Kent precluded them from offering immediate active resistance to the rebels.

---

[15] *Ibid.*, p. 6; *John of Gaunt's Register, 1379–1383*, ed. E. C. Lodge and R. Somerville, 2 vols. (Camden Soc., 3rd ser., lvi–lvii, London, 1937), ii, nos. 1186, 1187.

[16] *Polychronicon Ranulphi Higden*, ed. J. R. Lumby, 9 vols. (Rolls ser., London, 1865–6), ix, pp. 40–1, 189–90.

Gaunt, as is well known, was in the Scottish Marches.[17] The earl of March, lord of the Honour of Clare in Suffolk, was in Ireland;[18] the earl of Buckingham, an important landowner in north-west Essex, may have been in Wales but was more probably with the king;[19] the earl of Oxford was with the king and in any case probably did not receive livery of his inheritance until July 1381,[20] and the lands of the earldom of Norfolk were in the hands of Margaret Marshall, the aged countess of Norfolk who was in no position to muster a retinue and lead it against the rebels.[21] Of the more important Kentish landowners, Simon Burley was in Germany negotiating the king's marriage,[22] and Thomas Holland, earl of Kent, the king's half-brother, was with the king in London.[23] With the possible exception of the earl of Suffolk, the great lords of East Anglia, Essex and Kent were men with territorial interests in many different parts of the country; they were men accustomed to being with the king at court or to travelling abroad on diplomatic or military missions, and although they might exercise some degree of control over their estates through the kind of national and local management structure which emerges from, for example, John of Gaunt's Register, they were scarcely in a position to react with speed to a rising on one particular part of their estates.

In the last analysis, the deployment of military power against rebels at home depended upon the king's initiative. Only the king could instruct the sheriff and other leading men of the shire to deploy the shire levies;[24] only the king could issue a general appeal to men-at-arms to join him in resisting the rebellion; and, as the

---

[17] *Anonimalle Chronicle*, ed. Galbraith, p. 133.

[18] A. J. Otway-Ruthven, *A History of Medieval Ireland* (London, 1968), p. 315.

[19] The *Anonimalle Chronicle*, ed. Galbraith, p. 138, states that Buckingham was with the king; Froissart states that he was in Wales: J. Froissart, *Chroniques*, ed. S. Luce *et al.*, 14 vols. (Paris, 1869–1966), x, p. 106. He was evidently in London by about 28 June, for he took part in the suppression of the revolt in Essex: Walsingham, *Historia Anglicana*, ii, pp. 18–19. He was back in Wales by the end of July: Public Record Office (hereafter P.R.O.), Exchequer Issue Roll, E.403/484, m. 11.

[20] He was first styled earl on 10 July 1381: *Cal. Pat. Rolls, 1381–4*, p. 73.

[21] G.E.C., *The Complete Peerage*, ed. V. Gibbs *et al.*, 13 vols. (London, 1936), ix, pp. 599–600.

[22] T. F. Tout, *Chapters in the Administrative History of Medieval England*, 6 vols. (Manchester, 1920–33), iii, p. 368.

[23] *Anonimalle Chronicle*, ed. Galbraith, p. 138.

[24] The array was used to deal with the rebels in all the counties most seriously affected: *Cal. Pat. Rolls, 1381–5*, pp. 72–4.

pardon issued in the parliament of November 1381 shows, only the king could release men from the obligation to observe due process of law in depriving even rebels of their lives.[25] Once the king had recaptured the initiative in London after the death of Tyler, 'he sent messengers into the country asking all those who loved him and honoured the realm to hurry to him in London, well-armed and on horseback'. Walsingham says that 40,000 armed men answered this appeal.[26] In all probability scarcely a tenth of that number came to the king, but those who came were paid: on 25 June the Keeper of the Wardrobe received 2,000 marks from the Exchequer for the wages of men-at-arms and archers going 'to certain places by the king's order for the safeguard of the kingdom of England (*ad certas partes ex assignacione Regis pro salvacione regni Angliae*)'.[27] In this respect, the campaign against the rebels resembled other military campaigns for which the household took financial responsibility.

The military campaign against the rebels was followed by judicial proceedings which were marked, in general, by respect for due process of law. In stamping out the rebellion in London, William Walworth, Sir Robert Knolles, John Philpott and Nicholas Brembre received royal authority to deal with the rebels according to the law of the land and also according to their discretion, and under colour of this commission several rebels were executed without trial,[28] but neither the general proclamation to all sheriffs and justices issued on 18 June nor the commission to the sheriff and other officials in Kent issued two days later gave such sweeping powers: they were commanded to bring rebels to justice and punish them as they deserved according to the law and custom of England.[29] In the proceedings against the rebels, legal process was generally observed and punishments were lenient: a remarkably small number of rebels suffered death. There is no evidence of any pressure on the king or on the sheriffs and justices from the great nobles for more severe sentences. Indeed, if Walsingham is to be believed, the magnates and notables of Kent interceded with the king to prevent him leading a military campaign against the rebels in

[25] *Rotuli Parliamentorum*, 6 vols. (Record Comm., London, 1783), iii, p. 103.

[26] Walsingham, *Historia Anglicana*, ii, p. 14.

[27] P.R.O., Exchequer Issue Roll, Easter, 4 Richard II, E.403/484, m. 8.

[28] P.R.O., Chancery Patent Roll, 4 Richard II, part III, C.66/310, m. 4d; Walsingham, *Historia Anglicana*, ii, p. 14.

[29] P.R.O., Patent Roll, C.66/310, m. 4d.

Kent when it seemed that the rebellion was coming to life again despite the death of Tyler.[30]

In short, neither the great nobles nor the lesser landowners seem to have contemplated the use of arbitrary force to quell the rebellion. The bishop of Norwich alone stands out for his willingness to put rebels to death without due process of law or royal authority to dispense with normal legal formalities. When military force was used it was at the king's initiative, and the judgement of offenders rested on legal powers derived from the king's authority. The nobility who were with the king in the aftermath of the revolt supported him and took part in military action, but as in other military campaigns, ultimate responsibility lay with the king and his nobles did not seek to usurp that responsibility into their own hands.

The suppression of the revolt by military force and by legal process, however, was accompanied by measures on the part of individual lords to punish their tenants who had taken part in the rising, and to obtain compensation for damage done. But there is little evidence that the lords took a vengeful attitude towards their tenants, that they sought to place heavy or novel burdens on them as a result of the rebellion, or that in general they tried to procure legal or financial advantages for themselves from the wholesale destruction of estate and legal records that had accompanied the revolt. The lady of the manor of Mose in Essex used the destruction of court rolls by the rebels as an excuse to take all the lands of her villein tenants into her own hands and return them on payment of fines of 10*s.* or 20*s.*[31] But her attitude was not shared by the great nobles of East Anglia. On the duchy of Lancaster manor of Hilgay in Norfolk, where the rental had been destroyed during the rising, the tenants were merely instructed to make a new one before the next court under pain of a fine,[32] and on the earl of Buckingham's manors of Waltham and Pleshey in Essex tenants were fined for damage committed to the lord's property 'at the time of the rumour',[33] but there is no sign of any attempt to change their terms of tenure. The general policy of the duchy of Lancaster to the question of damage done during the revolt was set out in a letter

[30] Walsingham, *Historia Anglicana*, ii, p. 14.
[31] Essex Record Office, D/DGh M14, m. 2. A photostat of this document is included in G. A. Holmes, *The Later Middle Ages* (London, 1962), opposite p. 132.
[32] P.R.O., Duchy of Lancaster Court Rolls, DL.30/104/1459.
[33] *Ibid.*, DL.30/66/833, m. 17.

from Gaunt to his steward and receiver in Norfolk instructing them to inquire into the damage done by the rebels, bond and free, on duchy property, and to treat with them for compensation.[34] Gaunt was anxious to ensure that these officials should not get out of control: the outcome of these inquiries and negotiations was to be reported to his council in London, and no fines were to be imposed without reference to the council or without special mandate from Gaunt himself. Before this instruction was issued, the court of the duke's manor of Methwold in Norfolk had imposed fines on tenants for damage done during the revolt, but none of these fines was large: forty-nine tenants were fined a total of 35s. 7d. for destruction of hay and corn, and eleven tenants were fined 3d. each for damage to the duke's property at Thornholm.[35] There is no evidence from the duchy of Lancaster estates that officials took an unduly harsh or punitive attitude towards tenants involved in the rising, and Gaunt's instructions to his officials in Norfolk, especially his concern that they should not act without reference to his council, suggests that the nobility perhaps shared the Commons' view that the oppressive behaviour of local officials had been an important reason for the outbreak of the rebellion. In their dealings with their tenants, the evidence suggests that the great lords' reaction to the rebellion was studiously moderate.

In their analyses of the Peasants' Revolt, historians have generally argued that in the longer term the revolt achieved very little.[36] So far as the abolition of villeinage is concerned, this is of course true: Richard's charters of manumission were repealed, and the repeal was confirmed in the most forceful manner by the Lords and Commons in the parliament of November 1381.[37] The wording of the parliamentary declaration, however, requires careful examination. The essence of parliament's view was that the manumission of the serfs had been made without their agreement; serfs were the property of their lords, and to manumit them without the consent of the lords amounted to disinheritance.[38] The lords

---

[34] *John of Gaunt's Register, 1379–1383*, ed. Lodge and Somerville, ii, no. 1109.

[35] P.R.O., Duchy of Lancaster Court Rolls, DL.30/104/1476, m. 2d.

[36] See, for example, *Peasants' Revolt of 1381*, ed. Dobson, p. 27; C. Oman, *The Great Revolt of 1381*, new edn (Oxford, 1969), pp. 153–7.

[37] *Rotuli Parliamentorum*, iii, p. 100.

[38] *Ibid*.: 'These manumissions and freedoms were made and granted by coercion, in their disinheritance and the destruction of the kingdom (*Celles manumissions et franchises issint faitz et grantez par cohercion, en desheritance de eux et destruction del roialme*)'.

could not and would not agree to manumission of this kind, made without their agreement and contrary to their property rights. It does not follow from this, however, that each individual lord was determined to resist the manumission of serfs in all circumstances: merely that the disposal of property lay with the owner, and that the disposal of such rights could be a source of profit. If a lord was to manumit his serfs, he would expect to be able to exact payment for doing so.

It is difficult to argue on existing evidence that there was any general tightening of manorial authority in the years immediately after the revolt. There are particular instances in East Anglia of lords making greater efforts to enforce their legal rights,[39] and on both the Lancaster and March estates the lord and his council exercised a general vigilance over their manorial rights.[40] On the other hand it would be hard to show from the surviving evidence for the Lancaster and March inheritances that there was any fundamental change in manorial policy as a result of the rising.

It should not be assumed from this, however, that everything went on exactly as before, and that the nobility did not react at all to the rising. If it is accepted that the imposition of a third poll-tax in four years did much to precipitate the revolt, it must also be accepted that here the peasants achieved an important success. Parliament never again voted to levy such a tax, and in effect abandoned the attempt to broaden the social basis of taxation. This is a more substantial victory for the peasants than has sometimes been supposed. The tenths and fifteenths, the lay subsidy, had become very unpopular with the Commons in the 1370s: in 1380 they complained that it was 'in many ways oppressive to the poor Commons',[41] and in the 1370s they had proposed various fiscal innovations which would raise more money than the traditional tenths and fifteenths, and at the same time extend the fiscal burden more widely through the community and reflect more accurately the geographical distribution of wealth in the community.[42] The tax on parishes was intended to achieve this object, as were the three poll-

---

[39] Powell, *Rising in East Anglia in 1381*, pp. 64–6.

[40] R. R. Davies, 'Baronial Accounts, Incomes, and Arrears in the Later Middle Ages', *Econ. Hist. Rev.*, 2nd. ser., xxi (1968), pp. 211–29; G. A. Holmes, *The Estates of the Higher Nobility in Fourteenth-Century England* (Cambridge, 1969), pp. 115–20.

[41] *Rotuli Parliamentorum*, iii, p. 90.

[42] Oman, *Great Revolt of 1381*, introduction by E. B. Fryde, pp. xii–xvii.

taxes: the levying of the third poll-tax, which sparked off the 1381 rising, should be seen in the context of the Commons' preoccupation with fiscal innovation in the 1370s. The Peasants' Revolt ended any possibility of further experiments to move away from the tenths and fifteenths as the basis of direct taxation of the laity, and the Commons in the parliament of November 1381 were fully conscious of the effect the rising had on fiscal policy. They dare not, they said, grant a direct tax of any kind in this parliament, and they sought relief for the collectors of the poll-tax from any additional charges imposed by the commissions appointed to inquire into the levying of the tax.[43] This petition was granted, and was put to the test when the collectors of the poll-tax in Suffolk appeared before the Exchequer to account for £184 7s. 0d. imposed by the special commissioners. £128 6s. 4d. had been received by the collectors separately from various individuals during the period of disturbances, and this was paid into the Exchequer on 23 October 1381; but the collectors stated that they dare not levy the balance of £56 0s. 8d. 'because of fear of death (*propter metum mortis*)'. Their case was postponed until the quindene of Easter 1382, and they then sought to be exonerated of the £56 0s. 8d. 'on the pretext of the king's pardon and grace made to the community of his realm of England in his parliament held at Westminster on the morrow of All Souls (*pretextu perdonaciones et gratie Regis factarum communitati regni sui Anglie in parliamento suo tento apud Westmonasterium in crastino Animarum*)'.[44] This 'pardon' was evidently the Commons' petition seeking relief from charges imposed by the special commissioners, and the Exchequer accepted this as sufficient warrant to exonerate the Suffolk tax-collectors.[45] There are no other similar cases amongst the Exchequer records, but it is clear that the government had decided to write off the sums of money imposed by the special commissioners and not yet collected. The peasants' success assumes even greater significance in the light of recent work on the pressure of royal financial demands on the peasantry in the first half of the fourteenth century, and the willingness of the

---

[43] *Rotuli Parliamentorum*, iii, pp. 104, 116.

[44] The petition from the Suffolk collectors is in P.R.O., Exchequer Bill, E.207/6/11. The case is enrolled on the Exchequer K.R. Memoranda Roll, Michaelmas 1381–Trinity 1382: P.R.O., E.159/158 fines etc., m. 3.

[45] The petition of the Commons is enrolled on both the K.R. and the L.T.R. Memoranda Rolls, and described on the latter as a 'pardon': P.R.O., E.368/154 Communia, Easter 1382, m. 14.

government on several occasions in the 1330s and 1340s to give way in the face of popular pressure.[46] Seen in this context, the Peasants' Revolt was the most successful of all movements of resistance to the demands of the crown, and served to ensure that the system of direct lay taxation remained essentially unchanged until the sixteenth century. Fiscal innovation after 1381 was limited to such experiments as the baronial income tax of 1436,[47] and (apart from expedients such as benevolences) attempts to change the social or geographical basis of taxation came to an end.

The oppressive behaviour of the special commissioners appointed to inquire into the evasion of the poll-tax was the most glaring instance of a problem which, in the eyes of contemporaries at least, was a potent cause of discontent – the misconduct of officials. It was this, rather than a desire for liberty, which the Commons believed had brought about the revolt. In the parliament of November 1381 Speaker Waldegrave, who had himself been one of the special commissioners in Essex, complained of the 'grievous oppressions throughout the country because of the outrageous multitude of embracers of quarrels and maintenance, who act like kings in the country so that justice and law are scarcely administered to anybody'. He went on to complain of the activities of the purveyors of the royal household, the burden of subsidies and tallages, and 'other grievous and outrageous oppressions' suffered by the Commons 'from various servants of our lord the king and other lords of the realm'. Waldegrave believed that 'the said outrages . . . made the said poor commons feel so hardly oppressed that they caused the said mean commons (*menues communes*) to rise and commit the mischief they did in the said riot. And greater mischiefs are to be feared if good and proper remedy is not provided in time for the above mentioned oppressions and mischiefs.'[48] An explanation of social unrest in terms of malpractices by dishonest, greedy and violent officials was attractive to the Commons, who had a long tradition of complaining about such matters, and it is paralleled by explanations of social unrest in other periods.[49] It had the advantage

---

[46] See especially J. R. Maddicott, *The English Peasantry and the Demands of the Crown 1294–1341* (Past and Present Supplement no. 1, Oxford, 1975).

[47] T. B. Pugh and C. D. Ross, 'The English Baronage and the Income Tax of 1436', *Bull. Inst. Hist. Research*, xxvi (1953), pp. 2, 13.

[48] *Rotuli Parliamentorum*, iii, pp. 100–1.

[49] See, for example, J. Walter and K. Wrightson, 'Dearth and the Social Order in Early Modern England', *Past and Present*, no. 71 (May 1976), pp. 22–42.

for the Commons that it not only deflected attention from the problem of villeinage, but also made it possible to propose and implement remedial measures.

On the question of livery and maintenance, remedial measures were almost certain to be frustrated by the great magnates, who strongly opposed any attempt to regulate retaining by law. In the Salisbury parliament of 1384 the Commons' proposal for legislation was resisted by the duke of Lancaster, who insisted that lords could discipline their retainers without the need for legislation,[50] and an even firmer response from the Lords greeted similar proposals from the Commons in the Cambridge parliament of 1388.[51] On the other hand the Commons' complaints in the 1381 parliament may have borne some fruit when, in December 1382, the J.P.s were deprived of the power to determine cases involving felonies, armed conventicles, ambushes, livery and maintenances, trespass and forestalling. J.P.s might hear such cases, but their determination was to be a matter for the royal justices.[52] The J.P.s were more susceptible to influence and pressure than the royal justices, and this measure may have been designed to persuade the Commons that the government was reacting to the complaint that 'justice and law are scarcely administered to anybody', but there is little sign that it made any difference to the administration of law in the localities, and the J.P.s' powers to determine these cases were restored in 1389.[53]

Both nobles and Commons, in rather different ways, thus showed a certain sensitivity in the immediate aftermath of the revolt to complaints about the conduct of officials. However, another, more authoritarian, analysis of the revolt was possible. In the parliament of October 1383 Sir Michael de la Pole, newly appointed chancellor, said that

> the acts of disobedience and rebellion which men have recently committed and which continue from one day to another towards the lesser servants of the king, such as the sheriffs, escheators, collectors of the subsidies and others of the same type, were the source and chief cause of the treasonable insurrection recently made by the commune of England within this realm.[54]

[50] *Polychronicon Ranulphi Higden*, ed. Lumby, ix, pp. 40–1.
[51] *Ibid.*, pp. 189–90.
[52] *Proceedings before the Justices of the Peace in the Fourteenth and Fifteenth Centuries*, ed. B. H. Putnam (London, 1938), pp. xxiv–xxv.
[53] *Ibid.*
[54] *Rotuli Parliamentorum*, iii, p. 150.

But instead of going on to propose measures to control the behaviour of such officials, Pole used his explanation of the reason for the rebellion as the occasion for a homily on the duty of obedience to the king and his servants, obedience which was 'the foundation of all peace and quiet in the realm itself'. The view that peace could be ensured by the better performance of the obedience due from subjects to their king may well have formed part of the thinking of those round the king in the mid-1380s, and it was to become of considerable importance in the political crisis of 1386–8.[55]

The king probably shared Pole's view of the importance of obedience, for it is most unlikely that Pole would have put forward in his first address to parliament as chancellor ideas with which the king disagreed. It has been suggested that the king's attitude to the demands of the rebels in 1381 was more conciliatory than that of most of the rest of the governing class,[56] and it has been suggested that Richard was prepared to continue manumitting serfs even after the charter of general submission had been revoked. There is some evidence to support this hypothesis: the dating of charters of manumission and pardon to the men of Somerset on 2 July can hardly be dismissed merely as bureaucratic routine,[57] and the placing of Pole and Arundel in the household 'to advise and govern (*pur conseiller et governer*)' the person of the king suggests some parliamentary suspicion of the king and those round him.[58] Yet both the *Anonimalle Chronicle* and the chronicle of the monk of Evesham, perhaps the best authorities for the events in London during the revolt, suggest that the king was not so much conciliatory as distressed and fearful, preoccupied with the immediate problem of dispersing the rebels.[59] Whatever his real feelings, a conciliatory attitude was much more likely to persuade the rebels to disperse than a hard line, which in any case could not at that moment be supported by military force. It is not easy to see what else the king could have done in face of the rebels' strength in London, and his

---

[55] See, for example, R. H. Jones, *The Royal Policy of Richard II* (Oxford, 1968), pp. 143–6.

[56] B. Harvey, 'Draft Letters Patent of Manumission and Pardon for the Men of Somerset in 1381', *Eng. Hist. Rev.*, lxxx (1965), pp. 89–91.

[57] *Ibid.*

[58] *Rotuli Parliamentorum*, iii, p. 104.

[59] *Anonimalle Chronicle*, ed. Galbraith, p. 143; *Historia Vitae et Regni Ricardi Secundi*, ed. Stow, pp. 64–5.

actions inevitably lay open to misinterpretation by nobles and ministers. Furthermore, the king's position as a landowner was, of course, different from that of the great nobles, lay and ecclesiastical, and the lesser gentry. The form of tenure on the ancient demesne of the crown was superior to villeinage, and the plea that land was ancient demesne of the crown was used to support claims for relief from the burdens of serfdom.[60] Not all ancient demesne was under the king's direct lordship in 1381, and much land that was not ancient demesne passed in (and out) of the king's hands through forfeiture and the operation of the feudal incidents. None the less, the king saw this land more as a source of patronage than of long-term income, and the management of crown lands differed in many respects from the management of most seigneurial estates. Thus the king might not see the problem of villeinage in quite the same light as other landowners, great and small, and he was more likely to analyse the revolt in terms of the relationship between king and subjects. He thus might well be sympathetic to a reaction to the revolt which laid stress on the subject's duty of obedience to his sovereign, and, perhaps under the influence of Pole and Burley, Richard undoubtedly moved towards a more authoritarian view of kingship in the years following the Peasants' Revolt.[61]

There is little sign, however, that the authoritarian view put forward by Pole in 1383 was shared by the Commons in parliament. As social unrest continued after 1381, so the attitude of the Commons was shaped by a desire to avoid provoking another rising, and to remedy the grievances which they believed underlay the 1381 rebellion. The possibility of further unrest, and the need to avoid it, thus became probably for the first time an element in the political calculations of the Commons, and this is nowhere better illustrated than in their attitude to taxation. Not only did the parliament of November 1381 refuse a subsidy, but the parliaments of May 1382 and February 1383 also refused a grant in spite of considerable pressure from the lords and the council.[62] This unprecedented unwillingness on the part of the Commons to grant taxes made it impossible for the lords to implement their plans for a royal expedition to France, and the bishop of Norwich's proposal for a 'crusade' in Flanders commended itself to the Commons not so much

---

[60] B. P. Wolffe, *The Royal Demesne in English History* (London, 1971), pp. 24–6.
[61] Jones, *Royal Policy of Richard II*, pp. 18–27.
[62] *Rotuli Parliamentorum*, iii, pp. 122–3, 144–6.

because of the bishop's martial reputation but because it appeared to be cheaper than a royal expedition.[63] It is clear, too, from the pressure exerted on the Commons to grant taxes in these years that the great lords did not share the Commons' fear of the possible consequences of taxation; their attitude was determined much more by a desire to take advantage of the political weaknesses of France in the years after the death of Charles V. The Commons' parsimony frustrated their purposes and, as has been rightly said, the years after the Peasants' Revolt 'mark a turning point in the war'.[64]

The Commons accompanied their parsimony over taxation with continued agitation about law and order and the oppressive behaviour of officials. Their concern reached a climax in the two parliaments of 1388. In the spring of 1388, as the Lords debated whether the sentence of death passed by the Merciless Parliament on Simon Burley should be carried out, news came of a movement in Kent pressing for his execution. Fear of a rising in Kent if Burley were reprieved evidently made those nobles who had hitherto laboured to save his life feel that it was not worth it, and they allowed him to go to his death.[65] Rumours of a rising in Kent reawakened memories of the 1381 revolt, and a petition submitted to the same parliament drew attention to the same grievances which, the Commons believed, had provoked the rising seven years earlier and perhaps underlay the movement in Kent. The Commons warned of the damage that would be done to the realm if the grievances were not remedied, but, preoccupied with high politics, the government took no action on the petition, and it was not even enrolled on the parliament roll.[66]

In the next parliament, which met at Cambridge in September 1388, the Commons showed for the first time since the rising of 1381 a wish for legislation directed specifically against those sections of the community which had been implicated in the Peasants' Revolt.[67] Both the labour legislation of this parliament and the Commons' request for the abolition of guilds and fraternities were

---

[63] *Ibid.*, p. 146.
[64] J. J. N. Palmer, *England, France and Christendom, 1377–79* (London, 1972), p. 11.
[65] T. Favent, 'Historia Mirabilis Parliamenti', ed. M. McKisack, in *Camden Miscellany* (Camden Soc., 3rd ser., xxxvii, London, 1926), xiv, p. 21.
[66] *Chronicon Henrici Knighton*, ed. Lumby, ii, pp. 266–70.
[67] For this parliament, see J. A. Tuck, 'The Cambridge Parliament, 1388', *Eng. Hist. Rev.*, lxxxiv (1969), pp. 225–43.

intended to impose a greater degree of control and supervision on the labouring class; and the request for the suppression of guilds almost certainly sprang from a belief that they provided a cover for seditious gatherings. The Commons had to be satisfied with an inquiry into guilds, and the whole matter was subsequently dropped;[68] but their petitions about the control of labour were embodied in a statute.[69] If the labour legislation of the Cambridge parliament was a reaction to the 1381 rising alone, it is difficult to see why, even allowing for the political upheavals of 1386–8, the Commons waited seven years before bringing their proposals to parliament. It is more likely that both the labour legislation and the petition against guilds arose from a continuing, and probably growing, concern about social unrest in the years after 1381. For despite the suppression of the revolt in June and July 1381, rural unrest continued throughout the 1380s. In Kent the rebellion continued to smoulder throughout the summer of 1381, culminating in the armed assembly of rebels under the leadership of Thomas Hardyng at Broughton Heath on 30 September.[70] There were conspiracies, or rumours of conspiracies, in Norfolk in 1382 and 1384, in Sussex in 1383, and Kent again in 1388;[71] while concern about unlawful assemblies in the southern counties generally led to government action in 1387.[72] In these circumstances a greater degree of control over those sections of the community likely to become involved in social unrest came to seem as important as remedying the misgovernment which had, in the Commons' eyes, done much to provoke the rising of 1381.

In their reluctance to grant taxation, their complaints about misgovernment and their pressure for legislation on the question of law and order, the Commons received no support from the Lords, and indeed they were acting in a manner quite contrary to the wishes of the great magnates. Nor did they enjoy any backing from the king until the Cambridge parliament of 1388 when, for political reasons, Richard chose to support the Commons' demand for the abolition of liveries.[73] Even on the question of heresy, the Com-

---

[68] Ibid., p. 237.        [69] Ibid., pp. 228–9.

[70] Peasants' Revolt of 1381, ed. Dobson, pp. 323–4; W. E. Flaherty, 'The Great Rebellion in Kent of 1381 Illustrated from the Public Records', Archaeologia Cantiana, iii (1860), pp. 95–6.

[71] Walsingham, Historia Anglicana, ii, p. 70; A. Réville and C. Petit-Dutaillis, Le soulèvement des travailleurs d'Angleterre en 1381 (Paris, 1898), p. cxxxiv; Favent, 'Historia Mirabilis Parliamenti', p. 21.

[72] Cal. Pat. Rolls, 1385–9, p. 323.

[73] Tuck, 'Cambridge Parliament, 1388', pp. 236–7.

mons took an independent line. It has traditionally, and rightly, been assumed that the pressure from the clergy to intensify measures against heresy arose from the belief that Lollard preachers had been implicated in the Peasants' Revolt, and that there was a connection between social unrest and movements against the authority of the church.[74] Clerical initiative procured the adoption by parliament in May 1382 of a new procedure to deal with heretical preachers and their supporters under which the Chancery was empowered to issue commissions to sheriffs and other officials to arrest and imprison such preachers.[75] But this did not meet with the approval of the Commons, and in the next parliament, at Michaelmas 1382, they petitioned for the repeal of the statute, saying that they had not known anything about it and in any case they did not wish to see the prelates' influence over them enlarged.[76] The Commons' reluctance to support a firmer stand against heresy requires explanation, since if they were motivated by a general fear of subversion of all kinds as a result of the Peasants' Revolt they might have been expected to support the new procedure. Perhaps Wycliffite ideas enjoyed more support among the lesser gentry than has sometimes been supposed;[77] perhaps the Commons had misgivings about the way in which the new procedure might be administered by sheriffs and other officials; but perhaps the petition should be taken at its face value and interpreted in the light of the anti-clerical attitudes so strongly displayed by parliaments in the 1370s. The Commons were reluctant to allow general alarm at social unrest to be used as an excuse to widen the powers of the prelates.

The reaction of the Commons to the Peasants' Revolt thus differs markedly from that of the great secular lords, the prelates, and the king himself. The great magnates, even those such as Gaunt whose property suffered considerable damage during the revolt, saw the problem in a rather different light from the Commons. They dealt with their own tenants where necessary, but they do not appear to have taken a fundamentally different attitude to the question of manorial authority in the years immediately after the rising. Their

[74] M. Aston, 'Lollardy and Sedition, 1381–1431', *Past and Present*, no. 17 (Apr. 1960), pp. 1–5.

[75] H. G. Richardson, 'Heresy and the Lay Power under Richard II', *Eng. Hist. Rev.*, li (1936), pp. 5–9.

[76] *Rotuli Parliamentorum*, iii, p. 141.

[77] See, for example, K. B. McFarlane, *Lancastrian Kings and Lollard Knights* (Oxford, 1972), p. 225.

reaction seems to have been considerably cooler than that of the Commons. The prelates were not unnaturally moved to demand stiffer measures against heretics, but even on this question the ruling class was not of one mind. The reaction of the Commons perhaps had the greatest impact on political developments over the years between 1381 and 1388: their fears about taxation decisively inhibited the English war efforts in these years, and their complaints about misgovernment provide an important reason for their growing distrust of the king and the court. The political consequences of the Peasants' Revolt were of rather greater importance, in the short run at least, than the impact of the revolt on manorial authority.

# Index

*Note:* All entries refer to England unless otherwise stated. Counties are given in their pre-1974 forms.

# Past and Present Publications

General Editor: PAUL SLACK, *Exeter College, Oxford*

*Published also as a paperback
**Published only as a paperback
†Co-published with the Maison des Sciences de l'Homme, Paris